ARCHBISHOP OSCAR ROMERO

A DISCIPLE WHO
REVEALED THE GLORY OF GOD

UNIVERSITY OF SCRANTON PRESS SERIES

PEACE, JUSTICE, HUMAN RIGHTS,

AND FREEDOM IN LATIN AMERICA

In Honor of Archbishop Oscar Romero, Martyr and Prophet

Robert S. Pelton, C.S.C.

General Editor

Other titles in the series:

Vessel of Clay: The Inspirational Journey of Sister Carla
Jacqueline Hansen Maggiore

Archbishop Oscar Romero:
A Disciple Who Revealed the Glory of God
Damian Zynda

The Surprising Adventures of Balthazar
Claudio Orrego Vicuña
Translated by Christine Cervenak and Alejandra Méndez

ARCHBISHOP OSCAR ROMERO

A DISCIPLE WHO
REVEALED THE GLORY OF GOD

Damian Zynda

University of Scranton Press

Scranton and London

© 2010   University of Scranton Press

All rights reserved.

Library of Congress Cataloging-in-Publication Data

Zynda, Damian, 1956-
  Archbishop Oscar Romero : a disciple who revealed the glory of God /
Damian Zynda.
    p. cm.
  Includes bibliographical references and index.
  ISBN 978-1-58966-211-7 (cloth)
  1. Romero, Oscar A. (Oscar Arnulfo), 1917-1980. 2. Catholic Church--
El Salvador--Bishops--Biography. 3. Psychology, Religious. I. Title.
  BX4705.R669Z96 2010
  282.092--dc22
  [B]

                                                          2010034611

Distribution:
University of Scranton Press
Chicago Distribution Center
11030 S. Langley Chicago, IL 60628

PRINTED IN THE UNITED STATES OF AMERICA

TO RONALD MERCIER, S.J.

CONTENTS

ACKNOWLEDGMENTS

I am indebted to Margaret Brennan, I.H.M., and Joseph Schner, S.J., master disciples both, whose encouragement and steady faith supported me in the various phases of writing this book; to my dear friend and colleague, Mary Lou Mitchell, S.S.J.; Ph.D., who dreamed more for me than I did for myself; to Daniel Brent whose generosity of heart and literary skill made this book a pleasure to read; to Julian Filochowski and Robert Pelton, C.S.C., whose affection for Archbishop Romero inspired this project to completion; and to my editor Jeff Gainey and copy editor John P. Hunckler and the staff of the University of Scranton Press for seeing this book to the light of day. Finally, I am profoundly grateful to Robert, my husband, whose steadfast love encircled and accompanied me through the many years of writing this book.

INTRODUCTION

Early on in his doctoral studies, Oscar Romero wrote, "I've been think-ing of how far a soul can ascend if it lets itself be possessed entirely by God." Romero's life is a story of discipleship framed by this inquiry. It is a moving love story of his radical spiritual and psychological con-version, a process that took place little by little throughout his life. As we examine the struggles he lived with, caused mainly by his scrupu-losity and obsessive-compulsive personality disorder, we are better able to appreciate how Romero came to be possessed entirely by God. His graced desire motivated his gradual transformation into the likeness of the Son of God, freeing him to be available to whatever God asked of him.

This book is about Romero. It is the witness of how Romero could not say no to God, regardless of what God desired for him or from him. This is a study of how one man took discipleship seriously—to the point of accepting the mantle of prophet and martyr. Oscar Romero is a master disciple who merits our attention for his spiritual conversion—from one formed in a seminary system in the 1930s and 1940s to an archbishop who modeled what it means to take the Gospel seriously. This is the story of his psychological development, how he was able to grow beyond the constraining patterns of his obsessive-compulsive per-sonality disorder, to becoming an authentic human being.

How I study Romero here is through the unique theological lens of the second-century pastoral theologian, Irenaeus of Lyons. Most have reflected on Romero's story, life example, and gifts to the Church and world through the eyes of Western Christian theology, but Irenaeus provides a template with which to look at Romero through the eyes of the Eastern Christian perspective.

Irenaeus wrote that the glory of God is the living human being and that the human person has true life only in the vision of God. I find Irenaeus inspiring. As a pastoral theologian, his theology provides a foundation for a dynamic and meaningful contemporary spirituality, a spirituality of conversion.

Exploring a spirituality of conversion grounded in Irenaean theology offers important insights for Christian spirituality today. While Irenaeus did not write explicitly about discipleship and formation, his thinking can be fruitfully advanced in those directions. Irenaean theology relies on grace and encourages a priority for God's mercy and compassionate understanding of human nature. Irenaean anthropology suggests a greater appreciation of God's desires for our human flourishing than familiar Western emphases—inspired by Augustine—on sin, and frames spirituality in developmental terms. Irenaean soteriology proposes that, while the healing vector of the grace of conversion motivates us out of sin, the elevating vector animates our struggle in the life of grace to discover divinely endowed gifts and gradually to heal and liberate us from the constraints of our woundedness.

When grace is offered as gift to call forth unnoticed gifts and/or to reorient us in our woundedness, love impels a response. Our response, of course, can only happen if we know God and, in knowing God, desire God all the more. To respond to grace invariably gives rise to tension between our longing for God and our drive toward human progress and the limitations imposed on us by human nature. The struggle to be faithful to grace in this tension has the potential to convert disciples into the likeness of the Son of God—or, what Irenaeus termed "master disciples."

Since conversion is a phenomenon best studied through careful observations of human beings, I enter into dialogue with the life and ministry of Oscar Romero in this effort to deepen the conversation between doctrine and the practice of faith. Archbishop Romero is a particularly promising dialogue partner in my efforts to develop a fuller spirituality because he is a contemporary Christian, whose radical features of conversion make the shifts in his spiritual development more observable. Also, Romero invites a fuller dialogue with some strands of psychology and psychotherapy because of their roles in his life.

Drawing on selected aspects of Irenaeus's theology and his commentators, in dialogue with available records and commentaries on Romero's life and certain strands of psychology, in the quest for a fuller understanding of spirituality, I will sketch a framework of spiritual conversion and development which highlights the transformative operations of grace. This helps to make sense of Romero's development, and offers advantages in contemporary spiritual direction more generally. The human and spiritual struggles which challenged Romero to move forward as a person and disciple of Christ transformed him from one whose search for holiness was motivated by a scrupulous fear of sin to a man whose quest for holiness led him to embrace his finite human nature and, eventually, his martyrdom. This book represents the fruits of my probes into Oscar Romero's witness in dialogue with Irenaeus and strands of contemporary psychology which played an important role in his own discernment and development, indeed, what appear as truly radical shifts—conversion—in allegiance and action.

Even though the historical context of Romero's life (El Salvador in the midst of massive state-sponsored terrorism against the people) may differ from ours, considering his conversion through the lens of Irenaean theology gives contemporary Christian disciples a renewed appreciation for how we can experience salvation through being faithful to love in the normal circumstances and ordinary events of life.

CHAPTER 1

THE LIFE AND MINISTRY
OF
OSCAR ARNULFO ROMERO

Oscar Arnulfo Romero was Archbishop of El Salvador when he was assassinated in 1980. At the time of his death he was a controversial figure, regarded by the international community as a prominent advocate for human rights. His courageous defense of the rights of indigenous Salvadorans won him a nomination for the Nobel Peace Prize in 1979 from members of both the British Parliament and the United States Congress.

In the El Salvador of the 1970s, the wealth and power were largely in the hands of an oligarchy, the Fourteen Families. They and the military and government of El Salvador held Romero responsible for provoking military action and jeopardizing national security; the campesinos and victims of the repression acclaimed him a saint. Within ecclesial ranks, Romero, while maintaining his objectives, had been encouraged by Paul VI, misunderstood by John Paul II, opposed by four Salvadoran bishops and the Apostolic Nuncio to El Salvador for his pastoral policies and decisions, and revered by some Latin American bishops, priests, religious, and laity as a prophet and martyr whose lifetime of conversion into the likeness of the Son of God disclosed the imminence of God. Following his death, Romero's vicar general, Ricardo Urioste, captured the contentious Romero well: "You must understand. Archbishop Romero was the most loved person in the country. And the most hated."[1]

The Vatican's choice of Romero as Archbishop was not well received by the presbyterate because of his well-known ties to certain members of the Fourteen Families and his theological conservatism. Yet, three years later, his funeral drew thousands of clergy and laity from all over the country and the globe. To what can we attribute this radical change in the last few years of Romero's life? What happened to him to effect such a pronounced shift?

Who we knew Romero to be at the end of his life reflects a pattern of psychological and spiritual changes he sustained throughout his life and ministry. To better appreciate these radical changes that affected Romero, we need to pay careful attention to the details of his entire life, his presbyteral formation, his psychological and spiritual development, and the people, events, and circumstances that affected him. Such study provides valuable insights into the man and his dynamic process of conversion.

When Romero was thirteen years old, his father, Santos, arranged for him to apprentice as a carpenter with Alfonso Leiva in Ciudad Barrios. While his father intended to provide his son with an opportunity to learn a skill that would provide a livelihood, Romero wanted to be a priest. So while both parents encouraged neither further education nor his dream of becoming a priest, Oscar sought out the town's mayor to intercede on his behalf. Santos Romero relented and allowed his son to attend San José de la Montaña, the minor seminary in San Miguel.

As a child, Oscar Romero was naturally attracted to prayer and solitude. The Claretain Fathers who staffed the minor seminary recognized this and built the foundation of his priesthood. As a young seminarian, Romero adhered to the schedule of prayer prescribed by his formation directors and added nightly prayer in the silence and solitude of the seminary chapel before the Blessed Sacrament. Already, at this initial stage of formation, he demonstrated a need to exceed the norm.

In the minor seminary, Romero established a reputation as an above average student who was prayerful, virtuous, and concerned with service to others. Graduating in 1937, he was sent to the major seminary in San Salvador for six months. This was Romero's first encounter with Spanish Jesuits and Ignatian spirituality. Here he was exposed to the formative principles of Dom Joseph Columba Marmion on priesthood and the theology of the ascetical and mystical sacrifice of the Eucharist. He also studied the great paragons of discipleship, Sts. Augustine, Teresa of Avila, and John of the Cross.[2]

In Romero's formative years, holiness was equated with perfection and rigid observance of spiritual and ascetic practice, and, as a young seminarian, he devised a plan and method with which to hold himself accountable for his spiritual progress. The following excerpt from his *Spiritual Diary* offers insight into his earnest care for his spiritual life. It also reveals a need for order, method, and rigidity:

PROGRAM OF PRAYER AND MORTIFICATION SUBJECT TO AN EXAMINATION OF CONSCIENCE

1. Pray matins at night. Pray the remainder of the breviary at the assigned hours.
2. Meditate for an hour. If not completed in the morning, complete it in the afternoon.
3. After Mass, spend fifteen minutes in thanksgiving.
4. Read the Gospels, *The Imitation of Christ*, and Fr. Rodríguez for fifteen minutes.
5. Make a short examination of conscience at midday; complete it in the evening.
6. Rosary—all three mysteries each day if possible.
7. Do not go into San Salvador unnecessarily; if need be, stay in religious houses and flee anything threatening.
8. Separate from street life completely.
9. Keep careful vigil and control all desires and memories that arise at any given moment, anytime of the day.
10. Fast on Fridays, no sweets on Sundays, wear a hair shirt for a half hour daily, take the discipline on Fridays (33 lashes in honor of Jesus).[3]

Biographer Delgado does not give a specific date for this entry but places it between Romero's minor seminary and his studies in Rome.

At midyear 1937, Bishop Dueñas of the Diocese of San Miguel sent Romero to Rome for studies. Romero lived in Europe during the rise of fascism and the consolidation of Stalin's control of the Soviet Union. Here he shared the fears, austerities, and privations experienced by many during World War II. He resided at Pio Latino Americano and studied at the Gregorian University, staffed by Jesuits who further formed Romero's theological, spiritual, and ministerial life. Of all his

Jesuit professors, Romero was most influenced by Fr. Güenechea who was instrumental in facilitating Romero's desire for understanding Ignatian spirituality and the practice of the *Spiritual Exercises*. The *Exercises* provided Romero with a program of prayer and asceticism that appealed to his need for method and predictability. They also contributed to his burgeoning scrupulosity.

During this time, Romero exhibited the understanding of priesthood one would expect of a man trained in the 1930s and 1940s. In an in-house newspaper, he published an article offering insight into his theology of priesthood: "This is your inheritance, priest: the cross. And this is your mission: to share the cross. Carrying pardon and peace, the priest runs to the dying, a cross in the right hand is the key which opens heaven and closes the abyss. Be with the crucified Christ who redeems. With Christ resurrected, be resurrected and share his resurrected life."[4]

As the contours of Romero's spiritual life began to take more definitive shape, so too did features of his personality and physical demeanor. Romero was a perfectionist. He was easily agitated, naturally nervous, temperamental, emotionally uneven, and demonstrated little tolerance for people who exhibited any form of weakness. Physically, he had a frail constitution, attributed to a mysterious illness he sustained at age four that left him physically and socially debilitated.[5]

Concluding the 1940–41 academic year, Romero graduated *cum laude*, received a licentiate in theology, and was ordained on April 4, 1942 in the college chapel. He began a doctoral program in ascetical theology, planning a dissertation on Christian mysticism and asceticism based on the sixteenth-century Jesuit, Luis de la Puente.[6] During his research, a moment of insight and inspiration captured him and inspired his lifelong dedication to prayer and discipleship. As we will see, this is what motivated his heroic surrendering of himself, little by little, to be totally united with God. Romero wrote, "In recent days, after reading some of Fr. La Puente at the curia, principally the life of Father Alvarez, the Lord has inspired in me a great desire for holiness. *I've been thinking of how far a soul can ascend if it lets itself be possessed entirely by God.*"[7]

Due to the war, Romero's bishop called him back to El Salvador. Unfortunately, he never had an opportunity to complete his dissertation.

Following his first brief parochial assignment in the mountain town of Anamorós, Romero was assigned secretary to Monseñor Miguel Angel Machalo, Bishop of San Miguel. Since the Ordinary possessed few qualifications for leadership, he gradually delegated increasing responsibilities for the direction, organization, and governance of the diocese to Romero. Administratively, Romero utilized his organizational strength to create pastoral plans, and he implemented them with energy and enthusiasm. He governed with a firm sense of authority, successfully accomplishing multiple tasks. Interpersonally, his rigid, overly demanding temperament made him highly critical of priests for their moral failings. It also led to misunderstandings and his increasing isolation from the presbytery. Manuel Vergara, who was later interviewed by María López Vigil, recalled his experience of the young Fr. Romero:

> "He's a stickler, that priest! You have to walk on eggshells with him!" Father Romero was a stickler, a *guishte*. Like one of those sharp slivers of glass that will cut you. Very, very strict. But then, how could he have been any different when the Diocese of San Miguel was such a disaster? "Those sloppy priests that go around without their cassocks!" he would agonize. "Better they go without their cassocks since they're just chasing after prostitutes anyway!"
>
> And he'd agonize more. It was true. There were womanizing priests. And liquor flowed faster than communion wine among them. Pastoral plans? They all went up in smoke. There was no interest. There was no effort. And the bishop? Bishop Machado didn't give orders and he didn't give advice. What he gave were loans at outrageous interest rates. Everybody knew those stories, and Father Romero knew them best because he saw all the drama from the inside.
>
> Since the clergy in San Miguel did whatever they pleased, it was up to Romero to do what they didn't do. He took responsibility for everything and more. He handled several parishes, all of the religious organizations, all the movements, the work in the schools, the files, the jails, and, on top of all that, he had to give the irresponsible priests a good chewing out.[8]

Romero was eventually named pastor of the cathedral parish and completed its construction. He was also chaplain of the little colonial church of San Francisco, where the venerated image of Our Lady of Peace, patroness of El Salvador, was housed. At both parishes, he initiated and facilitated several pastoral organizations including catechetical classes, Legion of Mary, Knights of the Holy Sepulcher, Alcoholics Anonymous, Cursillos de Cristianidad, Apostleship of Prayer, Guardians of the Blessed Sacrament, the Rosary Association, Third Order of St. Francis, and the diocesan branch of Caritas (an association that provides food for the poor).[9]

By the time he left the diocese, Romero had earned a reputation as a charismatic and effective preacher who focused on the need to integrate prayer and action in a Christian life. Romero insisted that religion could not simply be associated with acts of sentimental piety. By 1966, Romero earned notoriety as a gifted spiritual director and confessor to several consecrated men and women. He had also been the editor of the diocesan paper, *Chaparrastique*. He had served as rector of the seminary and governed the diocese in the absence of the Ordinary.

Despite this active and demanding ministry, Romero compulsively tried to maintain the same spiritual practices he learned in the seminary. As if that were not enough, he presided each evening at a Holy Hour, in the presence of the Blessed Sacrament, which included a rosary and a sermon. Once again, he exceeded the norm. Romero practiced the *Exercises* and, in 1954 or 1955, made the Ignatian thirty-day retreat directed by Miguel Elizondo, the Master of Novices for the Jesuit Central American province.[10] Although we have no record from this thirty-day retreat, subsequent journal entries indicate it had a profound effect on Romero.

In 1966, Romero made another important retreat in Mexico at the Franciscan Retreat House, Planes de Randeros. While there, he had access to his Opus Dei spiritual director, Fr. Juan Izquierdo, and a psychiatrist, Dr. Dárdano, with whom Romero seems to have had an established relationship. This was a seminal retreat for Romero for several reasons. First, at forty-eight years of age, on the threshold of midlife, repressed issues of sexuality and feelings of lack of intimacy and painful loneliness had emerged. Second, Vatican II had called the Church to renewal, and it expected the clergy to reframe their identity in accord with the directives of the Council. This was a threatening prospect for Romero who had been secure in his isolated, hierarchical role as a traditional pre–Vatican II priest. Third, after nearly twenty-five years of active priesthood, Romero felt physically and mentally depleted by the demands of his responsibilities and the consequences of his administrative decisions. Fourth, he acknowledged his rigidity and the demanding attitude that provoked animosity in the priests, together with his frustration regarding his inability to control his temperament. Romero presented these concerns—together with his intensified fear, interior tensions, conflict with others, agitation, obsession with perfection, having a grim outlook on life, and his lack of flexibility—to the two men. The psychiatrist diagnosed him as an obsessive-compulsive perfectionist and the spiritual director told him he was scrupulous. The two problems are intimately linked.

The American Psychiatric Association designates the following characteristics as probable features of the personality disorder:

> The obsessive-compulsive personality disorder [OCPD] displays a pervasive pattern with orderliness, perfectionism and mental and interpersonal control, at the expense of flexibility, openness, and efficiency, beginning by early adulthood and present in a variety of contexts, as indicated by four or more of the following:

(1)   is preoccupied with details, lists, rules, order, [and] organization of schedules to the extent that the major point of the activity is lost;

(2)   shows perfectionism that interferes with task completion (i.e. is unable to complete a project because his or her own overly strict standards are not met);

(3)   is excessively devoted to work to the exclusion of leisure activities and friendships (not accounted for by obvious economic necessity);

(4)   is overly conscientious, scrupulous, and inflexible about matters of morality, ethics, or values (not accounted for by cultural or religious identification);

(5)   is unable to discard worn-out or worthless objects even when they have no sentimental value;

(6)   is reluctant to delegate tasks or to work with others unless they submit to exactly his or her way of doing things;

(7)   adopts a miserly spending style toward both self and others; money is viewed as something to be hoarded for future catastrophes; shows rigidity and stubbornness.[11]

Clinical researchers interested in the relationship between scrupulosity and obsessive-compulsive disorder generally describe scrupulosity as an anxiety disorder provoked primarily by fear and intolerance of uncertainty. For the religious individual, boundaries between normal religious behavior and obsessive-compulsive symptoms are blurred. People who suffer with scrupulosity focus on "seeing sin where there is none." They dramatically overreact to falling short of the impossibly high standards they set for themselves, focus on the minor details of religion to the exclusion of more important areas, and take religious behavior to the extreme. Sufferers are tortured by the intensity of their doubts about their goodness and they believe, therefore, that they are simply bad.

Scrupulosity consists of persistent, irrational, and unwelcome beliefs and thoughts about not being devout or moral enough, despite all evidence to the contrary. Sufferers believe they have sinned or will sin, disappoint God, and be punished for failing.

In response to these disturbing thoughts, victims of scrupulosity try to calm themselves by using a host of compulsions. Their discomfort makes it difficult to dismiss their thoughts which become sticky and hard to chase away. The persistence of these thoughts, and the frequency and anxious intensity with which they return, turns those irrational thoughts to obsessions. They feel they must get rid of the obsession at any cost and the result is a compulsion.[12]

This diagnosis provided Romero with an explanation for his behaviors and a language with which he could begin to understand the complexity of the features of OCPD particular to him. While an intellectual comprehension of the disorder was a critical step, it was still too early for Romero to do the work of therapeutic integration. Still thinking he could control the features of the OCPD and scrupulosity, Romero attempted to "correct" the OCPD with another strategy.

This was a strategy that only perpetuated the cycle of unhealthy attitudes and behaviors that kept him unfree and miserable. With an eye toward strengthening his spiritual life and diminishing feelings of insecurity, Romero created this plan:

Considering all this, and after a genuine reexamination of my life, I propose the following reform:

To strengthen my interior life:

A. Sincerely return to piety:

1. Daily meditation (I will follow the liturgy or return to the eternal truths in times of temptation.)
2. Examination of conscience (after siesta, and a brief one after lunch). I'll make the particular examination on my problem with protection and the general examen on my way to reform.
3. Breviary and spiritual reading. Continue as usual.
4. Go back to saying the rosary in church. Invite those in the house to The Rosary Association . . .
5. Go back to making the monthly spiritual retreat . . .
6. Thanksgiving after Mass.
7. Weekly confession. I'll go see Fr. Damián. I'll decide on a day and be better prepared—Saturday, when I am going to or coming back from hearing confessions of the Hospital Sisters, or whenever Father chooses.

B. To regain a sense of penance and mortification to my duties.

1. Organize my time better concerning all my duties: parish, diocesan office, printing shop, seminary, [and] other work associations.
2. Get my accounts in order. Get them up to date and pay off my debts this year. Especially to the Soler family.

3.   Charity and humility. I will not speak ill of anyone and refrain from self-praise. Refrain from any idea of vanity. Love and pray for those who do not love me or who I think wrong me. At the least, observe some common charity. Have a sense of hope for reconciliation and union.

4.   Overcome my harsh and grim disposition. Be kind to those who come to see me, especially the priests, seminarians, the poor, the sick. Even a refusal can be given with kindness.

5.   Custody of the eyes: newspapers, the confessional, and the streets.

6.   On Fridays and Saturdays, do some small fasting or mortification at table in honor of Christ's passion and of the Blessed Virgin. Abstain from sweets.

7.   Wear a penitential chain from rising after siesta until after prayer.

8.   Discipline on Friday nights.

Providing a Secure Environment:

A.   Do not travel alone to San Salvador—nor stop in dubious lodgings.
B.   Let someone else take care of answering the door.
C.   Confide my problems to my confessor.
D.   Keep certain persons at a distance.
E.   Wait and see what the future holds.
F.   Avoid being alone.
G.   Go out with friends or seminarians once a week.[13]

That same year, 1966, the American Franciscan, Lawrence Graziano was first appointed auxiliary Bishop of the Diocese of San Miguel and later became Ordinary. Graziano was aware of Romero's history and reputation in the diocese and the tension between Romero and the clergy. The new bishop's administrative style was quite different from his predecessor, Monseñor Machalo. Graziano had more energy and assumed greater responsibility and participation in the governance of the diocese. He was sensitive to Romero and did not want to hurt or offend him. But he had been appointed to alleviate the tension and bring order to the diocese. This episcopal appointment was a prelude to Romero's eventual separation from the diocese.

The need to resolve these tensions, coupled with Romero's reputation as a hard worker and perfectionist, led to his appointment as secretary-general of the Salvadoran National Bishops' Conference. This was a bittersweet experience for him because, although it was an advancement, he perceived that the change was manipulated by the priests, Bishop Graziano, and Archbishop Chávez y González to remove him from the diocese. Painful as it was, he accepted the position in a spirit of obedience and moved to San Salvador where he resided with the Jesuits at San José de la Montaña Seminary.

It was not long before Romero's hard work with the Conference resulted in his appointment as executive secretary of the Central American Bishops' Secretariat in addition to his duties with the national conference. Soon after, the Archbishop petitioned the Holy See that Romero be made an auxiliary bishop. On April 21, 1970, the Apostolic Nuncio telephoned Romero to notify him of Paul VI's desire that Romero be consecrated bishop.

Overwhelmed by doubts, confusion, and fears, Romero consulted Dr. Dárdano and either Fr. Juan Izquierdo or Fr. Fernando Sáenz Lacalle. (It is unclear which of these Opus Dei priests served as his spiritual director at the time.) The psychiatrist and spiritual director affirmed and encouraged Romero to accept this invitation to greater responsibility. They also cautioned that the appointment could easily be a temptation to arrogance. They counseled him to remember that the ministry of bishop carries great responsibilities and demands tremendous personal sacrifices to properly attend to the souls entrusted to him. "It is, after all," one reminded him, "the Good Shepherd who gives his life for his sheep."[14]

A man accustomed to making himself available to God, Romero responded with characteristic generosity and took *Sentir con la Iglesia* (to be of one mind with the Church) as his episcopal motto. The motto, *Sentir con la Iglesia*, comes from the "Rules for Thinking with the Church," one of the appendices to the *Spiritual Exercises*.[15] The motto is emblematic of a relationship to the official hierarchy that was much like Ignatius's own: respectful, attentive, accountable, but also contextualized within a broader sense of God's presence and activity in the world, of which the Church is called to be a sacrament.[16]

On June 8 and 9, 1970, Romero made a retreat in preparation for his episcopal consecration. It was here that Romero began to formulate his identity as a bishop. "I desire to distinguish myself for this: to be a bishop with the heart of Jesus."[17] And so he chose the Sacred Heart of Jesus as his model and dedicated his episcopal ministry to that same heart. From these choices, we glean insight into how Romero understood the office and ministry of bishop.

During the retreat, he prayed over the "Principle and Foundation" from the *Spiritual Exercises*. In this exercise, he would have reflected on the gracious generosity of God, God's desire to be in relationship with human beings, and the correct use of persons and things. He resolved to do all for God's glory and to further his own holiness. To that end, he wrote, "God created my nature, and God authors my new being through the grace of baptism and ordination. In my episcopacy, let your Spirit give me a tremendous new power." Romero sensed this "new power" was a call to do something different for El Salvador. He continued, "I feel I am called to be a leader, to plan a new phase, to confirm a delicate change."[18]

It is interesting, though not unexpected, that he identified a purgative dimension to this new call, noting his ministry was a continuous reparation for his sins and the sins of other people. Choosing the Sacred Heart of Jesus as the patron for his episcopal life, he was united with other men and women of the world whose sins have lacerated the Heart of Jesus.[19]

Discovering new dimensions of his identity and ministry, Romero composed a strategy to guide this new phase in his spiritual and pastoral life. In his *Spiritual Notebook* he wrote,

> For Mary, my Mother, to the Heart of Jesus, guest and eternal priest, Shepherd, and Bishop of our souls. I synthesize my consecration in these words: *To be of one mind with the Church*. According to the encyclical, *Ecclesiam Suam*, and after examining my life, I make these three categories for the glory of God and the eternal health of my soul.

1. To increase my self-awareness:

A. Each day gain more knowledge of the Church and my job and obligations.

B. Fidelity to the magisterium. Her doctrines are my priority.

C. Keep updated on Church documents, news of the Holy See and the universal Church.
D. Meditate daily on my episcopal responsibilities. The circumstances, critics, and conversations in my life will convey these to me . . .

2. Renewal:

The Church demands holiness, and conversion is always necessary. I have examined many things in myself that require penance, precaution, and reform:

A. My sensuality:

Penance for my excesses:
1. First of all, the circumstances of my life will determine my purgatory.
2. In eating, take on the diet of a diabetic. Some privation at each meal, some fasting on the principle vigils (as did the Apostles).
3. Hair shirt. One hour daily.
4. Take the discipline on Fridays.
5. Short rest (one half-hour). Sometimes sleep on the floor. Matins at midnight.

B. Precautions:

1. Sever all relations with people who are threatening to me . . .
2. Do not go out at night unless absolutely necessary, and in each case, be accompanied.
3. Organize my evening activities. Go to bed early (no later than ten o'clock).
4. When traveling, seek lodging in houses associated with the Church.
5. Do not accept dinner invitations. Lunches are better.

C. My bad example:

1. Share my life of reparation with those who have been hurt. Master of souls, have pity on them.
2. Never do anything that could be scandalous. Set a good example.

D. My sacrileges:

1. I will celebrate Mass with greater fervor. Prepare and execute with grace, never with negligence. Even when on vacation. Have more dialogue about executing obligations to celebrate Mass in respect to the laws of bination.
2. Be better prepared for my confession. Weekly, fixed. Spiritual direction.
3. I will be faithful to my breviary. Matins at midnight. Safeguard a dispensation for truly impossible cases.

E. My disorganization, tepidity, tardiness, abruptness:

1. Organize the tasks assigned by the Archbishop. Do them punctually. Process the agenda.
2. Save time for my spiritual exercises.
3. Prior to accepting new commitments, think it over, prioritize them. Know when to say no when I cannot help.
4. Each day, mark off tasks completed.

F. Disorganized accounts:

1. Organize my responsibility and account for the day.
2. Repay debts. Work. Alms for the poor.
3. Help poor priests, the seminary.

G. My arrogance:

1. Bring a real sense of simplicity to my ministry.
2. Do not be preoccupied with my appearance . . .

3. Dialogue

The Church is self-reflective and is being renewed, not for itself, but to redeem the world and attract others. Act with purpose. I also need to dialogue with others.

A. With the bishops:

1. Concerning the Archdiocese. I have an obligation to the Holy See. I will uphold these as a priority. My personal worth comes from taking part. I will win their confidence and will consult them. I will work together with the Archbishop.
2. With CEDES. Confidence, frankness, integrity. Relate to individuals.
3. With the Church. I will live collegially forming warm relations with other bishops, sharing in their extraordinary circumstances.

B. With priests:

My worst fear!

1. Genuinely love them—offer my friendship and mediation.
2. I will visit them when there is an opportunity or take interest in the important circumstances of their lives. Naturally and supernaturally . . . caution when they feel inferior to me.

C. With religious communities:

Take interest in their concerns. Encourage holiness . . . through them. How much spiritual work . . . how much social work!

D. With the laity, with society:

I will help them when I know I can. Be socially tasteful. Always seek the glory of God, not my own.

E. With those on the margins:

These are also Jesus' sheep . . . a Bishop is responsible for them.

F. With my family:

Love them with a priestly love . . . do not discard their relationships . . .

G. With the poor:

Love them as Christ would. Encourage works of charity in their favor and for their promotion. Visit infirmaries, hospitals, slums. Encourage the laity to serve them.

Make my examination of conscience regarding conversations, especially with priests and the areas the Archbishop assigns me.[20]

Times of transition are times of vulnerability, and vulnerability surface deep fears. Grief over personal loss gets tangled in the web of anxieties over what the future holds. Romero was in the thick of transitions. Vatican II changed the secure and only world he knew. He moved from one diocese to another, and his ministry shifted from pastor to administrator. Having gained greater insight into the dynamics of his complex psyche, he worked to integrate new, healthier behaviors. And Romero was, by virtue of his new office, thrust into the political and ecclesial spotlight. He was placed in a position he neither desired nor was prepared to undertake. Immersed in a tidal wave of transition, Romero walked into his new future—confident that this was God's desire for him, and well aware of his fragile human condition.

While the authority of his office positioned Romero to effect change, it also exposed him to dark forces and powers he had heretofore not encountered. Perhaps former United States Ambassador to El Salvador Robert White's words were a prophetic utterance in this regard: "I have always contended that there was no more radicalizing experience than for a priest to become Bishop in Central America and all of a sudden become, at first hand, acquainted with the political considerations and the influence of the people."[21] Romero soon encountered these radicalizing forces.

Oscar Romero was consecrated bishop on June 21, 1970, in the Liceo Salvadoreño, a Marist Brothers High School. He selected this particular day because of his great devotion to the Virgin of Peace, whose feast all of Catholic El Salvador celebrated on November 21—and remembered on the twenty-first of each month.

Immediately following the consecration, a Pastoral Week was held to discuss the implementation of Medellín in El Salvador. The city of Medellín, Columbia played host to the second General Conference of Latin American Bishops (CELAM) in September 1968. This meeting was to further the agenda of the first CELAM meeting in Rio de Janeiro (1955) and to discuss various applications of Vatican II to the Latin American Church. The Medellín Conference gave new vitality to responding to the need for justice and meeting the material and spiritual needs of the poor in these countries. The Conference also confirmed the decision of many European and North American religious communities to dedicate their apostolates to the Latin American Church.

The Pastoral Week was a national event that involved the bishops, priests, religious, and laity responsible for church leadership. Archbishop Chávez, and his other auxiliary bishop, Arturo Rivera y Damas, coordinated the week, and although all pastoral leaders were expected to attend, Romero registered for the entire week but only attended the first day. Romero feared change, and the trajectory that the meeting at Medellín accepted for implementation terrified him. Since Archbishop Chávez and Bishop Rivera wholeheartedly supported Medellín, it put a noticeable strain on their relationship with Romero.

During Romero's four-year tenure as auxiliary bishop, three events—his psychoanalysis, his personal crusade to safeguard ecclesial orthodoxy, and his association with Opus Dei—played significant roles in his life and ministry.

The three months spanning November 1971 to February 1972 was a critical period in Romero's life. He began with a retreat at Our Lady of the Angels Monastery in Cuernavaca, Mexico. An excerpt from his *Spiritual Notebook* indicates he was wrestling with some of the features of the OCPD. He wrote the following:

Examine my principal defects:

- Avoiding socializing with others and getting to know them
- I worry about being criticized by others
- Perfectionism
- Disorganization in my work
- I have few austerities: visits, desires, eating, rest . . .
- Little courage at our bishops' meetings . . . defending my opinions at those meetings

In my particular examen, I will focus more on relationships.[22]

Perhaps following through on his proposed particular examen, Romero spent three months in psychoanalysis after this retreat.

Following this psychoanalysis, Romero stayed in Mexico to make a Lenten retreat at the Casa del Actor. The entries made in his *Spiritual Notebook* during this week reflect a subtle shift beginning to occur in his theology and newly acquired self-understanding as a result of the psychoanalysis.

Romero came to three key insights regarding his personality and family background. He recorded (1) his immaturity when he vowed celibacy and his lack of understanding of the full ramifications of this commitment; (2) a fear of intimacy which prevented him from establishing wholesome and nurturing friendships, based upon an unconscious transference from his family; (3) the manner in which his fear unconsciously dominated his life and contributed to his rigidity, immaturity, stubbornness, irrational behavior, harshness, and demanding attitude. The dream analysis included in the psychoanalysis confirmed the immediate changes needed to take place in his life.

Romero reflected on the history of his spiritual life and on recognizing God's grace and fidelity throughout the years. With this awareness, he recommitted himself in love to God. He articulated that his initial desire to seek God, to serve the Church, and work out his own salvation had not changed. As for his episcopacy, Romero stated that he had no desire to be bureaucratic. He wanted to execute his office faithfully with the sensibilities of a pastor under the light of the Church and his spiritual director. This meant cultivating an interior freedom so as to see with the eyes of Christ and judge with the standard of Christ, not his own. At the conclusion of this retreat, he noted that his conversion was incomplete and, acknowledging the mercy of God toward him, he elected to follow Christ more intimately and devote himself more completely to God's desires for him.

Of all the discoveries Romero made in those three months, the most important was that he saw clinical psychology as a supplement to theology and morality to define and explain his personality disorder and its consequences. Psychoanalytic self-discovery entailed great risk to Romero's ecclesially defined self-concept. Psychoanalysis gave him a new context for understanding his complex personality and accepting his humanity; it was an opportunity to put his uncertainties and fears into perspective. The experience helped clarify the dimensions of his personality and his soul, which, though distinct, intersected and affected each other. The psychoanalysis played a significant role in further advancing his theological, Christological, anthropological, soteriological, and ecclesial thinking.

The pain and frustration that drove him to Dr. Dárdano indicated that Romero intuited something fundamental was missing from his personhood, priesthood, and ministry. Working diligently and compulsively, meticulously adhering to ecclesial discipline and liturgical norms, and being faithful to prescribed spiritual exercises, which had heretofore satisfied him, could no longer assuage his suffering. Perhaps his experience of darkness, disillusion, and disappointment roused in him a need to attend seriously to his personal needs and reorder his priorities. Whatever the case, it was obvious that a shift had occurred following the psychoanalysis.

Lest we forget, these discoveries were just that, discoveries—new awareness, new patterns of thinking and perception. Romero's "recovery" was fragile. The time needed to absorb this fresh knowledge and experience, let alone experiment with new behaviors, was lost in the chaos of El Salvador and the church to which he returned. Now in a position of leadership, exposed to the public eye, he was vulnerable and more frightened then ever. It was desperation and fear that drove him to return to his former patterns of thinking and defensive behaviors in search of the security he seemed to have found in orthodoxy. His intensified efforts toward some restored sense of security reawakened the preexisting tensions in his life.

Oscar Romero had a tumultuous history with the Salvadoran Jesuits, and when the Jesuit superiors of Latin America called the Society to establish centers for social study and action throughout Latin America, Romero was adamantly opposed to them. The Jesuit provincials had advised,

> In all our activities, our goal should be the liberation of humankind from every sort of servitude that oppresses it: the lack of life's necessities, illiteracy, the weight of sociological structures which deprive it of personal responsibility over life itself, [and] the materialistic conception of history. We want all our efforts to work together toward the construction of a society in which all persons will find their place, and in which they will enjoy political, economic, cultural and religious equality and liberty.
>
> We are counting on you as we undertake this effort to divest ourselves of any aristocratic attitude that may have been present in our public positions, in our style of life, in our selection of audience, in our dealings with lay co-workers, and in our relations with the wealthy classes.[23]

Romero interpreted this as a Marxist ideology, which he believed had no place in the Church. Recall that Romero was not alone in his thinking. Many powerful groups like the United States Government and Opus Dei claimed that the Jesuits were Marxist and atheists. Regardless, it seems that the Society's shift toward conscientization and social justice did not yet fit Romero's ecclesial framework.

In 1971, Archbishop Chávez appointed Romero editor of the diocesan newspaper, *Orientación*. Romero used the paper to educate the faithful in ecclesial matters and as an extension of *L'Osservatore Romano*, the Vatican paper, whose articles he frequently reproduced. He also used the paper to battle the Jesuits and others committed to social justice.

On May 27, 1973, he printed an editorial attacking the Jesuit High School, Externado San José, for practicing demagogy and promoting Marxist ideologies. Romero's editorial was incendiary. He accused the Jesuits of providing a "falsely liberating education" and of lacking charity toward former teachers, most notably the Spanish Jesuits. This situation illustrated the internal tension between European Jesuits and Latin American Jesuits. This shift toward independence was intentional on the part of the Latin American Jesuit leadership. In 1972, a Nicaraguan was named principal of the school, and a Salvadoran was named Provincial, replacing European (predominantly Spanish) administrators. Regarding this particular situation, it appears that a few parents, affluent and wealthy friends of Romero, convinced him that the new administration no longer honored the more conservative Jesuits who had been administrators with whom the parents were sympathetic.

Orientación applauded the support of the Medellín Conference for liberating education but not the demagogy and Marxism it found in the pamphlets and literature. The "Marxist ideologies" Romero found so threatening had their source in the Jesuit Provincial's directives:

> Education, for example, is a major factor for social change. We think it is most important that our schools and universities accept their role as active agents of national integration and social justice in Latin America. We will not have development for all until we have integral education for all.
>
> We should also do what we can to see to it that our students engage in some real social service before graduation. This service should form part of the school's curriculum. In this way the families of our students will commit themselves to working with us in our concern for societal problems.[24]

The administration of the High School added evening and weekend classes to educate youth of the poorest sections of San Salvador. Sociology classes incorporated field trips to the barrios so students could have personal experiences of poverty in their own city. To add to this, the school magazine printed articles in which conflicts surfaced between the students' experiences on the field trips and the values their families instilled in them.

The Jesuits received full support from Bishop Chávez and the conference of religious. Bishop Chávez, concerned that the public might misinterpret Romero's opinions as the official position of the Church, appointed a commission of priests to conduct an internal investigation of the charges against the school. The commission exonerated the Jesuits and Bishop Chávez asked Romero to print the commission's conclusions. Romero obeyed the Archbishop and on the last page of the paper printed the article "Archbishop Chávez Defends Externado San José." In the same issue, Romero attacked the commission as persons who followed questionable opinions instead of the sure teachings of the Church.

Romero also used the cathedral pulpit to extend his crusade. He exposed and condemned primarily young Jesuits involved in social action, supporters of Medellín, and liberation theologians. In subsequent issues of the paper, he reprinted articles on the evils of "certain fashionable theologies" that invoked "dangerous Marxist positions"—along with selections of Church condemnations of Marxism.

In the August 12, 1973 issue of *Orientación,* Romero wrote an article entitled "Medellín, Misunderstood and Misinterpreted" asserting his belief that the vision of Medellín had been subverted and maliciously misinterpreted, misleading the faithful with Marxist ideologies. Before Romero left the paper, he had the last word on the issue:

> What we do regret, more with an understanding silence of tolerance and patience than with an attitude of polemical resentment, is the explicitly worldly, violent, and uncontrolled conduct of those who have tried to make use of religion to destroy the spiritual basis of religion. In the name of faith, those who have lost their faith have tried to struggle against the faith. And this is very sad, truly sad. For our part, we have preferred to adhere to that which is certain, to cling with fear and trembling to the Rock of Peter, to seek assurance in the shade of the Church's teachings, to put our ears to the lips of the Pope, instead of leaping like reckless and foolhardy acrobats to the speculations of the imprudent thinkers of social movements of dubious origin.[25]

Increasingly in conflict with the progressive sectors of the Church in El Salvador and the Jesuits' option for the poor and support for social action, and frustrated by his inability to control diocesan clergy and by the impact of liberation theology in Latin America, Romero became more involved with Opus Dei. From his days in San Miguel, Romero did not hide his admiration for Opus Dei and its founder, Monseñor Escrivá de Balaguer. In 1975, he even wrote to Pope Paul VI on behalf of Fr. Escrivá, advocating for his beatification: "Personally, I owe deep gratitude to the priests of the Work to whom I have confided with great satisfaction the spiritual direction of my life and that of other priests."

He sought out Opus Dei priests to serve as his spiritual directors and noted in his *Spiritual Notebook* his participation in three retreats directed by Opus Dei priests: Fr. Juan Izquierdo (November 10–14, 1969), Fr. Fernando Sáenz (November 13–17, 1972), and Fr. Juan Izquierdo (sometime in February 1974).

Since Opus Dei does not reveal the identity of its members, we must leave unanswered the question of whether Romero was a member or how closely he was associated with the organization. Based on his unrelenting defense of orthodoxy and deference to papal authority and his reluctance to make independent decisions for himself, I can see why he found the secular institute so attractive. While it is clear that Romero was influenced by Ignatian spirituality, his membership in Opus Dei is tenuous. Regarding this, biographer Jesús Delgado asserted, "Msgr. Romero's spirituality was cultivated by two branches of the same river: Jesuit spirituality and the ecclesial obedience of Opus Dei."[26]

On October 15, 1974, Romero was named Ordinary of the young rural diocese of Santiago de Maria. After the public battle with the Jesuits and his efforts to expose and condemn liberation theologians, Romero understood his election as bishop to be the voice of the Vatican affirming his position. In an editorial in *Orientación*, he wrote, "This trust of the Pope in its editor must be interpreted as the most solemn backing of the Church's magisterium for the ideology that has inspired the paper's pages under this editorship. This silent approval from so high a source constitutes the best reward and satisfaction for all of us who work together for this ideal, at the same time that it determines the route to follow."[27]

Archbishop Gerada presided over Romero's installation as Ordinary on December 14, 1974. Santiago de Maria had been separated from the diocese of San Miguel in 1954, making Romero only the second Ordinary in its history.

· Since the priests of the diocese held Romero's predecessor in contempt because they felt he was self-absorbed, accomplished little in the diocese, and was preoccupied with members of the intellectual elite and the wealthy, they generally affirmed and appreciated Romero's pastoral style: "The new bishop, by his actions, demonstrates that he is a bishop of the campesinos, with a sense of the people, especially the poor."[28] The priests also sensed a growth and maturity in Romero— which they respected: "He was no longer the Romero of San Miguel, full of fear of the young priests. Now he was open to them, lovingly embracing the details of their lives which touched his heart, especially those who were the weakest."[29]

As Bishop of Santiago, Romero, while obviously changed, nevertheless had some distance yet to go. He was still blind to the magnitude of the repression in El Salvador and to his own political inclinations. Since some of the oligarchs were close friends, he denied their greed and participation in and responsibility for the bloodshed in El Salvador. He supported government policies and denied the government's involvement in torture, murder, and widespread disappearances of persons. In contrast, he held politicized priests—the Salvadoran Jesuits and liberation theologians, whom he accused of compromising the mission of the Church—responsible for endangering the lives of innocent people.

In May of 1975, Romero was appointed to the Pontifical Commission for Latin America. This commission functions to coordinate relations between the Vatican and the Latin American bishops. Most of the membership is comprised of Vatican officials, but one member and three consulters are Latin American bishops. Meetings were held in Rome where Romero became familiar with upper level ecclesial governance.

On November 5, 1975, while in Rome for one of these meetings, he attended a conference given by Bishop Alfonso Lopez Trujillo, an ecclesial conservative who was secretary-general for CELAM. Trujillo's conference, "Priests' Political Movements in Latin America: Present Situation, Dangers, and Proposals for Remedies," led Romero to write an unsolicited confidential brief, "Three Factors in the Priests' Political Movement in El Salvador—Very Confidential—For the Bishops of Latin America."

In the report, Romero stated that a liberation theology promoted by the Salvadoran Jesuits in the Society's high school, their catechetical centers, seminary, and Central American University all contributed to the politicization of priests. He stressed that the country's bishops did not sanction the Jesuits' new theology and pastoral plan. He objected to the "Marxist ideology" which he accused the editor of the publication *Justice and Peace* of advocating in the paper. He said the articles were subversive and incendiary, which provoked the government to condemn the Church as subversive. And Romero claimed that the catechetical centers were staffed by politicized priests, nuns, and lay catechists.

These centers, he objected, operated without the support or permission of the bishops. Defending the perspective of the Salvadoran bishops, Romero insisted that their greatest pastoral concern was "spiritualizing the clergy" through prayer and conversion so they could work more collaboratively with the government. The nature of Romero's brief reveals his obvious captivity to the perspectives of groups like Opus Dei and the Salvadoran government.

Romero's myopia began to dissipate, however, when on June 21, 1975, the National Guard terrorized and massacred the villagers in Las Tres Calles, a small rural village in his diocese. Guardsmen shot and hacked to death six men from the Astorga family, then proceeded throughout the village ransacking homes in search of weapons.

Upon hearing this news, Romero went to Las Tres Calles to console the families of the victims and to celebrate liturgy with them, condemning the massacre in his homily as a violation of human rights. According to the official government version of this incident, the deceased were members of an underground political military organization and had opened fire on the National Guard. Other sources indicated that these campesinos, catechists trained at Los Naranjos, were taken violently from their homes, brutalized, tortured, and killed.

Los Naranjos was a center for the evangelization and catechesis of the campesinos. It was already established by the time Romero arrived in Santiago, and it was no surprise that he was dubious of and anxious about the center's theology. Yet, he felt it had some value because it offered pastoral activities beyond the weekly liturgy and routine dispensing of sacraments, the usual extent of pastoral service throughout the diocese. Romero, however, was not pleased with what he interpreted as the political overtones associated with the center's evangelical activities; he also knew the government regarded it as subversive. He was aware that the Papal Nuncio was suspicious of the political tone of the center's mission and of the Passionist priest, Fr. Juan Macho, who was the center's director. The Nuncio wanted Romero to take some action, preferably to close the center.

Still unable to see beyond his own prejudices, Romero maintained that the military and government were not responsible for these atrocities. But he did protest to the Guard commander. Nevertheless, the priests of the diocese pressured him to publicly denounce—in compliance with Medellín's directives—the Las Tres Calles massacre. He did. But worrying that some of the victims may have been subversive, and fearful of potential embarrassment to the Church if this was so, he wrote a letter of protest to President Molina.

The massacre at Las Tres Calles enabled Romero to see a bit more clearly the source of violence in the country. His personal experience of the massacre helped him confront more directly the reality of the brutal military violence and its indiscriminate targeting of many innocent people. This situation contributed to the chipping away of Romero's emotional attachments to his powerful friends. But he still was not free enough to respond with the full authority of his office.

Perhaps what finally helped Romero recognize his political biases was when the military opened fire on unarmed students who were protesting the government's occupation of Santa Ana University on July 30, 1975. The fatalities numbered forty. In protest of this massacre, many groups, including priests, religious, and pastoral leaders, occupied the cathedral. Fr. Macho, the director of Los Naranjos, was among them.

This incident provoked Romero to action. Administratively, he addressed the center and its director. To gain clarity, he suspended functions at the center and called Bishop Marco Rene Revelo, who chaired the bishops' catechetical commission, to join him in a meeting with the priests who staffed Los Naranjos. The meeting was difficult for Romero because the priests accused him of obstinately opposing the policies of Medellín and obstructing their efforts to implement Medellín's directives. Romero and Revelo maintained that the training at the center was manipulating Medellín directives for political purposes.

To resolve the situation, Romero suggested that the courses offered by the center be taught by their teachers but take place in the parishes where the campesinos lived. The compromise would alleviate some of the intensity of indoctrination for the campesinos and would let Romero and the parish priests observe the full process. Romero was emphatic about changes he wanted at the center—"more attention to the social teaching of the Church, less political ideology; more importance of the Eucharist, less liberationist indoctrination; fewer songs of protest, more piety and prayer."[30] Romero named a new director for the center who worked more closely with him than Fr. Macho had previously done.

The incident also led Romero to a serious study of the Medellín documents—while simultaneously studying *On Evangelization in the Modern World*. In the encyclical, Romero was surprised to find papal affirmation of the more radical thinking taking place in his diocese. He found there that the Church's mission of evangelization, if it is to be authentic, must be concerned with the material needs of all people and engaged in the struggle for human liberation from forces which contribute to the oppression of human beings. The document also affirmed base communities as an important component in the evangelization process.[31] Romero came to see the apostolic exhortation as a key source of inspiration for the Medellín documents. He acknowledged he had not previously understood Medellín and that he had been reacting based on the distortions of its contents in his own thinking.

Romero's ideas and positions were shifting. As Bishop, he came closer to the brutality of El Salvador's military. His own experience with psychological intervention offered him a new lens with which to place human limitations in perspective, complementing his theological framework of sin and grace. Romero's life experience as priest and Ordinary, the theology and direction of Vatican II and Medellín, the growing threat of an increasingly violent repression and destructive civil war, and escalating persecution of Christians active in the struggle for social justice conspired to chip away his former assumptions.

As all this whirled around him, interiorly Romero seemed to have become more understanding and supportive of his priests and protective of the defenseless people under his care. Gradually exposed to life struggles from the perspective of the poor, Romero began to recognize the truth of the poverty, suffering, and repression around him, and the deeply Christian motives of so many of those struggling for a better world. Certainly, Romero's personal experience, psychological development, and spiritual conversion prepared him to assume leadership as Archbishop of El Salvador.

Archbishop Chávez presided over the Church of El Salvador from 1939 until 1977. Oscar Romero succeeded him as the sixth Archbishop on February 22, 1977. He was widely believed to be the firm conservative endorsed by the oligarchs and ecclesial right who was expected to rein in politicized priests, squelch liberation theology, and bring order to the archdiocese. Ambassador Robert White noted, as did many, that, Romero was not the favored candidate for the position. Bishop Rivera y Damas, who succeeded Romero in 1980, had also been an auxiliary bishop to Chávez since 1960. He was the favored candidate by more progressive elements in the Church and proved to have a very impressive record of intellectual excellence and commitment to social change.[32]

During his tenure as Archbishop, Romero underwent an unanticipated change that, since he was the official head of the Church in El Salvador, had profound implications for the image of the whole Church. The most dramatic factor that appears to have crystallized Romero's radical conversion was the assassination of Rutilio Grande. While his struggle with Grande's assassination had a profound impact on him, Romero's struggle born of the tension with opposing Salvadoran Bishops, the renewal of his Christology, and the acceptance of his own potential martyrdom contributed to complete his conversion.

Jesuit Rutilio Grande was a friend whom Romero respected and admired. A former teacher and rector of the national seminary, Grande was responsible for the spiritual formation of two generations of Salvadoran clergy and was perhaps the most respected priest in the archdiocese. Grande "was partially responsible for changing the entire Jesuit philosophy in Central America with his 'primary and fundamental option' for the poor which envisaged 'a pastoral team working in either rural areas or in a slum to promote Christian conscientization.'"[33]

In 1972, Grande assumed the pastorate of a rural parish in Aguilares working with a team of young Jesuits among thirty thousand campesinos, forming "delegates of the Word," preaching a gospel of justice, and administering the sacraments. The mere fact that the peasants were organizing threatened the landowners who accused the Jesuits of being subversives and Communists.

On Saturday afternoon, March 12, 1977, en route to El Paisnal, Grande, seventy-two-year-old Manuel Solorzano, and sixteen-year-old Nelson Rutilio Lemus were ambushed and murdered by the Salvadoran military. Rodolfo Cardenal identifies the suspected gunman as Benito Estrada and gives a fairly complete account of Grande's murder. He also notes that, on March 21, 1985, Col. Roberto Santibáñez, a former colonel of the Salvadoran Army, declared in a press conference in Washington, DC, that one assassin was Juan Garay Flores, a member of a group of officers that had trained at the International Police Academy in Washington with Major Roberto D'Aubuisson and Santibáñez himself.[34] Three other children were also in the car, but their lives were spared and they ran to safety.

Having received the news, Romero left San Salvador immediately and arrived in Aguilares at 10:00 PM. He spent hours praying beside Grande's body in the presence of the other corpses wrapped in white sheets. Afterwards, Romero concelebrated a liturgy with the priests and people of the Aguilares church. Responding to this heinous crime, Romero acted collaboratively and swiftly. He wrote a firm letter to President Molina demanding an investigation into the assassination, excommunicated those responsible for the murders, and refused to participate in forthcoming government ceremonies until the murderers were brought to justice. In collaboration with the Jesuit provincial, César Jerez, and other advisors, Romero decided there would be only one Mass on Sunday, March 20th, on the steps of the diocesan cathedral as a communal expression of mourning and in protest of Grande's murder.

Romero's biographers agree that the death of Rutilio Grande was the singular event that crystallized Romero's conversion. Ignacio Martín-Baró noted Romero's own recognition of how Grande's death affected him. "He himself often recalled that it was the blood of Fr. Grande that brought on a profound spiritual crisis that he resolved through an increasing identification with the God of Jesus, who lived in the poor of El Salvador."[35]

Martín-Baró also described how Grande's death served to expose truth for Romero:

> This situation represented an unmasking of the true nature of
> this particular conception of religion, behind which the sin-
> fulness of oppressive structures, and in the end, the idolatry
> of wealth and private property, was hidden. This unmasking
> was so complete that Monseñor recognized with complete
> confidence the fallacious nature of official explanations.
> Those explanations, he saw, promised an investigation of Ru-
> tilio's death, but hid those responsible, pretended to affirm a
> desire for justice, but continued the violence against anyone
> who followed Rutilio's path, or simply showed a religious
> identification with him.[36]

Romero's response to the assassination shocked the Church in El Salvador to its foundation, and marked the beginning of a sustained, systematic, and overt persecution of the progressive Church by the military.

The White Warriors Union, a right-wing vigilante group, announced that they would murder the remaining forty-seven Jesuits if
they did not leave the country by July 21, 1977. The Jesuit University
of San Salvador was bombed six times and the Union warned parents
that any student attending a Jesuit school might be killed. But the Salvadoran oligarchy underestimated the power of the Jesuits. From Rome,
the Jesuit Superior General Pedro Arrupe warned, "They may end up
as martyrs, but my priests are not going to leave (El Salvador), because
they are with the people."

Spokesman for the Archdiocese of San Salvador, Fr. Víctor
Guevara, further stated, "If we have to die for the truth, to defend the
poor, human rights, and justice, we believe that our Lord will give us
sufficient strength to accept the consequences." Further, the Jesuit sec-
ond-in-command, Vincent O'Keefe, warned the government of El Salvador that they would be excommunicated if they did not cease the
persecution of the Church. Penny Lernoux recounts, "As if by magic,
President Romero (no relation to the Archbishop) was suddenly stricken
with concern for the country's Jesuits, and on the day set by the White
Warriors for them to leave the country, government troops were on hand
to protect the Jesuit schools and seminary."[37] El Salvador's government
did not anticipate the greater activity and force of the converted Church,
which wielded such power and influence.

Romero grieved the death of his friend, Rutilio. He also grieved
the disharmony among the country's bishops due to their differing the-

ological and pastoral positions.[38] The Salvadoran Bishops' Conference was split between Archbishop Romero and Bishop Rivera y Damas on the one hand, and the four remaining prelates, Alvarez, Aparicio y Quintanilla, Barrera, and Revelo on the other. Although Romero inherited this division from Chávez, it was aggravated by the four bishops who bitterly opposed his movement to disengage the Church from any appearance of alliance with the state.

The more Romero insisted that the Church was under persecution, citing increasing numbers of assassinations, the more adamantly the four denied any such persecution, insisting that the sources of conflict were disobedient and subversive clergy and religious, the Jesuits who propagated Marxist ideologies among the people, and Archbishop Romero himself, whom they accused of being the Jesuits' puppet, unable to control politicized priests in his archdiocese. Romero's decision to celebrate a single liturgy and close diocesan schools for three days—to mourn the death of Grande and to offer the people an opportunity to express their outrage—further widened the discord.

The opposing bishops carried their animosity into the public arena, publishing newspaper articles criticizing Romero's pastoral plan and questioning his authority at every turn. They wrote letters to Cardinal Sabastiano Baggio, Prefect for the Congregation of Bishops in Rome, distorting Romero's motives, accusing him of inciting military repression against the people, and compromising the Church and its mission in El Salvador.

After only a month as Archbishop, Romero was summoned to Rome by Cardinal Baggio. On March 26, 1977 he met with Baggio to brief him on the situation in El Salvador and to discuss the allegations made by the bishops. Those allegations asserted that "Romero surrounded himself with untrustworthy priests who flattered him and made him think that he was a prophet. He disappointed those who backed his appointment expecting serenity and prudence. He allowed priests to become politicized. He marginalized Bishop Marco René Revelo, who had been assigned as auxiliary in San Salvador. He denied the Nuncio the use of the cathedral for a quasi-diplomatic function with government officials causing 'an almost irreparable scandal.' He was criticized for homilies that were very long and very concrete, although they were found to be without doctrinal error. Baggio was 'terrified' to think of the sort of priests who would emerge from the seminary."[39]

Romero also met with Cardinal Agostino Casaroli, secretary of the Council for Public Affairs of the Church, to explain the situation in El Salvador and to clarify and defend his pastoral decisions.

Lastly, he met with Pope Paul VI in a private audience to give an account of his stewardship. He explained that what he was doing in his archdiocese was trying to put into practice what Vatican II, *On Evangelization in the Modern World*, Medellín, and Paul himself had taught. Romero accounted for his preaching which consisted of calling the people in his country to conversion, peace, and respect for human rights. He also indicated disappointment that the misinformation sent by some of the Salvadoran bishops and the Papal Nuncio to Cardinals Baggio and Casaroli seemed to have cast Romero in a dubious light.

Romero wrote in his *Diary*, "It seems that a negative judgment prevails that coincides exactly with that of the most powerful forces that there, in my archdiocese, try to stop and discredit my apostolic effort." Romero reassured the Holy Father, "You can be sure of my faithfulness to you as the Successor of Peter and of my unconditional allegiance to the magisterium." The Pope took both of Romero's hands in his and urged him with a voice of affirmation, "Courage. You are the one in charge!"[40] After the disheartening experience with Baggio and Casaroli, Paul VI's affirmation was a source of encouragement and support that sustained Romero's vision and ministry.

Romero experienced deep heartache because of the opposing bishops' refusal to acknowledge that the Church was being persecuted. He grieved over their public opposition to his authority. An incident of March 1978 illustrates the magnitude and intensity of their opposition— and his pain.

A group of clergy and religious authored an open letter of exhortation to the Papal Nuncio holding Bishop Gerada accountable for openly supporting a repressive and unjust government and for publicly opposing Romero's pastoral plan which he had developed in communion with the clergy and lay apostolic movements.[41] Infuriated, the Nuncio sent a copy of the letter to the Bishops' Conference as a top priority item for their March 15th meeting.

Bishop Aparicio reacted by announcing the immediate suspension of ten priests from the San Vincente diocese who had signed the letter. He, along with Barrera, Alvarez, and Revelo were indignant and called an emergency meeting to secure approval of their statement against the open letter. The statement was entitled, "Condemnatory Statement of the Bishops' Conference of El Salvador in Regard to a Letter Sent to His Excellency, the Apostolic Nuncio, and Statement of Allegiance to the Representative of the Holy Father, Pope Paul VI." They condemned:

> with all the energy of our mission as pastors this haughty and irreverent posture as unjust, anti-evangelical, and disrespectful of the Holy See in the person of the Supreme Pontiff's representative. They rejected the charges against Gerada and deplored "the effrontery of publishing the letter in the press of the country in violation of canon law." The zeal of many of the persons who signed the letter "does not agree with the witness of their lives as Christians, ecclesiastics, or religious." The bishops pledged their fidelity to the Nuncio and the Pope and prayed for "these children who have caused so much sorrow."[42]

Romero attended the meeting against his better judgment if only to support the ten priests who were denied due process. His diary entry for that day captures the depth of his anguish:

> The Bishops' Conference of El Salvador called an urgent meeting. My first impulse was not to go, since the invitation arrived only on Monday morning. I was advised to go, however, and I did because it had to do with the matter of the priests to the Nuncio, and I could, therefore, by going give an opinion in defense of the priests.
>
> As I expected, when I arrived at the meeting, I found everything had already been decided prior to the meeting. Bishop Rivera's telegram—saying that he could not come because of a meeting in Guatemala and asking them to wait since the topic required a meeting at which all the bishops would be present—was not heeded, even though I seconded Bishop [Arturo] Rivera's request. With the vote, naturally, four bishops against my one vote, the meeting was held. I also protested that the document to be discussed had been prepared in advance. They told me that there was always a draft document presented, but I could see that it was not just

a draft, since it was not discussed. Rather they began right away to sign it in spite of my giving reasons against it.

My reasons were these: The priests have written a letter to the Nuncio, so what should happen now is that the Nuncio should invite the priests to talk with him. Another reason is that the document of the bishops against the priests accuses them of offending the Holy See. I made a distinction between the Holy See—mainly the person of the Pope with whom these priests feel themselves united in the faith—and the person of the Nuncio who represents the Pope but does not always do so effectively. In order to show this, I pointed out some things that have made the Nuncio an unpopular figure here and in Guatemala. Another reason is that the document written by the priests should itself be analyzed, not just to criticize the composition or the inadequacy of expression, but rather to see concretely what the Nuncio has done to cause them to say that his witness is less than Christian. The priests should not be accused without a hearing, and it seems to me that publishing this document will only foment division among the bishops since I would not agree to sign it.

In spite of these reasons, the document was already being passed around so that the four bishops could sign it: Bishop Aparicio, president of the Conference; Bishop Barrera, bishop of Santa Ana; Bishop Alvarez, bishop of San Miguel; and Bishop Revelo, auxiliary bishop of San Salvador.

The document was approved, and I was subjected to many false accusations by the other bishops. I was told that my preaching is subversive, violent; that my priests provoke a climate of violence among the peasants; and that we should not complain about the abuses that the authorities are committing. The archdiocese was accused of interfering in the other dioceses, causing division among the priests and pastoral unrest in other dioceses. The archdiocese was accused of sowing confusion in the seminary, and they said that it was urgent that the archdiocesan offices leave the building of the San José de la Montaña Seminary. And other calumnious and false accusations to which I prefer not to respond.

It has been a bitter day because of this event and I lament that the division among the bishops will be worsened with this step, which seems to me not to be very wise.[43]

Romero sustained yet another painful humiliation and disappointment. In December, Gerada informed him that Cardinal Baggio assigned Bishop Antonio Quarracino of Avellaneda, Argentina as apostolic visitor to San Salvador. This was a significant blow because the appointment indicated that Rome was questioning Romero's leadership. Romero respectfully cooperated and provided Quarracino with unbiased studies of the situation in the country and the archdiocese, correspondence about Romero's turbulent relationship with his auxiliary, Bishop Revelo, statistics and documentation on violations of human rights, letters of solidarity received by the Archbishop, press clippings on the division among the bishops of the country, all the bulletins and statements published by the archdiocese under Romero, and transcripts of his homilies. Interestingly enough, Romero did not hear anything official about Quarracino's visit until his trip to Rome in April 1979.

Romero wrote in advance of this trip requesting appointments with Cardinal Baggio and Pope John Paul II to update them on his situation. The Vatican secretaries made it very difficult for him to obtain those appointments. Romero wrote of those frustrating days:

> I am still very concerned about the attitude they show to the pastor of a diocese, considering that I asked for this audience some time ago. They keep delaying the response, and I am afraid that they are not going to grant the audience because there are many bishops in *ad limina* visits. And there are also other reasons they could give preference to other requests.
>
> I have put it in God's hands. I told him that I have done everything in my power and that, in spite of everything, I believe in and love the Holy Church, and with his grace, I will always be faithful to the Holy See, to the teaching of the Pope; and that I understand the human, limited, defective part of his Holy Church, which is the instrument of the salvation of humankind and which I want to serve without any reservations.[44]

Romero finally received an audience with Pope John Paul II on Monday, May 7, 1979, but left the meeting disappointed because he recognized how Gerada, Quarracino, and the opposing Salvadoran Bishops' letters had misinformed the Pope. He was also discouraged to think

that the Pope was planning to appoint an administrator for the archdiocese. These combined to heighten his sense of disillusionment, a normal
response for any person. Yet, for Romero, the sense of scandal may have
been intensified because of his perfectionist self-criticism and the
canonical-administrative inference of questioning a bishop's judgment,
which would lead the Vatican to possibly appoint a diocesan administrator. Romero's entry regarding this papal audience reflects the depth
of his disappointment and his insight into ecclesial politics:

> He [Pope John Paul II] said the unity of the bishops is very
> important. Recalling his time as a pastor in Poland, he said
> that keeping the bishops unified was the main problem.
> Again, I clarified, telling him that this is also something that
> I want very much, but that I was aware that unity cannot be
> pretended. Rather, it must be based on the Gospel and the
> truth.
>
> He referred to the report on the apostolic visitation of
> Bishop Quarracino. He realized that the situation was an ex-
> tremely delicate one, and he had recommended that, to re-
> solve the deficiencies in the pastoral work and the lack of
> harmony among the bishops, an apostolic administrator *sede
> plena* be appointed.
>
> And I left, pleased by the meeting, but worried to see
> how much the negative reports of my pastoral work had in-
> fluenced him, although deep down I remembered that he had
> recommended "courage and boldness, but, at the same time,
> tempered with the necessary prudence and balance." Al-
> though I did not feel completely satisfied with the meeting, I
> think that the audience and our conversation were very useful
> because he was very frank. I have learned that one cannot ex-
> pect always to get complete approval and that it is more use-
> ful to hear criticism that can be used to improve our work.[45]

Romero returned to El Salvador discontented but not deterred
by Vatican politics. The Vatican, in a last attempt to unify the Salvadoran
bishops, appointed Archbishop Lajos Kada, papal nuncio from Costa
Rica as apostolic administrator for El Salvador. Whether or not the Vatican actually intended to unify the bishops is debatable; accommodating
the Salvadoran and United States governments may have influenced

their position. Archbishop Kada showed no sympathy for Romero. He came to San Salvador on March 11, 1980 to review the situation. But his assignment was terminated shortly after Romero's assassination, just two weeks later.

The public contempt for the bishops who opposed him was demonstrated at Romero's wake and funeral and is evidence of the understanding the people had of Romero's struggle with the opposing bishops and the Papal Nuncio:

> Hostile remarks from bystanders, however, had greeted Bishop Aparicio on Tuesday in the basilica when he came to view Romero's body. During the week a group of priests, nuns, and grass-roots ecclesial community members began a fast in the cathedral and hung a large banner over the entrance proclaiming that Aparicio, Revelo, Alvarez, Freddy Delgado, the junta, and the United States ambassador should stay away. Monseñor Urioste, as acting head of the archdiocese, sent a trusted seminarian to demand that the banner be taken down. But the fasters refused, and in those hectic, busy, and tense days, further efforts to remove it were unsuccessful. It remained as a sign of the division of the Salvadoran church; of the Salvadoran bishops, only Rivera came to the funeral mass.[46]

Romero's disheartening experiences with the opposing bishops and Vatican officials was profoundly frustrating. Instead of finding understanding and support among his colleagues, they were the source of agony.

As bishop, ordained to preach and teach, his suffering—shared with the people and at the hands of his brother bishops and ecclesial hierarchy—and solidarity with his people deepened his courage and commitment to the Gospel. I attribute this to the formation of a new Christology that grew and guided Romero to his final days.

> People say that a Democratic Congressman from the United States, Tom Harkin, who was passing through El Salvador, went to Mass one Sunday at the Cathedral. The church was filled to overflowing.
>
> He was moved by the piety of all the poor people and by the archbishop's homily. But what really made an impression

on that gringo's heart was the lousy shape the Cathedral was
in.

It needed paint. It was only half-finished. It was full of
scaffolding and patches. Birds were flying around inside the
sanctuary, coming in through broken windows and out
through the open door frames with nonexistent doors.

"This church doesn't give a good impression," Harkin
lamented in broken Spanish. "Doesn't Monseñor Romero
take care of his most important church?"

"Monseñor Romero spends his energy taking care of others."

They told him that when Monseñor had become archbishop, he'd begun a plan to rebuild the Cathedral, but that
soon he'd changed his mind.

"This is not the most important thing," he said, convinced.

For Monseñor, people came first. And that's why he said
the Cathedral would remain that way: halfway done, as a
monument to the people who don't have a roof over their
heads or land to plant on, people who have neither bread nor
peace.[47]

Oscar Romero came to recognize the poor, suffering Christ in
the faces, lives, and circumstances of the people he called "my brothers
and sisters." His homilies, speeches, and pastoral letters indicate that
he began to see Christ incarnate in the suffering poor. As his Christology
shifted, so did his ecclesiology. In opting for the poor, Romero became
like Bartolomé de las Casas centuries before, a defender of God, a defender of the poor.[48]

At his academic investiture as a Doctor of Humanities, *Honoris
Causa*, given by the University of Louvain, Belgium, Romero articulated this development in his Christology, a shift that inspired the mission of the Church in El Salvador:

The Church has not only incarnated itself in the world of the
poor, giving them hope; it has also firmly committed itself to
their defense. The majority of the poor in our country are oppressed and repressed daily by economic and political structures. The terrible words spoken by the prophets of Israel
continue to be verified among us. Among us there are those

who would sell others for money, who sell a poor person for a pair of sandals; those who, in their mansions, pile up violence and plunder; those who crush the poor; those who make the kingdom of violence come closer as they lie upon their beds of ivory; those who join house to house, and field to field, until they occupy the whole land, and are the only ones there.

This defense of the poor in a world deep in conflict has occasioned something new in the recent history of our Church: persecution.

Real persecution has been directed against the poor, the body of Christ in history today. They, like Jesus, are the crucified, the persecuted servants of Yahweh. They are the ones who make up in their own bodies that which is lacking in the passion of Christ. And for that reason when the Church has organized and united itself around the hopes and the anxieties of the poor it has incurred the same fate as that of Jesus and of the poor: persecution.[49]

Romero's compassion increased as he struggled to listen to heartbreaking stories of widows, mothers, and daughters as they described episodes of fathers, husbands, brothers, and sons taken from their homes, tortured, mutilated, or killed in front of them, or abducted in the middle of the night, never to be heard from again. He listened to accounts of women brutally gang-raped by soldiers and pregnant women whose breasts were cut off or whose bellies were cut open and the infants ripped from their bodies, then used as target practice. He listened to campesinos tell how the military decimated their entire village with fire to terrify them, displacing them in the mountains. For Jon Sobrino, people knew their only recourse was Romero whom they trusted to advocate for them. "It was not that they came to him simply as a friend, seeking consolation. They came to him as a protector who was in duty bound to put the full weight of his episcopal authority at the service of the poor and oppressed."[50]

Exposing himself to the suffering around him also contributed to the shift in his theology. It was no mere coincidence. The influence of Vatican II and liberation theology enabled Romero to see Christ more visibly in those who participated in the paschal mystery through their own baptism, suffering, and martyrdom. It is no wonder then, that in his first pastoral letter as Archbishop, "The Easter Church," Romero developed the Second Vatican Council's theme of the paschal mystery as a paradigm for the Church and its mission. He described the Church in El Salvador as experiencing its own "paschal hour," that final moment of transformation on the cross, that final passing from death to life. It was also, he pointed out, a time of the superabundant power of faith, hope, and love of the risen Christ. In that letter, Romero wrote, "The Church is the body of Christ. Through baptism, all those who belong to it live out that paschal tension, that 'passage' from death to life, that 'crossing over' that never ends and is called conversion, that continual demand upon us to destroy whatever is sin and to bring into being ever more powerfully all that is life, renewal, holiness, justice."[51]

Awakened to Christ incarnated in the people, Romero revealed a new pastoral aspect of his vocation as Archbishop: protector of the defenseless. This role seemed to have rounded out his ministry and given him deep joy: "With people such as this, it is not difficult to be a Good Shepherd. These are people who impel to service those who have been called to defend their rights and to be their voice. For me, even more than a service that has merited such generous praise, it is a duty that fills me with profound satisfaction."[52]

Romero's renewed Christology and theology influenced his spirituality. No longer was there a separation between serving God and serving the people. The two converged, and Romero came to identify serving God with serving the poor. This conviction seemed to revive his passion as he committed himself resolutely to use the authority of his office to bring about the reign of God in El Salvador. With this vision, Romero, claiming to speak on behalf of the Archdiocese, opted for the poor and pointed the Church in a new direction. Such a bold move, Romero already knew, would one day be sealed with his own blood.

Archbishop Romero lived knowing he was marked for elimination. Since the Salvadoran government and the opposing bishops contributed to persecuting the Church, he celebrated the martyrdom of his people and priests. In the funeral homily for Fr. Rafael Palacios, Romero affirmed the solemn dignity martyrs share with Christ: "The priesthood in our diocese can bear the seal of Jesus: 'If they persecuted me, they will also persecute you.' We can present along with the blood of teachers, of laborers, of peasants, the blood of our priests. This is communion in love. It would be sad, if in a country where murder is being committed so horribly, we were not to find priests also among the victims! They are a testimony of a Church incarnated in the problems of the people."[53]

Romero received so many death threats in the mail that at one point he instructed his secretaries to stop passing them on to him. As they increased, however, and the violence escalated, Romero began to consider seriously his own assassination. His outlook became more somber when the nuncio in Costa Rica advised him of the danger of threats against him and he told him he should be careful. The following day, in his homily, Romero said,

> I hope that this call of the Church will not further harden the hearts of the oligarchs but will move them to conversion. Let them share what they are and have. Let them not keep on silencing with violence the voice of those of us who are trying to achieve a more just sharing of the power and wealth of our country. I speak in the first person, because this week I received notice that I am on the list of those who are to be eliminated next week. But let it be known that no one can any longer kill the voice of justice.[54]

Scheduled to leave for Guatemala to make his annual retreat, Romero and a group of priests were persuaded by archdiocesan officials to modify their plans and not leave the country—for security purposes. They went to the Finca Lourdes House, run by the Passionist Sisters, and Fr. Fabián Amaya led the retreat. Romero's Jesuit confessor and spiritual director, Fr. Secundo Azcue, visited Romero during this retreat and subsequently reflected on the depth of Romero's struggle. Azcue's interpretation offers theological insight into Romero's experience: "I dare to consider this last retreat of his as prayer in the garden. Archbishop Romero foresaw his very probable and imminent death. He felt terror as did Jesus in the garden. But he did not leave his post and his duty, ready to drink the chalice that the Father might give him to drink."[55]

Romero recorded his experience of the same meeting with Azcue, noting his fears about death. He wrote,

> I find it hard to accept a violent death, which in these circumstances is very possible. The nuncio to Costa Rica even warned me of imminent dangers I would face this week. Father gave me strength by telling me that my disposition should be to give my life for God, whatever might be the end of my life. The circumstances yet unknown will be lived through with God's grace. God assisted the martyrs, and if it is necessary, I will feel him very close when I offer him my last breath. More important than the moment of death is giving him all of life and living for him.[56]

One significant meditation exercise during that week had been on the reign of God and the following of Christ, from the *Spiritual Exercises*. Following his prayer, Romero composed his consecration based on the offering Ignatius prescribes for the retreatant.

> Thus do I express my consecration to the heart of Jesus, who was ever a source of inspiration and joy in my life. Thus also I place under his loving providence all my life and I accept with faith in him my death, however hard it may be. I do not want to express an intention to him, such as that my death be for my country's peace or our Church's flourishing. Christ's heart will know how to direct it to the purpose he wishes. For me to be happy and confident, it is sufficient to know with assurance that in him is my life and my death, that in spite of my sins I have placed my trust in him and I will not be confounded, and others will continue with greater wisdom and holiness the works of the Church and the nation.[57]

Romero's anxiety persisted even though he made his offering to God and was confident in God's grace. Roberto Cuéllar offers a glimpse of the terror Romero lived with:

> After the assassination of Mario Zamora, the governing junta did nothing to investigate, but it did announce that it had discovered a list of people who were threatened with death. The first person on that list was Mario Zamora, and the second was Monseñor Romero. Monseñor called some of us to an urgent meeting.
>   "Did you hear the news? I'm the next one . . ."

We recommended that he be calm, that he be prudent, and that he take care of himself. Everyone had the same advice for him: "Don't go anywhere this weekend. Stay here. Prepare your homily. Stay calm. All of this is very new. Let's wait and see what happens . . ."

He listened to us, nodding his agreement. At the end, he finally came out with a "but . . ."

"But I've been invited to visit the community of Sonzacate . . ."

"You're going to have to let that idea go. How can you think of going so far away at a time like this?"

We insisted he should not even consider going and that he should send his regrets.

That same night, all of us and a few more came back to have a working dinner at the *hospitalito*. By 8:00 PM, he still hadn't shown up. All of us were eating dinner thinking the same thing: the man had gone to Sonzacate.

"Why do we even bother to give him advice? He doesn't do anything we say!"

When it was really late and several of the people had already gone home, Monseñor arrived, walking with defiant strides and an angry face. He knew we were the angry ones, but he didn't say anything. People turned in their reports for the week and there was hardly any conversation. The whole meeting lasted less than 15 minutes.

Everyone else left, and I was the only one there, chatting with the sisters. Monseñor approached me.

"Are you angry, too?" he said.

"Frankly Monseñor, we talked about it all this morning, but you refuse to listen to what people tell you."

"It's my work. It's my job. . . . They called me from that community of Sonzacate, and how could I tell them no? Besides, don't you argue with me! You're the ones responsible for this."

"We are? Responsible for what?"

"For making me afraid. After talking to you, I started to see assassins in places where there were only pigeons!"

It wasn't until then that I realized that he had fear painted all over his face. It wasn't anger, it was fear!

"What happened? Tell me . . ."

We sat down. He wanted to talk.

"Roberto, today I was really at the breaking point!"

"What happened?"

"Well, we were celebrating Mass in an open field in front of the church because there were so many people that I had to take the altar outside. Up until then, everything was fine, but when the offertory started and I was lifting the bread, I saw two men climbing up the bell tower of the church. Step by step, just climbing. I froze! I was thinking, 'what are they doing? They're going up there to kill me. They're going to get their aim just right and . . .' and right away I thought about Moreno and all of you guys. 'They warned me!' I thought. I was praying, and counting the steps my assassins had left to climb."

"What happened when they got to the top?"

"I saw them doing something, but I couldn't tell what, and I started shaking. And believe it or not, Roberto, I even heard the shot being fired!"

He was sweating now, as he talked openly about his fear.

"Later, I asked about it, and they told me that those 'killers' were probably a couple of kids who usually climb the bell towers to get the pigeons out from under the eves."[58]

There was a definite shift in Romero's soteriology. The graces he received, peace and calm, fruits of his sustained struggle, are evident in the interview he gave two weeks prior to his assassination.

I have often been threatened with death. I must tell you, as a Christian, I do not believe in death without resurrection. If I am killed, I shall arise in the Salvadoran people. I say so without boasting, with the greatest humility.

As a pastor, I am obliged by divine mandate to give my life for those I love—for all Salvadorans, even for those who may be going to kill me. If the threats are carried out, from this moment I offer my blood to God for the redemption and for the resurrection of El Salvador.

Martyrdom is a grace of God that I do not believe I deserve. But if God accepts the sacrifice of my life, let my blood be a seed of freedom and the sign that hope will soon be a reality. Let my death, if it is accepted by God, be for my people's liberation and as a witness of hope in the future.

You may say, if they succeed in killing me, that I pardon and bless those who do it. Would, indeed, that they might be convinced that they will waste their time. A bishop will die, but God's Church, which is the people, will never perish.[59]

In 1943, Romero had asked himself the question: "How far can a soul ascend if it lets itself be entirely possessed by God?" The witness of his conversion and the transformation of his life lead me to believe this question animated and directed his spiritual life. Indeed, it led him to accept, in this final phase of his archepiscopacy, God's call to prophetic leadership and martyrdom. Based on a conversation with Dr. Jorge Lara-Braud two days before his murder, Romero found the answer to that lifelong question. Lara-Braud wrote,

There was a full moon. A little breeze gave some relief to the heat of the day's work. We were coming back exhausted from a busy day, a day full of visits to the communities. We were headed back to San Salvador. Barraza was driving, and I was sitting in back with Monseñor. I was leaving the country the next day. It was the last time I would see him, and perhaps that's why I dared to ask him:

"Monseñor, I've heard many people asking you to take care of yourself. Have the threats increased?"

"Yes, they have. Everyday there are more, and I take them very seriously . . ."

He was quiet for a few moments. I felt a kind of air of nostalgia come over him. He leaned his head back, half-closed his eyes and said to me:

"I'll tell you the truth, Doctor: I don't want to die. At least not now. I've never had so much love for life! And honestly, I don't think I was meant to be a martyr. I don't feel that calling. Of course, if that's what God asks of me, then there is nothing I can do. I only ask that the circumstances of my death not leave any doubt as to what my true vocation is: to serve God and to serve the people. But I don't want to die now. I want a little more time."[60]

Oscar Arnulfo Romero, sixth Archbishop of El Salvador, was assassinated while celebrating the Paschal Sacrifice, on March 24, 1980. Decades later, contemporary Christians in general and Catholics in particular, are left to ponder what Romero's amazing life and generous death teach us about contemporary discipleship. One way to understand discipleship and explain what happened to Romero is through developing a conception of conversion as a response to grace— a rich and real process which generates growth into the likeness of the Son of God. Such transformation is two-pronged: growth toward human authenticity and growth toward deeper intimacy with the Triune God (rather than simply a movement out of sin). It is to this process of conversion, interpreted through the pastoral theology of Irenaeus of Lyons, that I now turn.

CHAPTER 2

THEOLOGICAL RESOURCE:
IRENAEUS OF LYONS

In Romero's pondering, "I've been thinking of how far a soul can ascend if it lets itself be possessed entirely by God," a dynamic, progressive spirituality is implied. Most categories of Western Christian spirituality have inherited distortions from an overemphasis on sin most evident in Augustine's framework, from failure to address the whole life cycle, and from an insufficient sensitivity to the complexities of internal psychodynamics as addressed in the modern discourses of psychology and psychoanalysis.

Reading the pastoral theologian Irenaeus of Lyons from the second century, I found inspiration for another approach to spirituality which emphasizes grace, frames spirituality in developmental terms, and suggests a more inclusive, holistic approach—including lifelong personal struggles with the wounds incurred in life as well as blessings yet to be developed.

Inspired by Irenaeus, my approach to articulating a contemporary spirituality that is real and meaningful is based on his theology. In this chapter, I will probe his resources for insights, clues, and sensibilities that resonate with my concerns about the promising possibilities for renewal as called for in the encyclical *Lumen Gentium*.

While Irenaeus offers a fresh way to consider Christian spirituality, I recognize that there are many important issues involved in interpreting a figure across time and cultural distance. These would rightly be addressed in a more intensive and focused study of Irenaeus. My purpose is more modest, however. I am beginning a dialogue with Irenaeus in the quest for insights to reframe spirituality in a more holistic, comprehensive, and developmental way. I will ground that dialogue in Irenaeus's anthropology and soteriology, suggesting that his framework offers a new paradigm for understanding conversion in a more integrative and positive light.

Irenaeus's anthropology interprets a person in terms of a totality. The human person is created in the image of God and is called to grow into the likeness of the Son of God. Irenaeus's soteriology maintains that human beings are created with a capacity to receive God and can gradually grow in intimacy with the Triune God. According to Irenaeus, grace is mediated through life experiences, and our response to grace is what propels us further into union with God. As I interpret Irenaeus, he places human and spiritual development at the heart of his soteriology.

Yes, we are saved because we share in the "recapitulation" of Christ. By that he means the fresh start given the human race by Christ whose victorious struggle gave humanity a new foundation and regained the righteousness lost by Adam and Eve. But in concert with that, we are saved also through our personal and communal daily struggles to be faithful to grace. Irenaeus's anthropology and soteriology therefore forms the theological framework for a spirituality of conversion that emphasizes the transforming power of grace operative primarily within the context of our blessed and wounded humanity.

Irenaean teleological anthropology is best understood within the broader context of his systematic theology. Although I am constrained by the limits of my topic, and am not able to pursue a thorough presentation of the Irenaean synthesis, it is important to sketch his doctrines of God and the Trinity. To that end, I will first consider the importance Irenaeus gives to human beings created in the *image* of God. Second, I will consider his view of our *similitude* to the Creator, who, through the gift of free and rational choice, invites us to growth and responsibility. Third, I will attend to Irenaeus's developmental notion that humanity, although created in original innocence and ignorant of God, has the potential to mature in strength, knowledge, and experience of God. Finally, I will discuss Irenaeus's developmental notion of growth into the *likeness* of the Son of God.

Irenaeus's theology developed in dialogue with Scripture, particularly the Johannine corpus. Influenced by Greek philosophy, Irenaeus drew upon the Platonic distinction between Being and Becoming.[1] For him, only God exists independently. It follows that the uncreated God is absolutely free and stands alone in timeless eternity while the rest of creation is in a dynamic process of struggling to become. He explained the distinction:

> In this respect God differs from man, that God indeed makes, but man is made; and truly, He who makes is always the same; but that which is made must receive both beginning, and middle, and addition, and increase. God also is truly perfect in all things, Himself equal and similar to Himself, as He is all light, and all mind, and all substance, and the fount of all good; but man receives advancement and increase toward God. For God is always the same, so also man, when found in God, shall always go on toward God. For neither does God at any time cease to confer benefits upon or enrich man; nor does man cease from receiving benefits, and being enriched by God.[2]

Out of love and absolute goodness, God created humanity from nothing so that humanity might share in divinity. Since God is immediately present to creation and creation is in God's hands rather than separated from God in a hierarchal chain of being, creation is constituted with a capacity to receive and grow in God. According to Irenaeus, the two "hands" of God, the Word and Wisdom, are always involved in creation with God.[3] It is God who brings all things into being, and "makes them beautiful" when humanity cooperates with grace through docility to the Spirit and obedience to the Creator.

Irenaeus is visually oriented. He communicates in images, visions, and impressions. His writing incorporates two standards: truth and beauty, logic and aesthetics. "The demand that the created image should resemble the divine artist is the governing principle that orders the world. God must be allowed to draw out of himself the beautiful form of created things and the devising of the beautiful ordering of the world."[4]

Despite God's immediate presence to humanity, God's transcendence remains absolute, since God in Godself cannot be grasped in essence or comprehended entirely by human beings. Irenaeus insisted therefore that we use our powers of reason to be constantly aware of God's grandeur and diversity in the world around us because creation reveals the presence of God in a way that makes possible our human capacity to know God. Because we are limited and cannot take in God's glory all at once, the Triune God gradually and incessantly communicates Godself to us until we are finally taken up in our development toward God.

An Irenaean doctrine of God affirms that we are created in God and are in the process of struggling to grow toward union with God. This developmental process is possible because humans are created with a capacity to receive God and the freedom to respond or refrain from responding to the actuation of grace. The struggle that results from God's unrestricted call of grace and our finite ability to respond is *the* central dynamic in the process of conversion.

Irenaeus emphasized that the God who brought creation into existence is the God who created and who continues to create with the Word and the Spirit, each having distinct roles in the economy of salvation. So that we could enjoy participation in the life of God, God revealed Godself and elevates creation to God. For Irenaeus, it is through the Word and Wisdom that God becomes available and tangible to our finite human capacities to know and love God. It is through their touches and grasps that these two hands shape and mold us according to God's divine plan.

Irenaeus was preoccupied with how we know God and the ways in which each divine person participates in revealing God and divinizing humanity. This long developmental process originates with God and is culminated in seeing God face to face. For him, this "seeing" was not an inner seeing or some mystical vision, but rather a seeing with human eyesight, the visible God, Jesus, for those who did not live in the time of Jesus.

Irenaeus articulated this in terms of the economic Trinity: "For those who bear the Spirit of God are led to the Word, that is to the Son, while the Son presents them to the Father, and the Father furnishes incorruptibility. Thus without the Spirit it is not possible to see the Word of God, and without the Son one is not able to approach the Father, for the knowledge of the Father is the Son, and knowledge of the Son of God is through the Holy Spirit, according to the good pleasure of the Father, the Son administers the Father's will as He wills."[5]

For humans to grasp God's self-revelation, God communicates through our experience of being human. God's self-communication was accomplished most immediately in Jesus, who in the Incarnation reveals God who is now seen and heard. Jesus is God searching out God's own creation and carrying it home on God's own shoulders. Irenaeus emphasized Jesus' words, "The person who has seen me has seen the Father," (John 14:9) and acknowledged that the Word knows God, for the Son is what is visible of God, while God is what remains invisible of the Son.

For Irenaeus, the role of the Spirit is critical within the saving economy of God since the mission of the Spirit is to guide us toward salvation. Regarding each person's salvific journey, Irenaeus has us look to Jesus. At his baptism, the Spirit was graciously poured out on him and anointed him, and guided him into the wilderness of his own humanity where he had to discover for himself his own human authenticity and way to God. Irenaeus interpreted that what the Spirit began in Jesus was only the foretaste of what the Spirit would do in the life of future disciples. Arousing a desire for God and leading disciples through the mystery of fullness in Christ is the work of the Spirit who anoints, liberates, and deifies.

Irenaeus's pneumatology is intimately linked to his ecclesiology since the Church is where the living Spirit of God resides. He says, "Where there is the Church, there is the Spirit of God; and where the Spirit of God is, there is the Church, and all grace: for the Spirit is Truth."[6] For Irenaeus, there was no other way of ascent to God than through the Church. Terrance Tiessen formulates this intimate link: "Indeed, what the Church preaches is a faith ordered to the salvation of human beings. The gift of God, which is tradition delivered to the Church, was given for the purpose of bringing life to members of the Church. To the Church, God has given the Holy Spirit, who is the communion with Christ and the way of ascent to God. The Spirit is so identified with the Church that to be cut off from the Church is to be cut off from the life-giving Spirit (*AH* III.24.1).[7]

Irenaeus insisted that the Church is characterized by apostolicity, having an institutional character and a charismatic character.[8] The institutional dimension is the rich depository of truth, which Irenaeus classically identified by three criteria. First, the episcopacy, founded by the apostles and continued by their duly appointed successors, guarantees the validity of Church doctrine. In his view, the bishops handed over not only the faith or doctrine, but the *Church itself*. By that, he meant all those elements that make up the Church, including its doctrine and its original structure.[9] Second, the New Testament, written by the apostles, represented the authoritative and definitive witness to God's saving act in Jesus Christ.[10] Third, the "rule of truth," handed down by the apostles, provides a concise statement of the essentials of faith in the form of a creed.[11] For Irenaeus, these are found in all the churches, which are united in the Spirit.

Irenaeus defined the charismatic dimension of the Church as an assembly of disciples, who by adoption are gathered by the Son, and in whose midst God stands.[12] The Church of Irenaeus displayed an abundance of charisms. Yet, for him, the identifying charism of the community is love, present in the Church from the beginning: "[Love] is more precious than knowledge, more glorious than prophecy, and excels all the other gifts. Wherefore the Church does in every place, because of that love which she cherished toward God, send forward, throughout all time, a multitude of martyrs to the Father."[13]

Irenaeus saw the community as a means for mediating conversion. The Christian community shows, by teaching and example, how to grow toward God. Conversion is not private, nor are the graces received personal. The example of the martyrs and *master disciples* inspire nascent disciples and demonstrate concretely what it means to respond to grace. For Irenaeus, the martyrs—by their living and dying—demonstrated this charism of love, or true discipleship. In this way, through their commitment and example, they mediated the grace of conversion. Certainly, Irenaeus's ecclesiology can inspire a powerful new way of *being* Church today.

Irenaeus's ecclesiology flowed from his doctrine of the Trinity, and paved the way for his anthropology. He wrote, "By this arrangement, therefore, and these harmonies, and a sequence of this nature, man, a created and organized being, is rendered after the image and likeness of the uncreated God, the Father planning everything well and giving His commands, the Son carrying these into execution and performing the work of creating, and the Spirit nourishing and increasing (what is made), but man making progress day by day, and ascending toward the perfect, that is, approximating to the uncreated One. For the Uncreated is perfect, that is, God."[14]

God's benevolence bestows prevenient and incessant grace on humanity inviting us into participation in God, and only grace makes possible our response to God. As is apparent, Irenaeus's Christocentric anthropology suggests an understanding of the whole of human nature, both the constraints as well as the boundless potentialities inherent in us.

Irenaeus grounded his anthropology in Genesis. "Then God said, 'Let us make human beings in our image, after our own likeness'" (Gen. 1:6). This text provides the twofold foundation for Irenaeus's understanding that the human person is created in the image of the Son of God and is predisposed for transformation into the likeness of the Son of God. It is also the sum and summit of his soteriology. Given this, Irenaeus acknowledges profound respect for the dignity of the human body.

By situating the human person at the center of creation, Irenaeus placed great value on the *totality* of the human person. His anthropology reflected the Greek trichotomist scheme, maintaining that the fullness of the human person requires full development of body, soul, and spirit. The body is pure matter and its condition is to be animated. The soul is neither corruptible nor mortal, and is not the means of salvation. The spirit preserves and fashions humans, making progress into God's likeness possible. Irenaeus wrote,

> We do also hear many brethren in the Church, who . . . bring to light for the general benefit the hidden things of men, and declare the mysteries of God, whom also the apostle terms "spiritual," they being spiritual because they partake of the Spirit, and not because their flesh has been stripped off and taken away, and because they have become purely spiritual. For if anyone take away the substance of flesh, that is, of the handiwork of God, and understand that which is purely spiritual, such then would not be a spiritual man but would be the spirit of a man, or the Spirit of God. But when the spirit here blended with the soul is united to God's handiwork, the man is rendered spiritual and perfect because of the outpouring of the Spirit, and this is he who was made in the image and likeness of God.[15]

Irenaeus's esteem for the body is grounded in his understanding of the Incarnation. The flesh is the vehicle of Christ's saving act and is a vessel in and through which humans experience salvation. The Christ who is completely human saves the complete human being. Further, since human flesh has been nourished on the human body and blood of Christ and is the dwelling place of the Spirit, glory is in the human body of the Christian.

For Irenaeus, the Son of God became human for a twofold economic purpose. The first was to *accustom* humanity to God and God to humanity. "Being the Word of God who dwelt in man, He might *accustom* man to receive God, and God to dwell in man, according to the good pleasure of the Father."[16]

The theme of accustoming figures prominently in Irenaeus's soteriology. In the time between creation and the Incarnation, God accustomed Godself to humanity through the Patriarchs. God's people lived as strangers in the world and became accustomed to following the guidance of the Scripture. In the Incarnation, a new dimension of accustoming occurred. The Spirit's descent on the Son of God who became man enabled the Spirit to become accustomed to living in a human being to live and work among humanity. In Christ, humanity is able to see God, to contain God, to accustom itself to participate in God while God is accustomed to live in human beings.

The second reason the Son of God became human was to reveal God as visible and tangible. This reveals both God and the full dignity of the human person. In his often quoted statement, "God made Himself human, that humanity might become God," Irenaeus encapsulated his understanding of the nature, essence, and purpose of the Incarnation.[17] In the words of Vladimir Lossky, "The Fathers and Orthodox theologians have repeated Irenaeus's words in every century with the same emphasis, wishing to sum up in this striking sentence the very essence of Christianity: an ineffable descent of God to the ultimate limit of our fallen human condition, even unto death—a descent of God which opens to men a path of ascent, the unlimited vistas of the union of created beings with the Divinity."[18]

In Christ's humanity, limits are placed upon the infinite God that God might then become accessible to our finite powers of comprehension. Christ is the perfect image and likeness of God because, in his humanity, he established the paradigm for how a human being can be responsive to the creative touch of the Creator's fingers, a person vulnerable to and receptive of the transforming Spirit of God. Christ's obedience sets the perfect example of how we can discern and follow the presence and promptings of the same Spirit in our daily lives. Because of the Incarnation, one can more fully appreciate the importance Irenaeus gives to human beings created in the *image* of the Son of God.

The second dimension of Irenaeus's anthropology affirms that human beings are created in *similitude* to God. *Similitude* has two meanings for Irenaeus. The first refers to the similarity which human beings bear to God through the freedom and intelligence we possess. These enable us to perceive and engage in the purpose of God through the gift of free and rational choice. While Irenaeus maintained that the human person carries the image of the Son of God in the flesh, we are also similar to God in freedom. Humankind is free from the beginning because we are made in similitude to God who is free. For Irenaeus, while God created us in love and with freedom, the Creator, who is merciful and understanding of human nature, holds us accountable for the decisions we make. People are free to do good or evil, to accept or reject the gift of the Spirit who constantly invites us to divinization and maturity.

Similitude can also mean a growing into the likeness of the Son of God through obedience to the Spirit. The goal of the divine economy is to bring to perfection or wholeness the person being divinized. Human beings, created morally incomplete, have to grow in moral maturity and personal integrity. For Irenaeus, this maturation process is achieved through engaging in ethical and spiritual struggles, exercising freedom of choice, and taking responsibility for the consequences. Through repeated experiences of such struggles, a person gains through trial and error the knowledge of good and evil and the ability to discern and choose.

In the fourth book of *Against Heresies*, Irenaeus apportioned a notable section to freedom and the manner in which a person responsibly develops freedom. He addressed three interconnecting questions: Why did God make us free? Why were humans not created perfect from the beginning? Why must we exercise the knowledge of good and evil in the discernment process?

In answer to the first question, Irenaeus asserted that God created us with freedom because God is just. Those who are good by nature and not by choice could not value what they had won. On the other hand, those who struggle to achieve that which is valued can claim their hard-earned victory. In his own words, "The harder we strive, so much is it the more valuable; while so much the more valuable it is, so much the more should we esteem it."[19] Irenaeus insisted that even though God is merciful and compassionate, God's justice cannot be taken for granted. Key to Irenaeus is the sacredness and importance of human struggle in the process of developing responsible freedom.

Defending his position as to why God did not make humans perfect from creation, Irenaeus insisted that by definition a creature, who receives the beginning of existence from another, is inferior to the creator. The newly created are like infants who are not accustomed to exercising mature moral conduct. Adam's Fall is an example.

Irenaeus described Adam as "a child," "a little one," who was misled by the deceiver because his ability to discern was not yet developed. Adam's fall is an event that occurred in the childhood of the human race, an understandable lapse due to human weakness, ignorance, and immaturity. Irenaeus does not consider that human freedom was lost as a consequence of the Fall, but was merely "put on hold," until it was "recapitulated" by Christ. He affirms that the Fall appears not as something merely permitted by God, but almost directly willed, as something required for our development.

Irenaeus drew attention to the enslaved condition of humanity after the sin of Adam, and contrasts it with the recapitulation in Christ. Even with Christ's saving action, redeemed humanity still needs to struggle to grow into the fullness of the likeness of the Son of God. Moral, spiritual, and human maturity can only develop by responsibly exercising the gift of personal freedom.

So Irenaeus understood the Fall to be something required for human development. In this view, a "divinely appointed environment," which includes the coexistence of good and evil, is the context within which we can grow toward the attainment of the fullness of God's intentions for us. In order to choose the good, however, Irenaeus insisted that one has to exercise the innate human ability to know good and evil. To explain this, he used an analogy:

> For there is thus a surer and undoubted comprehension of matters submitted to us than the mere surmise arising from

an opinion regarding them. For just as the tongue receives experience of sweet and bitter by means of tasting, and the eye discriminates between black and white by means of vision, and the ear recognizes the distinctions of sounds by hearing; so also does the mind, receiving through the experience of both the knowledge of what is good, become more tenacious of its preservation, by acting in obedience to God. . . . But if anyone do shun the knowledge of both these kinds of things, and the twofold reception of knowledge, he unawares divests himself of the character of a human being.[20]

Since we possess this ability, Irenaeus would advocate that we exercise constant discernment between good and evil as a prelude to choosing the good. The spiritual discipline of discernment enables us to choose what is God's desire for us. Each choice for God transforms us a bit more into the likeness of the Son of God. As prayer increases our knowledge of and intimacy with God, discernment enhances and accompanies that knowledge made manifest in the realities of life.

The third dimension of Irenaeus's anthropology held that Adam and Eve, created innocent and ignorant, were not perfect from the beginning of creation. They were infants, inexperienced in the ways of God. God's glory, far too powerful for newly created humans to take in, is made accessible to us by the Spirit who enables us to increase in strength and understanding of God.[21] Our perfection is to be found in gaining closer proximity to the perfect God, in the sense that God's Spirit dwells in human beings,[22] and through the use of created things we can find our way, growing in maturity and finding immortality.[23] This is the dynamic process of "becoming"—that continuous creating sequence of transformation into the likeness of the Son of God that progresses into the eschaton. The whole concept of development is inherent in the creating act of God, a process that includes the whole created cosmos.[24]

Irenaeus illustrated this through Adam who, through the Spirit, possessed a likeness to God, but was nevertheless weak, and who, in his immaturity, lacked sufficient personal experience and knowledge of God. Had Adam been mature in relationship with God, he would have acknowledged the fact that he was a creature and God was his Maker, thus averting his fate. That not being the case, Adam lost his original righteousness, that is, his right relationship with God.[25]

John Hick offers a critical insight into original righteousness:

> Instead of the doctrine that man was created finitely perfect
> then incomprehensibly destroyed his own perfection and then
> plunged into sin and misery, Irenaeus suggests that man was
> created as an imperfect, immature creature who was to un-
> dergo moral development and growth and finally be brought
> to the perfection intended by his Maker. Instead of the fall of
> Adam being presented, as in the Augustinian tradition, as an
> utterly malignant and catastrophic event, completely disrupt-
> ing God's plan, Irenaeus pictures it as something that oc-
> curred in the childhood of the race, an understandable lapse
> due to weakness and immaturity rather than an adult crime
> full of malice and pregnant with perpetual guilt. And instead
> of the Augustinian view of life's trials as a divine punishment
> for Adam's sin, Irenaeus sees our world of mingled good and
> evil as a divinely appointed environment for man's develop-
> ment toward the perfection that represents the fullness of
> God's good purpose for him.[26]

Irenaeus did not clarify whether sin is hereditary or an individual experience, or a mixture of both. Moreover, he does not interpret
Adam's sin as the worst sin. The sin of Cain, who killed a man, who
acted without reverence or penitence and who persevered in wickedness,
drew the curse of God.[27] In contrast, Adam, having disobeyed God, immediately felt the shame and guilt of his actions and turned toward God.
And out of the depth of God's compassionate heart, God could not abandon Adam but reached out and offered salvation in Christ.

In creating us, God bestowed the faculty of increase on his own
creation, the final dimension of Irenaeus's anthropology.[28] Simply
stated, this is humanity's capacity for growth into the likeness of the
Son of God, which culminates in the eschaton. In framing this process,
Irenaeus wrote this: "Now it was necessary that man should in the first
instance be created; and having been created, should receive growth;
and having received growth, should be strengthened; and having been
strengthened, should abound; and having abounded, should recover
(from the disease of sin); and having recovered, should be glorified; and
being glorified, should see his Lord. For God is He who is yet to be
seen, and the beholding of God is productive of immortality, but immortality renders one nigh unto God."[29]

The capacity for growth into the likeness of the Son of God is a Trinitarian invitation to participate in God's glory. Although human beings are sinners, God, through Christ and the Spirit, draws us upward toward spiritual perfection. Since we are body and soul, incomplete until we share in the divine spirit, we have the capacity to intentionally choose whether or not to accept the invitation to participate in God. With each choice that leads to clearer truth and greater freedom, we choose God. Choosing God renders oneself available to be re-created through the Word and Spirit. It is the process of choice that advances us toward the fullness of life in God.

Christ's response to the divine invitation both redeemed us and set the paradigm for us to follow. Participation in the life of God requires familiarity with the Word, docility to the Spirit, and loving obedience to the Creator. It necessitates attentiveness to the indwelling Spirit, whose presence and direction can be discerned in and through the ordinary events and circumstances of daily life. This depends on grace. Once we recognize grace, freedom determines whether we respond, or not, to the grace revealed. Since human persons have this capacity to increase, we can exceed all possible expectations of self. This is the triumph of God's goodness and manifests God's glory.

Because of the Incarnation, Irenaeus recognized the great dignity of the human person. Since Christ's humanity was the vehicle of his act of salvation, then the human body is the vessel through which salvation is experienced. In Irenaeus's view, human beings are created in the *image* of God and are similar to God through the gift of freedom. Created in original innocence and ignorant of God and God's ways, we possess the "capacity for increase," enabling us to grow into full human and spiritual maturity, reflecting a bit more clearly a *likeness* of the Son of God. This lifelong process, initiated by the Creator and guided by the Word and Wisdom, together with our participation, transforms us to reflect the glory of God. Movement toward God's glory depends upon the *vision of God*, which is the heart of Irenaean soteriology.

In Irenaeus's interpretation, God created a divide between the uncreated God and creation, and affirmed God's desire that human beings participate in the life of the Triune God. Irenaeus's progress toward union with God is soteriological and consists of two central themes. The first theme is his theology of recapitulation. Irenaeus saw that Christ, through his obedience and human struggle, recapitulates—that is, corrects or rectifies creation and Adam. This sets an example for future disciples to follow.[30]

Irenaeus situated his understanding of recapitulation in Pauline theology: "He has let us know the mystery of his purpose, the hidden plan he so kindly made in Christ from the beginning to act upon when the times had run their courses to the end: that he would bring everything together under Christ, as head, everything in the heavens and everything on earth."[31]

To highlight God's continuous saving work through the Old and New Testaments, Irenaeus traced God's progressive saving work with humanity through a succession of covenants made since creation: first in the time of Adam, second in the time of Noah, third in the time of Moses, and finally the Incarnation of the Word, who renewed humanity and recapitulated everything in himself.[32] Irenaeus interpreted recapitulation as rectification and development of the human race. As a community, our common moral struggle in freedom is toward the good and serves as a catalyst to advance the human race.

Irenaeus explained a progressive developmental system where nature and grace interweave to compel growth. Recapitulation does not suggest a process of completion. Rather, the end experienced is integrated and moved forward to yet another horizon to continue the process of development. Note that Irenaeus's notion of recapitulation is distinct from that of Augustine who suggested a return to original innocence. Since Christ has recapitulated creation, things are not the same as they were at the origin of creation. Through him, creation, particularly humanity, is able to be strengthened, confident, more knowledgeable of God, self-possessed, and better able to withstand the deceitful cunning of Satan.[33] It is Christ's obedience and integrity as a fully human being that saves us from spiritual death.

Christ became human to reveal God and to set a standard for becoming accustomed to God. Irenaeus wrote, "For He came to save all through means of Himself—all, I say, who through Him are born again to God—infants, children, and boys, and youths, and old men. He therefore passed through every age, becoming an infant for infants, thus sanctifying infants; a child for children, thus sanctifying those who are of this age, being at the same time made to them an example of piety, righteousness and submission."[34] Christ also came to complete the conflict with Satan. Through his Incarnation, Christ took the work of salvation to the next horizon and, by his struggle, restored the original righteousness Adam had lost.

Since my interest is a reformulation of spirituality which centers on the struggle to be obedient to the grace of conversion, it is essential to focus on Christ's confrontation with evil and its power, especially his temptation in the wilderness. Irenaeus pointed out that Christ obediently followed the Spirit into the desert to renew the fight with Satan. Since Christ had come to full stature as a human being and could discern between good and evil, he was not deceived and seduced by Satan's lies.

This fight between Christ and Satan was justified because Satan had struck first when humanity was weak and immature, before Adam had the strength to bear the likeness to the Son of God.[35] While Adam was seduced away from true life by Satan's lie, Christ incapacitated the liar and restored humanity's true life through his struggle. Christ's victory over Satan in the wilderness was a moral and human victory which restored the potential for human beings to grow in the vision of God.

Although Irenaeus's exegesis of Christ's temptations in the desert pronounced a major victory for Christ, the final battle with Satan was waged in full measure during Christ's passion and crucifixion, bringing Christ's saving mission to completion. In Jesus' death, Satan's power was depleted, and with Christ's resurrection, Satan's reign of manipulation, destruction, and death ended. Because of Christ's redemptive struggle, death, and resurrection we are able to become accustomed to God. Christ's paschal mystery restored what was lost prior to sin entering the world. It became the means through which humanity can grow in union with God and reach the human fullness for which we were created.[36]

For Irenaeus, recapitulation is the work of Christ the Redeemer. As Adam was the first *caput* (head) and failed, thus passing on to the human race his fallen state, so Christ is the new *caput* and succeeded. As new head of the race, he incorporated us into salvation. I am indebted to William Loewe who captures well the essence of what was lost through Adam and recapitulated through Christ: "If what human beings need to be rescued from is forgetfulness of the true God, minds seduced and hearts gradually darkened by the practice of disobedience—if these are components of Satan's power, then Christ's victory must occur through recalling human beings to the truth, opening their hearts once again and drawing them back to the practice of obedience."[37]

Christ's tasks in the economy of salvation were accomplished through his obedience: humanity's enemy was defeated, the sin of disobedience was destroyed, and humanity's debt to God was canceled. Christ's struggle and suffering elevated human nature, enabling us to share in the vision of God.

Disobedience characterizes the archetypal and paradigmatic sin which, though overcome through Christ's struggle, still has the capacity to hold humanity captive. Although Christ had won the victory, Irenaeus insisted that each person must take up the personal struggle and make the moral decision to comply with grace and live obedient to grace.

Irenaeus emphasized Jesus' lengthy struggles in the desert temptations and in the crucifixion. He highlighted Christ's humanity, his vulnerability, and his weakness to make the point that Christ the human being confronted Satan. Refuting his Docetist opponents, who reduced Christ's humanity, suffering, and agony to a fiction, Irenaeus insisted that Christ's divinity in no way diminished his humanity nor did it exempt him from physical suffering or the emotional agony of fear.[38] Gustaf Wingren notes,

> Irenaeus speaks similarly and quite naturally of Christ as God without His humanity being thereby lessened. God is in the Incarnate, and it is for this reason that Christ defeats Satan and his power to create. But God is in a *man*, who is tempted in the wilderness and trembles in Gethsemane. The agony which He had to endure was not easier than ours because of His Godhood, but more terrible than any other man has suffered. If we are going to understand Irenaeus we must see this clearly, otherwise we may conceive of Christ's victory as being purely a logical consequence of His divine nature, when in actual fact it was achieved in the hardest conflict.[39]

Christ's temptation in the desert imaged Christ's struggle and victory over Satan where the disobedience of Adam was cancelled, Satan was bound, and Adam's race liberated.[40] Irenaeus affirmed that the purpose of human existence is the *making of character* by the mastery of difficulties and temptations throughout life. Christ, the prototype of humanity living the likeness of God, was not exempt from the dynamics of life within the crucible of the divinely appointed coexistence of good and evil. Irenaeus asserted,

> For as He became man in order to undergo temptation, so also was He the Word that He might be glorified; the Word remained quiescent, that He might be capable of being tempted, dishonored, crucified, and suffering death, but the human nature being swallowed up in it (the divine), when it conquered, and endured (without yielding), and performed acts of kindness, and rose again, and was received up (into heaven). He therefore, the Son of God, our Lord, being the Word of the Father, and the Son of man, since He had a generation as to His human nature from Mary—who was descended from mankind, and who was herself a human being—was made the Son of man.[41]

Irenaeus correspondingly highlights two fundamental benefits from life's difficulties, temptations, and struggles. First, God allowed the human beings a personal experience of the misery of evil and human powerlessness so that human pride might be redirected and we might learn through our own discipline and experience. Second, having experienced the misery of evil, we would come to appreciate all the more deeply the saving hand of God.

> This, therefore, was the (object of the) long-suffering of God, that man, passing through all things and acquiring the knowledge of moral discipline, then attaining to the resurrection from the dead and learning by experience what is the source of his deliverance, may always live in a state of gratitude to the Lord, having obtained from Him incorruptibility, that he might love Him the more; for "he to whom more is forgiven, loveth more:" and that he might know himself, how mortal and weak he is; while he also understands respecting God that He is immortal and powerful to such a degree as to confer immortality upon what is mortal, and eternity upon what is temporal. . . . For the glory of man (is) God, but (His) works (are the glory) of God; and the receptacle of all His wisdom and power (is) man.[42]

To be human is to be born innocent and inexperienced in the ways of God. Adam's choice resulted in a loss of original righteousness. Christ's obedience restored what was lost, leaving a paradigm for those who would come after him. That progressive paradigm is a movement from darkness to light which rests in our freedom to respond to grace. Participation in the life of God, or the *vision of God*, is a matter of choice, Irenaeus's second soteriological theme.

Irenaeus's vision of God is a schema of three progressive stages of "seeing God." These are degrees of growth and development into human authenticity and spiritual intimacy with the Trinity. Irenaeus beautifully synthesized the essence of his anthropology and soteriology in saying that the glory of God is the living human being and the human person has true life only in the vision of God.[43] Given that we are endowed with the "capacity for increase," human beings reach the fullness intended by God through a gradual "seeing" of God at various stages of our growth.

Irenaeus's theme of the vision of God is concerned with the manner in which God is manifested, and how we can, like Christ, recognize and respond to each revelation. Irenaeus focused on the intimately spiritual, mystical communion of participation in the mystery of sonship, which is only made possible by our adopted status as sisters and brothers of Christ. This vision is explained in Irenaeus's description of humanity's progressive integration into the mystery of God.

Irenaeus maintained that human beings shall see God so that we may live, being made immortal by the sight and having become accustomed to God.[44] Pivotal to his developmental notion of our gradually seeing God as a human race and as persons is the eschatological incorruption which enables us to enter fully into God. To illustrate, Irenaeus used the image of light: "Those who see the light are in the light and partakers of its brilliancy; even so those who see God are in God, and receive of His splendor. But His splendor vivifies them; those therefore, who see God receive life."[45] To accomplish this vivification, the invisible God became visible and the incomprehensible became comprehensible in creation and in the Incarnation. And the Spirit, who resides in the Church, leads the faithful disciple to the fullness of the likeness of the Son of God.

Irenaeus clarified what can and cannot be seen in the vision of God: "In respect to His greatness, and His wonderful glory, 'no one shall see God and live,' for the Father is incomprehensible; but in regard to His love, and kindness, and as to His infinite power, even this He grants to those who love Him, that is, to see God, which thing the prophets did also predict."[46] God is seen by those who look on God, who are turned toward God, and who are dependent on this vision for life. Irenaeus was firm; we cannot see God by our own powers. No, only when God pleases, is God seen by us. Who receives the vision, when and in what manner, is up to the discretion of a loving Creator who desires nothing more than for us to share in the life and saving activity of the Triune God. For these who desire God, Irenaeus lays out this three-part progressive schema for becoming accustomed to God.

The Irenaean vision of God is in harmony with his motif of the Trinity in the unending process of creating and re-creating. Where we are concerned, God entrusts our growth as a race and as individual persons to the *two hands of God*, the Word and Wisdom, who, present at the beginning of creation, continue the work of salvation. In the Old Testament, the Word, who has been the revealer of the Father to show God to humanity and to present humanity to God, spoke through the prophets.

The prophets of the Old Testament did not directly look on God but "as the Spirit suggests," and they communicated what they received in word, vision, conversation, and acts.[47] The prophets saw God in multiple ways: some saw the prophetic Spirit and the Spirit's works poured out in various gifts, some saw the coming of the Lord and the way he did the will of the Father on earth and in heaven, and some saw the glories of the Father adapted to the ones who saw.[48] Their experience was rooted in what alone gave meaning to all human life, the vision of God. Regardless of how they saw God and gave expression to what they received, the prophecy was always the same: they announced that we would see God, that God would be present in creation and live with us, inspiring us to serve God in holiness and justice so that we might progress into the glory of God.[49]

Irenaeus's prophetic stage of salvation history corresponds to the time prior to a person's conversion where the vision of God is vaguely seen through the events of life. This stage, in Mary Ann Donovan's reading of Irenaeus, is the time prior to the awakening of a person's call to deification.[50] In this sense, a person sees "prophetically" yet awaits Wisdom's guidance toward a personal encounter with the Word.

The adoptive stage in Irenaeus's schema refers to the human race's receiving a more comprehensive vision of God through the Word. As to how the Incarnation further reveals the vision of God, Irenaeus has this to say:

> For in no other way could we have learned the things of God, unless our Master, existing as the Word, had become man. For no other being had the power of revealing to us the things of the Father, except His own proper Word. For what other person "knew the mind of the Lord," or who else "has become His counselor?" Again, we could have learned in no other way than by seeing our Teacher, and hearing His voice with our own ears, that, having become imitators of His works as well as doers of His words, we may have communion with Him, receiving increase from the perfect One, and from Him who is prior to all creation.[51]

Emphasizing the continuation of God's saving presence throughout history, Irenaeus noted that, as God was seen prophetically in creation, the vision of God is clarified in the life and ministry of Christ. Irenaeus elaborated on the role of the Word in the divine economy:

> For this reason did the Word become the dispenser of the paternal grace for the benefit of men, for whom He made such great dispensations, revealing God indeed to men, but presenting man to God, and preserving at the same time the invisibility of the Father, lest man should at any time become a despiser of God, and that he should always possess something towards which he might advance; but, on the other hand, revealing God to men through many dispensations, lest man, falling away from God altogether, should cease to exist. For the glory of God is a living man; and the life of man is in beholding God. For if the manifestation of God which is made by means of creation, affords life to all living in the earth, so much more does that revelation of the Father which comes through the Word, give life to those who see God.[52]

Irenaeus made two points in this commentary which demand attention. First, participation in God increases when we encounter the Word in Jesus. The evangelists recount narrative after narrative of people who, upon encountering Christ, experienced profound shifts at the deepest levels of their being; their behavior bore testimony to the change. As *the* revealer of God, Christ did more than fulfill the prophecies of the previous Dispensation. He provided a clearer vision of God to those who love God and who love their neighbor as themselves. Irenaeus asserted that Christ came "for all men altogether, who from the beginning, according to their capacity, in their generation have both feared and loved God and practiced justice and piety toward their neighbors, and have earnestly desired to see Christ, and to hear His voice."[53]

Further, as Christ reveals God, he also protects God's mystery. Although we see God more clearly through the Word, relationship with God continues to be a mystery which eludes human comprehension. We are invited to participate more intimately in relationship with God, a relationship which requires an attitude befitting creatures before their Creator. It was Christ who illustrated right relationship with God in recapitulating the disobedience of Adam, who prematurely assumed likeness to God.

Donovan refers to this as the post-conversion stage, a period of fuller participation in God through adoptive seeing.[54] As we encounter Christ through prayer, relationships, life experiences, and indeed all creation, new dimensions of grace are mediated. Experiencing Christ firsthand, we are better able to exercise vigilance to discern not only the presence of God but also the redemptive grace of conversion in the particular dimensions of our personal life and the circumstances in which we live. Within the constraints of our graced and wounded human nature, Christ and the Spirit can lead us to greater freedom, and ultimately, greater love. Responding requires an exercise of personal freedom, the dimension of self-transcending love that sets conversion on its course. This phase brings with it a new, critical dimension of becoming accustomed to God—the struggle to be obedient to grace revealed.

Transformation into the likeness of the Son of God happens by "imitating his works and doing his words."[55] Participation in the adoptive seeing means becoming accustomed to Christ's ongoing struggle for truth and freedom played out on the fields of our bodies and souls in the here and now. Obedience to the grace of conversion, discovered and responded to in the woundedness of our humanity and set in time and place, is the catalyst that is both transformative and transforming of individuals and the world in which we are placed.

Irenaeus defined the twofold terms of adoptive seeing: turning toward God and reaching out in justice.[56] Over time, as our heartfelt knowledge of God revealed through Christ increases, we acquire a deeper and truer understanding of God. In addition, justice makes visible and tangible God's loving and compassionate presence to others. Our experience of God leads to praxis. Those who desire God and look inwardly on God are directed outward to work for justice. Discernment provides the means for participants in this adopted vision to perceive a little more clearly—with the eyes, ears, and heart of Christ—the cries of humanity that call out for liberation and justice.

Of those who have received the adoptive vision of God and responded through fidelity in prayer and justice, Irenaeus wrote, "These, then, are the perfect who have had the Spirit of God remaining in them, and have preserved their souls and bodies, blamelessly holding fast the faith of God, that is, that faith which is directed toward God, and maintained righteous dealings with respect to their neighbor."[57] These faithful ones, Irenaeus says, are welcomed into the fullness of the vision of God, and look on God face to face.

The final stage of Irenaeus's schema rested in the eschaton, where God will be seen "paternally." When we are faithful to the transforming grace to grow into the likeness of the Son of God, God "confers incorruption for life eternal, which comes to every one from the fact of his seeing God."[58] In the following passage, Irenaeus summarized a process of conversion, clarifying the criteria for attaining to the full vision of God:

> Therefore throughout all time, man, having been molded at the beginning by the hands of God, that is, of the Son and of the Spirit, is made after the image and likeness of God: the chaff, indeed, which is the apostasy, being cast away; but the wheat, that is, those who bring forth fruit to God in faith, being gathered into the barn. And for this cause tribulation is necessary for those who are saved, and having been after a manner broken up, and rendered fine, and sprinkled over by

the patience of the Word of God, and set on fire (for perfection), they may be fitted for the royal banquet. As a certain
man of ours said, when he was condemned to the wild beasts
because of his testimony with respect to God: "I am the wheat
of Christ, and am ground by the teeth of the wild beasts, that
I may be found the pure bread for God."[59]

As I interpret Irenaeus, his images of "tribulation, having been
after a manner, broken up and rendered fine, and set on fire (for perfection)," pertains to the intense internal experience of the awareness of
the call to conversion, and to making the choice to enter or not into the
struggle at the deepest core of human existence. When grace encounters
our human limitations and fears, struggle ensues. Engaging the struggle
can be liberating, causing a radical shift in our attitudes and behavior.
Irenaeus's use of these images distinguishes the principal role human
struggle plays in conversion. The struggle to be obedient to grace,
played out in the drama of each of our lives, is the catalyst which advances disciples into the mystery of God, culminating in the paternal
seeing of God.

God's gradual, loving self-communication seduces those who
love God with an increasing desire to see God more clearly. Having
glimpsed God, we desire all the more to know God more intimately. In
knowing God more intimately, we become accustomed to living in God
more completely.

Dialogue with Irenaeus's theology provides fresh insights into
conversion, and suggests a new framework for Christian spirituality.
Emphasizing the loving and self-giving relationship within the Trinity,
Irenaeus celebrated the progressive movement of Christian life etched
in the beautiful process of becoming accustomed to God.

Since we are born weak, innocent, incomplete, and inexperienced
in the ways of God, God reaches into our human condition and, being
accustomed to dwelling among us because of the Incarnation, the Word
and Wisdom can lead us from darkness into a glorious light, to the fullness of truth and beauty intended by God from the beginning of creation.
The movement from darkness to light, however, rests in our freedom to
respond to grace. Participation in the life of God is a matter of desire
and choice.

Participation in God can only take place in the reality of the circumstances of our lives. While that includes time and space, I am more precisely concerned with the influence of the grace of conversion on our psychological and spiritual growth and development, as articulated in dialogue with psychology and psychoanalysis. When the light of grace shines on our unnoticed gifts, and illumines the dark corners of our sinful, limited humanity and onto our narrow notions of God, struggle is inevitable. It is in the struggle that we are transformed into the likeness of the Son of God. Oscar Romero was one such disciple well acquainted with this salvific struggle.

While the particularities associated with Romero's struggles may differ in many important ways from ours, what remains the same is that, although grace is offered and we desire it, the ambiguities and complexity of human nature and our failed attempts to transcend our finite circumstances cause conflict and suffering. Thus, what happened in Romero's life serves as a dialogue partner in our quest for a fuller understanding of a spirituality of conversion—that, within the matrix of struggle, human authenticity and spiritual freedom develop.

To appreciate the value and complexity of a spirituality of conversion, in the following chapter I probe the relationship between Romero's prayer and his struggle with his personality disorder. I pay particular attention to Romero's response to grace within the constraints of his humanity and suggest how his response may have been connected to other dimensions of his life. Tracing his human development provides the necessary data to explore his spiritual conversion further in chapter four by weaving together Irenaeus's theology and Romero's life and ministry.

CHAPTER 3

THE DYNAMICS BETWEEN OSCAR ROMERO'S SPIRITUALITY AND HIS PERSONALITY DISORDER

Irenaeus's theology resonates with contemporary sensibilities concerning conversion. His pastoral theology suggests that if we accept times of crisis and transitions and cooperate with the grace of conversion operative in these events, they become catalysts of conversion. Such are the circumstances through which the Two Hands of God fashion us into the likeness of the Son of God. The dynamics between Oscar Romero's spirituality and personality disorder, a lifelong process that animated his growth toward spiritual maturity and human authenticity, merit our attention.

To facilitate a focused understanding of these dynamics, I make a few assumptions about conversion. Christian conversion is a developmental process that can, little by little or abruptly, advance us toward human authenticity and spiritual maturity. In the process, we are active participants who can determine how far we want to proceed. Conversion likewise stimulates change within continuity. We never actually change our underlying personality structure; we are converted within its continuity. Yes, there is change, but change in continuity. And conversion does not mean extracting or eliminating that part of our human condition that causes us sorrow or suffering and which we perceive as an obstacle to our growth and development. The experience of conversion produces an increasing acceptance of and harmonious coexistence with the finite dimensions of our human reality within an abiding interior peace and freedom. Finally, conversion happens in the struggle to be obedient to the grace of conversion manifested in the unique circumstances of our lives—and, more specifically, within the constraints of the human personality.

The human personality is influenced by factors too numerous to mention, all of which communicate powerful messages which shape the attitudes that determine our behaviors. Romero was diagnosed with Obsessive Compulsive Personality Disorder (OCPD). So, to situate an understanding of the dynamics of his complex psyche and appreciate the magnitude of his development, I examine the compulsive personality style, one possible etiology, and the manifesting features of OCPD. Engaging the discourse of developmental psychology in general will help expand the horizons of our understanding of spirituality to encompass the whole life cycle. This will also help expand our appreciation of personality disorders and lifelong wrestling with them in the course of spiritual development.

According to Theodore Millon, who chaired the American Psychiatric Association's task force on diagnostic criteria for personality disorders for the *Diagnostic Statistics Manuals* (III and IV), a personality is a complex pattern of deeply embedded, largely unconscious psychological characteristics, which cannot be eradicated easily and which express themselves automatically in most facets of a person's functioning.[1] Formed by various contributing factors, personality comprises an individual's distinct pattern of perceiving, feeling, thinking, and coping. Personality refers to the less overt, inner psychological qualities that lead to more observable attitudes, habits, and emotions.[2]

When everyday responsibilities are responded to with inflexibility or when a person's perceptions and behaviors display increased personal discomfort or curtail opportunities to learn and grow, a personality pathology develops. Since these pathologies are characterized by pervasiveness and duration, they cause subjective feelings of distress and/or significantly impaired social functioning. One such personality disorder is the "compulsive personality style." It is a personality disorder that Millon and associates believe is associated with the child-rearing attitudes and behaviors of overcontrolling parents.[3]

Millon contends that compulsive personality disorder is rooted primarily in early interpersonal experiences and reflects the behavior that children learn and internalize from their parents.[4] Overcontrolling parents are unreasonably demanding, punitive in response to minor transgressions, and usually exhibit attitudes of severity, firmness, and repressiveness. Children reared in such a hostile environment, with a fear of severe physical or emotional discipline, become restricted to the parent's narrow boundaries. They learn what must not be done so as to avoid punishment and condemnation. They are, in effect, shaped by fear and intimidation to be obedient and conforming to the standards set down by parents. To cope, these children develop internal ambiguity and ambivalence, and construct defense mechanisms to protect their vulnerability.

Overcontrolling child rearing sets the stage for pathological developments which can cripple a child's normal development, especially when children begin testing the boundaries of autonomy and are more assertive and resistant to parental admonitions. Due to their rigidity, parents construe the child's resistance as defiance of their authority and punish the child. Thus the child learns to abandon independent thinking and restricts behavior choice to those acceptable to authority. Curtailed autonomy truncates the development of competency skills, and the child becomes dependent on rules, firmly adhering to them because of guilt, shame, and fear of rejection or punishment.

In 1966, Romero was diagnosed with OCPD, a type of compulsive personality style. This personality disorder suggests one way of framing his thinking and behavior, enabling us to observe certain patterns. In Romero's case, this interpretive framework is promising because he accepted it. As I proceed, bear in mind that such a suggestion is only that—one plausible interpretation.

Drew Weston and Amy Kegley Heim note that, "The concept of *personality disorder* emerged in the 1930s and 1940s in the psychoanalytic literature, as clinicians and theorists discovered a class of patients whose problems seemed to lie less in circumscribed symptoms (such as phobias or obsessive-compulsive thoughts and rituals) than in their enduring ways of thinking, understanding themselves and others, regulating their impulses and feelings and interrelating to other people."[5]

Thus, OCPD consists in a certain content, style and structure of a person's thought processes. Personality disorders in and of themselves are fundamental and involve the entire person—the cognitive, emotional, and behavioral dimensions. Obsessive-compulsive patterns reflect assumptions persons with the disorder have about themselves and their world. These assumptions include that there are right and wrong behaviors. Decisions and emotions and anything outside the "right" domain are considered wrong. One must avoid mistakes in order to be considered worthwhile. Making a mistake is equivalent to failure. To make a mistake is to be deserving of criticism. At all times one must be in perfect control of one's environment and self. One is powerful enough to initiate or prevent the occurrence of catastrophes by magical rituals or obsessive ruminations. One acts only when certain of success. And, without rules and rituals, one will collapse into an inert pile.[6]

These assumptions contribute to maladaptive behaviors. Induced by anxiety, they can sabotage goal-directed conduct into activities designed to relieve or eliminate anxiety. OCPD itself exists on a spectrum between a character problem and a neurotic problem in which symptoms are manifest. What Romero struggled with was not unlike the personality struggles contemporary people live with today. In the words of Dean Brackley, "Romero was only a garden-variety neurotic, like most of us. He was not a mentally or emotionally sick person."[7]

The traits of Romero's OCPD were stress-inducing and caused him deep emotional, physical, and spiritual suffering. We can only speculate whether it was his initially rigid spirituality that fostered some of his distorted thinking or his distorted thinking that promoted his rigid spirituality, further intensifying his discomfort. Irrespective of the causal direction, in an Irenaean framework, the traits associated with the diagnosis of OCPD comprised Romero's "divinely appointed environment." This includes the constraints of his OCPD and his yet unrecognized gifts, which, through the grace of conversion and his response to grace, gradually transformed him into a greater likeness of the Son of God. With an eye toward understanding the effects of the grace of conversion on our human constraints and blessings, we are now poised to look at some widely recognized milestones in Romero's life as graced struggles of ongoing conversion.

Chapter one provided a sketch of Romero's evolving personality and his maturing spirituality. Drawing from and building on that information, it is time to engage the discourse between Romero's personality disorder and his theology and practice of prayer on the one hand, and his asceticism and pastoral practice on the other. This dialogue helps us appreciate more fully the reality and cost of his human and spiritual struggles. It also traces the concrete ways Romero's soul ascended until it was possessed entirely by God.

In a letter written to Cardinal Sebastiano Baggio, the Prefect of Bishops with whom Romero had a thorny relationship, Romero seems to have taken a long look back over his life. He eloquently and succinctly captures the history of his conversion and summarizes the dynamic commitment that compelled the conversion: "What happened in my priestly life I have tried to explain to myself as an evolution of the same desire that I have always had to be faithful to what God asks of me. If I gave the impression before of being more 'discrete' and 'spiritual,' it was because I sincerely believed that thus I responded to the Gospel, for the circumstances of my ministry had not shown themselves so demanding of a pastoral fortitude that in conscience I believe was asked of me in the circumstances under which I became archbishop."[8] Given that general overview, we can now explore more specifically the dynamics between Romero's personality disorder and his prayer, asceticism, and ministry.

Oscar Romero had always been a serious and reflective intellectual. His introverted temperament led him to find life's meaning and direction through interior resources. As is characteristic of the introverted temperament, Romero was disposed to pursue prayer and the spiritual life with a focus on interiority. It was from this deep and resourceful well that his dedicated ministerial service emanated. This disposition was cultivated in the context of predominantly Catholic El Salvador and further defined through a post-Tridentine hermeneutic which undergirded the presbyteral formation and spirituality of his day.

Earliest accounts note Romero's attraction to prayer, being at ease with solitude in one of the two hometown churches where he visited the Blessed Sacrament as a young boy. In the minor seminary, his formators impressed upon him the fundamentals of prayer associated with priestly life. They introduced him to the methodical and regulated approach to prayer that would characterize the years between his adolescence and young adulthood in the major seminary. Romero had so absorbed and internalized these fundamentals that he composed a lengthy "Program of Prayer and Mortification," his "Rule of Life," a plan of spiritual and corporal disciplines practiced to achieve spiritual perfection.[9] At the top of this list was the practice of getting up during the night for prayer, something he did even while home on vacation.

In the major seminary in San Salvador, Romero had a reputation for being a man of prayer who desired to know and do God's will. He demonstrated a preference for the obscurity of the night and the silence of the chapel where he could be alone with the presence of Christ in the Blessed Sacrament. The stillness of the night and the solitude of the chapel offered him a place to concentrate. While the external environment was conducive to contemplative prayer, his prayer was active, and in part, rote. His obligation, as he saw it, was to pray and, through prayer, discover God's will. Compared to what we will later see, Romero's earlier prayer was task-focused and obligation-fulfilling. Nevertheless, one thing is certain in this period: Romero accepted, internalized, and clung to the semi-monastic values and practices of his formation. These he struggled to maintain under the demands of an active ministerial life.

At this point in the seminarian's life, there is a natural predisposition toward an active prayer life and a generous and sincere desire to abandon himself to God in service. There are also traces of later developments that were subsequently interpreted as features of his OCPD. Let's look more closely at Romero's prayer.

This was an impressionable adolescent, who, driven by perfection and initial zeal, wanted to achieve the Christian ideal set before him, holiness. Completely isolated, a seminary was an environment conducive to encouraging his overzealous efforts toward a brand of sanctification that denied the needs of the body (sleep, for example) in favor of spiritual progress. Recall also that Romero was reading Augustine and the Spanish mystics, persons whose heroic odysseys toward holiness captured his religious imagination and powered his determination. Romero's prayerful orientation and desire to make himself available to God is obvious.

Conventional interpretations of OCPD point to its first overt manifestations in adolescence. In this light, there was Romero's pattern of getting up during the night. On the one hand, this may indicate the beginning of a conflict between his monastic mode of spirituality and the demands of seminary formation—and, later, active pastoral ministry and the impossibility of sustaining it. On the other hand, it may have been a manifestation of a distorted cognitive style. Persons with OCPD have a rigid, intense, sharply focused style of thinking. They are continuously being attentive and concentrating, rarely seeming to let their mind wander. They become distracted and disturbed by new information or external influences outside their narrow range of focus. They would be inclined to actively work to keep this distraction from happening. Why would an adolescent disrupt the natural pattern of sleep except to gain the optimal environment with the least amount of distractions for prayer?

The diagnosis of OCPD suggests looking for signs of the emergence of a punishing superego that insisted that his efforts toward holiness were not sufficient. In a related way, his ritually patterned behavior could be interpreted as an attempt to alleviate his anxiety about imperfect performance of prayer. Since a defining feature of perfectionism is the tendency to engage in overly critical self-evaluation, mistakes are equated with failure. Given Romero's formation, any mistake would be interpreted in terms of sin, something to be avoided at all costs.

During his studies in Rome, Romero became more acquainted with Ignatian spirituality. In the OCPD framework, the *Exercises* could be interpreted as, in part, meeting his need for structure. They may have also reinforced and intensified his rigidity and scrupulosity. The *Exercises*, as then given, were regimented and concrete. The "particular examen" emphasized focused vigilance over one's faults and failings. Romero's behavior, which thrived on routine and predictability, reflected an extreme, most strict, most military interpretation of Ignatian spirituality. Since prayer was understood as interior warfare with sinful human nature, the *Exercises* emphasized careful vigilance over one's thoughts, motives, and actions.

Scrupulosity, a feature of OCPD, is generated by fear. In religious terminology, a scruple is an unhealthy and morbid kind of meticulousness which obstructs a person's religious adjustment.[10] Scrupulous people are usually fearful of parental or authoritarian figures, and, in a religious context, they project onto God the images which establish fear, not love, as the foundation for their relationship. In the OCPD framework, Romero projected onto God the fears he had of his father. This, together with a theology that emphasized the transcendence of God and an anthropology that focused on the moral weakness of the human condition, unfortunately induced in Romero fears of an exacting and calculating image of God.

Drs. Greenberg, Witztum, and Pisante studied the relationship between religious orientation and practice, and obsessive-compulsive disorders from the Judaic and Christian traditions. They drew from Ignatius of Loyola, himself a scrupulous person, and offer one way to interpret this dynamic within Christianity:

> According to Ignatius, the basis for scrupulosity is an inclination in devout people to go too far in the right direction, to be too cautious, too safe, too sure about pleasing God and too anxious to be certain that they have not sinned. The fear of sin leads the religious person to endeavor to prove to himself that no sin occurred, for example, that the act was committed in error. If the person accepts this, then all is well. Scrupulosity begins, however, when the person decides that a sin occurred, and acts of penance must be carried out. When these acts fail to reassure, the doubts, fears, and rituals of scrupulosity increase.[11]

Romero's scrupulosity may have been motivated by an obsession with sin and a fear-induced desire to root out even the least semblance of faults perceived as human weakness. Accompanying this cognitive style were behaviors to dominate his passions and impulses. We also detect the genesis of his obsession to control. One can only wonder whether this was the unconscious psychological dynamic behind his penitential and physical asceticism.

What spiritually motivated Romero to fast two days a week, or wear a hair shirt or a penitential chain around his waist in the heat of the Salvadoran day, or sleep on the floor, or isolate himself from meaningful relationships, and to flagellate himself every Friday? While these practices may seem abusive by today's standards, they were at that time the suggested practices of penance which would help a seminarian progress toward fulfilling the obligation of spiritual perfection which accompanied ordination.

One possible motivation for Romero's rigorous penitential asceticism may reflect the goals of priestly formation: a bound duty to work toward spiritual perfection, the glory of God, and the sanctification of others through a priest's sacrifice and example of virtuous life. In the 1930s and 1940s, Romero's formation would have included exposure to ascetical and mystical theology, as interpreted by authors—such as Adolphe Tanquerey, who wrote the popular formation manual, *The Spiritual Life*, which was used around the world to guide the formation of seminarians and religious until Vatican II.[12] Citing a few salient passages on the nature of priestly obligations, we can appreciate the expectations and pressures placed on an impressionable seminarian. Tanquerey writes,

> Priests, in virtue of their function and of the mission which makes theirs the duty of sanctifying souls, are bound *to a higher interior holiness* than that of simple religious not raised to the priesthood. This is the express teaching of St. Thomas, confirmed by the most authoritative ecclesiastical pronouncements. The Councils, and particularly that of Trent, the Supreme Pontiffs, especially Leo XIII, and Pius X, so insist upon the necessity of *holiness* in the priest. . . .
>
> After describing interior holiness, he (Pius X) declares that only this holiness makes us what our vocation requires us to be, "men who are crucified to the world, who have put on the new Adam, men whose thoughts are fixed on heavenly things and who strive by all possible means to lead others to heaven."[13]

In celebrating the Mass, the priest, because he was in direct contact with the transcendent God, was to have some measure of holiness. "What holiness is required in order to offer up the *Holy Sacrifice*! How could he worthily represent Christ were he not *another Christ*, if his life be but commonplace, void of any aspirations toward perfection?"[14] To reinforce these solemn expectations, Tanquerey continues, "How would he have the audacity to mount the altar uttering those prayers of the Mass which breathe the most pure sentiments of sorrow, faith, religion, love, self-denial, if the soul had no part in these?"[15] Finally, sharing in the Eucharist confirmed the priest's obligations:

> To unite himself daily in Communion with an All-holy God without a sincere desire of sharing in His holiness, without striving daily to become more and more like Him, would not

this be a flagrant contradiction, a lack of loyalty, an abuse of grace and a lack of fidelity to the priestly vocation? Let priests meditate on and take to heart the Fifth Chapter of the Fourth Book of the Following of Christ: ON THE DIGNITY OF THE SACRAMENT AND OF THE PRIESTLY STATE. *"If thou hadst the purity of an angel, and the sanctity of St. John the Baptist, thou wouldst neither be worthy to receive nor to handle the Sacrament. . . . Thou hadst not lightened thy burden, but thou art now bound by a stricter bond of discipline, and are obliged to greater perfection of sanctity."*[16]

This style of presbyteral formation, together with obsessive tendencies, pushed Romero toward an extreme penitential asceticism in his pursuit of holiness. Drawing on psychoanalytic perspectives, we see it is plausible that another dynamic motivated his extreme self-denial and penances: ambivalence caused by unresolved feelings of shame and guilt—particularly when he failed to control the powerful impulses of his id (referring to instincts).

In this framework, Romero's scrupulosity may have also been driven by the intense interior struggles between his superego (the active, controlling, perceiving, learning function of the personality), and ego (the moral ideals and taboos a person acquires as that person grows and matures). According to Freud, the superego is the psychic agency that watches the ego and compares it with an ideal standard—the ego ideal. The superego serves as the agency of repression of those instinctual impulses not in conformity with the standards of the ideal. Often it represents the moral values of the parents or other agents of authority.

The superego also serves as a channel for powerful drives. The greater the control of the impulses against external objects, the more tyrannical the superego becomes. This tyranny is manifested in a sense of guilt or worthlessness or other self-punitive postures. In my reading of his journals, with particular attention to the lists he constructed for his spiritual reformation, it appears that Romero displayed a deep sense of guilt. It was guilt and worthlessness that provoked his extreme physical asceticism, these self-punitive behaviors.

His ego ideal, shaped by the high standards of his formation, fell under the constant scrutiny of his superego. Note that in his spiritual journals Romero frequently judged himself a failure for not achieving a closer representation to his moral and religious ideal. Further, it is easy to imagine that shame, a close co-conspirator with guilt, motivated his severe self-punishment. Correspondingly, shame for having failed to control or dominate his human impulses may have also motivated his body-denying asceticism. Since scrupulosity is generated by the fear of having sinned, guilt may have driven him to do penance to make reparation for what he perceived as offences committed. Romero's severe superego would have harshly judged his efforts at atonement unsatisfactory, thus giving rise to doubt, fears, and the need to punish himself even more to alleviate guilt. In this framework, there are many reasons for concluding that Romero's scrupulosity was driven by an unyielding superego that was the force behind his self-destructive behaviors.

It is possible that Romero was attracted to the Spanish Jesuit Luis de la Puente because de la Puente served as an icon of Romero's ego ideal, providing an image of priesthood and the type of priest Romero hoped to become. Likewise, his study of de la Puente gave Romero a theology of prayer and asceticism to pattern his life on in the seminary and as a newly ordained priest.

Little is recorded about Romero's prayer during his twenty-three years of ministerial service in San Miguel, the two years in Santiago de María, and his seven years in San Salvador except for the pious practices he tried to continue from his seminary days. Based on his retreat notes, the *Spiritual Exercises* shaped and influenced his prayer. We have already observed his attraction to Ignatian spirituality while he was a student in Rome. So too, the Ignatian examination of conscience and particular examen likely heightened his scrupulosity. Having made the thirty-day retreat, his subsequent retreat entries note his use of the *Exercises*, referencing specific concepts unique to the *Exercises* such as making an election, and selecting *Sentir con la Iglesia* (to think with the Church) as his episcopal motto. I concur with Richard Blake, editor of *Studies in the Spirituality of Jesuits*, who aptly notes that Romero was not a Jesuit, but he *was* Ignatian.[17]

The *Exercises*, prescribing a process which mediates the grace of conversion, began to influence some modification in Romero's prayer. While they provided security of structure and method, conventional approaches to the *Exercises* reflect a progressive pedagogical construct. In this framework, Romero would have been encouraged to venture out into different experiences of prayer heretofore unknown to him. As he articulated following his psychoanalysis, meditation might have been the catalyst that challenged him to reflect on the particular manifestations of grace and sin experienced in the unique circumstances of his life. The method of contemplation, of placing himself in direct proximity to Jesus in a Gospel scene, might have predisposed him to personal encounters with the Word, and invited him to make a choice to love and to follow Jesus more closely with added self-generosity.

Certainly his post-psychoanalysis retreat notes indicate his election to follow Christ more closely. Those notes also reveal the development of a relational Christology. The art of discernment would have challenged him to grow beyond his narrow, seminary-taught conceptions of God. Discernment would have helped him develop a more open mind so as to recognize and risk being vulnerable to the ubiquity of God in the midst of life laden with busy pastoral demands. Later, during an interview given as Archbishop, Romero clearly identified the *Exercises* as a "wonderful school of discernment."

The *Exercises* might well have provided a different framework for Romero's purpose of prayer. Where previously he prayed to know the will of God and to have the grace to do it, he made a shift to a more relational style of prayer. On the first day of a retreat prior to his episcopal ordination in June 1970, Romero wrote, "After several hectic days of work and fatigue, I feel the gentleness and intimacy of Jesus. How I would like to advance in this important, intimate relationship."[18] Romero also said he desired to "be a Bishop with the heart of Jesus."[19]

To be a bishop with the heart of Jesus is to be a leader whose ministry is marked by compassion, a virtue that is developed by being in relationship and solidarity with the suffering of others. Romero was beginning to understand that human relationships did not have to be framed in a hierarchical structure or exist for functional purposes. He was beginning to understand that mutual friendships were a natural part of adult relationships. This indicates, of course, initiating steps toward a more integrated personality.

As Romero made progress toward a more personal experience of the Triune God, he still lacked an internal flexibility to negotiate his Rule of Life. Retreat after retreat, he vowed a return to the piety he understood as prayer: daily meditation, saying Mass with greater fervor, thanksgiving after Mass, examination of conscience, praying all hours of the breviary, spiritual reading, saying the rosary, fidelity to weekly confessions with more careful preparation, and monthly spiritual direction and retreat. Reflecting on Romero's prayer, María López Vigil says it was "very traditional . . . a Catholic religiosity of piety, devotions, sacrifices, long sessions in the chapel . . . maintaining a very regulated routine."[20]

The former U.S. Ambassador to El Salvador, Robert White, casts a bit more light on Romero's piety at the time. He noted that the classic criticism of Romero by some priests of the archdiocese at the time of his nomination as Archbishop described him as "a man much given to the dressing and undressing of dolls." This was a reference to Romero's widely known devotion to the Infant of Prague and his preoccupation with changing the Infant's clothing color to coincide with the liturgical year.[21] With their intense focus on adhering to ecclesial and liturgical orthodoxy, it was little wonder that, as Ordinary of Santiago de María, Romero kept company with the more traditional and pious members of Opus Dei.

Romero was caught in the crossroads of change. He transitioned into, drawing on Irenaeus, an *adoptive seeing of God*. At this phase of spiritual development, having experienced the Word in a more relational and satisfying way, Romero yearned for still more. Responding then to the grace of a deeper relationship with God, Romero struggled to integrate this style of prayer with his former, more conventional prayer. Simultaneously, his desire for closer relations with his peers indicates a movement from isolation to relationality. From a developmental stance, this progression, together with the psychological struggles he endured at this time, moved him toward further integration of his powerful super-ego with his ego.

Characterized as socially timid, inhibited, affectively isolated, and fearful, persons characterized by OCPD conduct their interpersonal relationships on a continuum from respectful to ingratiating, relating to others in terms of rank and status.[22] They tend to be more authoritarian rather than egalitarian, and present a grim and cheerless demeanor to convey an air of austerity and serious-mindedness. In general, they downplay the importance of interpersonal relationships and avoid intimacy at all costs.[23] As his spiritual journals verify, Romero thought of himself in these terms. It is easy to imagine that he was deeply frustrated by his compulsive tendencies and ambivalence. Certainly some deep frustration, perhaps desperation, motivated him first to see Dr. Dárdano, then to undergo psychoanalysis six years later, and to regularly confer with Drs. Semsch and Dárdano.[24]

Romero's psychological suffering was a catalyst for his growth because his ambivalence forced two central issues associated with his OCPD to the fore, his fear of human relationships and his resistance to accepting the limitations of his human nature. Both were intricately linked and key thresholds to deeper conversion. To appreciate this more completely, we need only look at Romero's behavioral isolation.

In his work with obsessive patients, Freud thought that the persistent doubts that plague the obsessional person were extensions of ambivalence and an incapacity to love. The obsessive individual doubts her or his own capacity to love because of the hateful feelings toward a loved person. One's inability to love another is an aspect of the doubting and ambivalence, not the *result* of it. It is the feeling of danger in committing to another and abandoning the doubts about another that prevents the obsessive person from falling in love. As loving involves being concerned about the feelings and reactions of another person, the obsessive is threatened because the other is not under the obsessive's control. This doubting can stimulate more doubt and uncertainty about one's integrity and honesty unless interrupted by therapy.[25] While the therapeutic process can be effective in its own right, the experience of relationship between the therapist and patient can be a valuable source of modeling appropriate relationship leading to changes in a patient's living.

As a general principle of therapy with obsessive people, the therapist takes some risks with regard to exposing some of her or his own weaknesses or deficiencies. While keeping a certain measure of objectivity and separateness, the therapist, responding in terms of warmth and intimacy to the interpersonal exchange, demonstrates to the patient that being human and fallible and admitting to deficiencies need not result in rejection or humiliation. Recall that one of the distorted cognitive assumptions of OCPD is equating self-worth and value with perfection. Instead of rejecting the therapist, the patient may gain a heightened respect for her or him.

The results can be an important learning experience for the patient because a deeper relationship involves participation, which in turn implies some need or dependency, as well as the commitment and exchange that grows from some trust in the relationship. Romero's first experiences of adult vulnerability and relationship might well have been with his therapist and psychoanalyst. It seems that it was more than mere coincidence that movement toward greater intimacy with God was accompanied by increased yearning for the warmth and satisfaction of human relationship.

In addition to his behavioral isolation, Romero's theological and spiritual training instilled in him a distorted image of sanctity, one that focused on eliminating human imperfections. His OCPD may have intensified that distortion, making the possibility of not only reframing but embracing his own humanity an enormous if not impossible task. That which Romero was taught to despise as a potential agent of moral failure and sin, his vulnerability and weakness, became the avenues through which grace was mediated, propelling him toward greater healing, liberation, and integration.

There are two psychotherapeutic methods for treating persons with OCPD. The psychodynamic approach, pioneered by Leo Salzman, sees the ultimate goal of therapy as effecting a change in the patient's living. It focuses attention more on unconscious factors contributing to the disorder.[26]

The second and preferred approach, cognitive therapy, is insight-oriented. It focuses on educating the patient to see that the perceptions, assumptions, and meanings one ascribes to life events influence feelings and behaviors. Therapy is generally directed at correcting faulty assumptions, perceptions, and meanings using self-monitoring techniques and new thinking habits. Similarly, behaviors or defenses are identified. When these are clarified, the resulting insight can be directed toward altering or abandoning these behaviors, with notable changes in the character structures, productivity, and satisfaction of the person.

Romero's post-psychoanalysis notes indicate that his analyst used some form of cognitive therapy, since the focus was on insight into OCPD, the nature of the disorder, its genesis, and how unique features played out in his life. Therapy would have challenged him to modify his notions about perfection and reframe his personal goals so they might be more reasonably attainable.

Conversion involves personality development as a central feature, and—since Romero identified his psychoanalysis as an experience of grace—attention to his psychological development provides observable data to comprehend more fully the grace of conversion operative within some of the features of his OCPD. Attention to his psychological evolution helps identify those predisposing factors which made the final phase of his conversion seem so dramatic, but which were, in actuality, progressive movements on the same continuum.

Romero's personality, thus far, has been described as conforming, overly controlled, inflexible, well regulated, and highly disciplined. These behaviors indicate the use of *reaction formation* as his primary defense mechanism. Reaction formation is a process through which persons repress their undesirable impulses and form a diametrically opposite conscious attitude. Together they serve to maintain conformity and social acceptability and to sustain control over socially unacceptable impulses that threaten to disrupt psychological equilibrium. They allow an individual to display an image of reasonableness, calmness, maturity, and social acceptability when faced with circumstances that would normally evoke anger, dismay, or embarrassment.[27] Romero reached a critical point in his development when, in 1966, he sought a psychological perspective to explain his internal struggles.

Clinicians maintain that a patient's *desire* for change is fundamental to health. Lorrin Koran contends that at a patient's initial visit the germane questions posed by the therapist are these: "Why has the patient come to you, and why now?"[28] Romero went to Dr. Dárdano because he already had an established relationship with the psychiatrist. Responding to the *why now* question, Romero's presenting problems were loneliness and a lack of intimacy, physical and emotional exhaustion, rigidity, frustration with a growing inability to control his powerful emotional drives, increasing conflicts with others, depression, and a demanding perfectionism.

Other than Dr. Dárdano, Romero consulted Dr. Rodolfo Semsch professionally, and, since resources about these meetings are confidential, we rely on Romero's own notes following the psychoanalysis to gain a deeper insight into how his thinking and behavior were modified.

In those notes, Romero lists several features he identified. (Note: Each is numbered to match, in the paragraph below, a corresponding change in Romero's thinking.) (1) Romero noted that his fear of intimacy was "expressed in avoiding sociability," and that his self-centeredness may have been the motivating factor in his charity. (2) He acknowledged timidity, fear of others, lack of warmth, and his business-as-usual manner with people as an unconscious transference from his relationships with his parents. (3) He saw himself as being interiorly and exteriorly rigid, irrational, and authoritative, and acknowledged that "perfectionism takes away from human warmth." (4) He also noted that his "insecurity was another dominant characteristic . . . which evoked doubts, and doubts triggered more rigidity." Finally, (5) he admitted his workaholism and the trap of becoming caught by the flattery of others.

For persons diagnosed with OCPD, change is brought about by setting and prioritizing therapeutic goals. Ranking these goals is determined by the importance of each problem and how solvable it is. Behavioral change is divided into small steps to keep anxiety manageable, allowing a progressive approach to a goal, and illustrating to the patient that all-or-nothing thinking is not necessary for success. Risk taking is also encouraged. Continued therapy helps the patient identify and understand the negative consequences of these assumptions, perceptions, and meanings, and then identifies ways of refuting them so that they no longer control the patient's feelings and behaviors and lead to the problems that first brought them to therapy.

In his entry for each of the behaviors cited previously, Romero followed by identifying a new cognitive pattern and/or behavior. (1) Regarding fears of intimacy and self-centeredness, he wrote, "I must be converted to love. I must develop my tendencies for others. All my relationships must be motivated by love . . . to avoid all forms of criticism". (2) As an antidote to the second, perfectionism, he said, "I have learned that figures of parents and children can no longer regulate my relationship between men who are equal. I must be more natural and spontaneous with my affections." (3) To counter his rigidity, he noted, "Internally and exteriorly I must be calm. I do not have to be so authoritarian and irrational with demands, or compromise my moral principles and holiness, but need to have more confidence in the forces of redemption. I must be more mature. Do not get lost in details; it is better to cultivate friendships. It is more important to be human and generous than to be caught up in unimportant details." (4) To deal with insecurity and doubts, Romero noted, "If I am less rigid, I can be more natural. If I make a mistake, I can begin again. I must be humble and know it is safe to make corrections if it is necessary and good." (5) Toward correcting his workaholism, he said he needed "to do fewer things with a more human touch and to make time for the necessities of friendships. This toning up will make it possible to live with greater happiness and satisfaction."

Romero's entry indicates that cognitive therapy effectively helped him formulate a way of thinking about his excessive feelings of anxiety and insecurity. According to therapeutic practice, his analyst would have reflected back to him ways in which his thinking and behaviors interfered with or sabotaged his life. He would have been counseled and encouraged to abandon his attempts at perfectionism and to accept his human limitations. In the framework I am developing, we begin to see the grace of conversion operative within the constraints of Romero's unique psychic composition. Expressing vulnerability in his need for love was the means out of the vicious cycle of self-perpetuating destructive thinking and behaviors.

The shifts that psychology facilitated in Romero were reinforced by concurrent changes in ecclesiology. Paralleling Romero's personality adjustments were the renewal of Vatican II and an ecclesiology laid out in Pope Paul VI's encyclical *On Evangelization in the Modern World*. Despite his initial dissatisfaction with liberation theology and the pastoral plan of Medellín, Romero came to a new level of appreciation for these. Further, since the Church gained respect for psychiatry, Romero came to a greater appreciation of the contributions of psychology. As rector of the seminary, he had more frequent access to Dr. Semsch because the admissions procedure required psychological evaluations of all applicants. Given the tools for the task of integration and the permission to form friendships and to relax, Romero was well on his way to change, recognizing grace operative in his pursuit of a healthier personality.

Since, for Irenaeus, growth has soteriological dimensions, the grace of conversion was operative within Romero's humanity—his weakness and limitations. Grace touched the rawness of his personality and invited him to embrace his humanity, to accept uncertainty and unpredictability as part of life, and to relinquish absolute control of himself and others. Romero responded, no doubt with fear and trembling, yet with faith and humility. He struggled to be obedient to this grace to integrate his past with the present, even if he did not understand it completely.

What effect did this have on Romero's asceticism? After more than twenty years of demanding ministry, his January 1966 retreat entry indicated he still applied the severe standard he used in the seminary to evaluate himself: "The disorder of my piety and my activity and my character had almost made me lose hold of the ascetical fundamentals that I used to be so careful about. A profound examination of my life for my general confession offers me the pitiful spectacle of ruin after ruin—of time lost."[29]

At that time, he seems to have concluded that he deviated from his Rule of Life because of his active ministry, and that he neglected his responsibility toward perfection. Romero's response to this perceived transgression still necessitated penitential punishment. In the same entry, he outlined a program for renewal: custody of the eyes in the newspapers, confessional, and on the streets, fasting on Fridays and Saturdays, wearing the penitential chain and taking the discipline on Friday nights.

Now, six years later, there is a shift in the kind of asceticism he practiced. As previously observed, psychoanalytic theory suggests that Romero's former motives involved tendencies toward being self-punitive, disciplinary, and control-oriented. Following the psychoanalysis, his asceticism appears less dominated by an obsession with self-denial. Rather, his asceticism in 1972 seems more designed to deal with the strains of the tendencies of his OCPD. This demonstrates an effort toward applying new cognitive patterns indicating that his asceticism grew deeper and more interior. Such efforts served to liberate him from the former behaviors associated with OCPD.

In his journal entry following the analysis, we glimpse, for the first time, Romero's understanding, tenderness, and mercy—directed toward himself. His notes suggest that he experienced some new degree of self-love, perhaps facilitated through an understanding of himself to be a sinner loved by God, the central insight fostered in the first movement of the *Exercises*. The observable growth that occurred in Romero's prayer and asceticism can further be detected in his ministerial life.

From the time of his ordination until somewhere in the middle of his tenure as bishop in Santiago, Romero's ministry was a charitable extension of his prayer and his earnest desire to be faithful to the pastoral responsibilities entrusted to him. Key to his spirituality, and the spirituality he tried to inspire in his charges, was contemplation and action. "'He was always concerned about the whole person's welfare,' said one woman who worked with him for years in various activities in San Miguel. Salvador Barraza, who became Romero's good friend, similarly recalled that, in preaching, Romero insisted on a religion that dealt with daily life and not mere piety."[30] For him, prayer and action were essential, but not integrated as yet into a union.

The motive for Romero's ministry before his conversion movement may have been a sincere effort to respond to God's will, or the means through which he attained the success that gained him attention and affirmation from his superiors, or the means through which he appeased his superego, or a combination of all three. Motives aside, Romero's initial period of ministry was task-oriented. The convergence of the needs of parishioners and administrative duties, limited meaningful relationships, and his own internal inclinations drove him to exhaustion.[31] He was all things to all people: dispenser of sacraments, confessor, spiritual director, coordinator of charitable outreach programs, pastor, builder, rector, editor, teacher, secretary to a powerful ecclesial body, Vatican liaison, and popular preacher. By all measures, Romero wielded considerable power and maintained ample control over his ministerial situations. Not withstanding his diligence and efficiency, his perfectionist tendencies placed unrelenting demands on him, his colleagues, and the poor who received assistance from him.

Psychologists suggest that compulsions occur in order to decrease anxiety and are linked to the avoidance of discomfort or future harm. One diagnostic feature of OCPD, excessive devotion to work and productivity to the exclusion of leisure activities and friendships, is easily detected in Romero during these years. What was the source of his anxiety? Most likely, it was related to his fear of making a mistake. Recall that the diagnosis of OCPD links making mistakes to feelings of being bad, worthless, or a failure. Since persons diagnosed with OCPD generally exhibit symptoms of low self-esteem to begin with, making a mistake diminishes their remaining self-esteem. María López Vigil validates this: "I believe he struggled against the fear of not doing well, perfectionism. . . . And his fear of not doing things well was part of his personality and his psychology."[32]

In due course, making mistakes evokes feelings of guilt, depression, shame, loss of pride of status, weakness, or deficiency—feelings which persons with OCPD want to avert at all costs. Therefore, to diminish their anxiety, they construct safeguards to maintain control over interior and exterior environments, to guarantee a dependable degree of certainty and predictability. "Psychoanalytic writers believe that the need to control masks yearning for dependence and nurturance, and that anxiety over being in control prevents the OCPD patient from achieving mutual nurturance in a satisfying intimate relationship."[33] This said, we can better understand the links in that period between Romero's anxiety and his controlling behaviors.

From a spiritual perspective, Romero's anxiety may have been reinforced by his theological and spiritual education and formation. His scrupulosity, reinforced by a fear of offending God and sinning, was exaggerated and distorted, leaving little room for the experience of God. Furthermore, as a newly ordained priest, Romero was sent to a diocese where there was plenty of pastoral work to be done and where, for all intents and purposes, the Ordinary of San Miguel had been delinquent in his responsibilities. Placing an inexperienced priest in a neglected diocese would have induced ample anxiety in the dutiful young cleric. Romero was dedicated to his ministry and did what he could to meet the pastoral, spiritual, and corporal needs of his people in San Miguel. His initial approach to ministry was certainly commendable according to the standards of his seminary formation.

We recognize a slight shift in his purpose and approach to ministry in his years as Ordinary of Santiago. Perhaps this shift occurred because Romero did not hide behind administrative safeguards. Rather, he stepped out in the other direction, positioning himself a bit closer to the tragic reality of the lives of his poorest charges. Affirmed by his priests as a "bishop of the people," he listened to the campesinos and saw firsthand the brutality of military action against some priests and catechists in his diocese. In Romero's response to the National Guard's attack in Tres Calles, his pastoral demeanor was different. Fr. Pedro Ferradas, Romero's secretary, described Romero's response:

> The sun was coming up when I saw Monseñor Romero arrive. He already knew.
> "Father, let's go to Tres Calles!"
> We were too late to see the bodies. By the time we got to the village, they'd already been buried, and the people could only tell us how they'd found them—mutilated, tortured almost beyond recognition. We went inside their little houses. The boards still held the stench of blood. In the years to come, we would become accustomed to those cruelties, but back then we were new to it.
> We spent almost three hours there, but our words failed us. Monseñor Romero didn't say anything. He just listened to everything and watched everything. As we were about to leave the village, we saw a group of campesinos off in the distance. We approached them. They'd found another body of another one of the people they had been looking for. It had been thrown in a ditch that ran alongside the road. He was just a kid, at the bottom of the ditch, face up. You could see the bullet holes, the bruises left by the blows, the dried blood. He was practically naked.
> Monseñor Romero mingled with all of them and prayed a slow responsorial psalm. He didn't say anything else.[34]

Romero's somber and wordless comportment indicated he was either overwhelmed by the incredible horror he witnessed or was trying to figure out an appropriate response in his newly acquired role as bishop. Observation, assessment, and discernment of how best to respond to a situation is a feature of the introverted temperament and is characteristic of scrupulosity: "People underestimate the strength of people with scrupulosity. Because they ponder what they do, they may come across as weak or ineffective. In reality, they are struggling with a thousand issues they must resolve before they act. Once they make up their minds, they are capable of taking strong stands."[35]

Note Romero's constrained posture. He is hesitant about confronting and holding the government responsible for the murders in a public forum. Jesuit Father Rafael Moreno, who attended a memorial Mass for the deceased of Tres Calles, presided over by Romero, interpreted Romero's reserve in these terms: "That Monseñor Romero made me mad. He was so wishy-washy! He talked about 'the dead' instead of the people who had been 'murdered' and he preached a sermon condemning violence, which practically suggested that those poor men had been killed because they were violent, that they somehow had it coming to them. I remember going home with a truckload of campesinos from Aguilares, all people who were participating in grass-roots organizations. They went back from that Mass disillusioned."[36]

Romero was constrained by his ambiguity and fear of making a mistake, and/or the fear of being attacked by other ecclesial officials or killed by the government. Judging from the number of his public confrontations with the Jesuits, liberation theologians, politicized priests, and even Archbishop Chávez during his tenure as Auxiliary in San Salvador, Romero's courage was in no small supply when it came to causes he defined as defending the Church. So what can account for his reticence at Tres Calles? Romero's ecclesiology had not as yet shifted.

Romero's notion of Church as the People of God was still just that, a notion. According to the psychological theory that persons with OCPD only act when certain, Romero doubted the innocence of those murdered. Since he still maintained close ties with member families of the oligarchy, he was not convinced of their culpability, nor was he willing to suffer their disfavor. As Bishop, he wielded greater authority and responsibility, and now, accountable to Rome, he would not allow himself to compromise the Church by making a fatal error in judgment which would incur Vatican disapproval.

Whatever light these reflections may shine on understanding his complex motives, one thing is certain: in this period, Romero displayed signs of painful growth. His prayer seemed less consumed with performance and self-preoccupation, showing signs of a deeper relationship and intimacy with God. His asceticism seemed less self-deprecating and penitential and more focused on integrating his human limitations with his idyllic notion of holiness. And his ministry seemed less task-oriented and more person-oriented. In psychoanalytic terms, by the time he was appointed Archbishop, Romero had achieved some integration of his ego and superego. This affected his psychological well-being and readied him for the final phase of conversion.

The assassination of his friend, Rutilio Grande, was a personal tragedy for Archbishop Romero. Moreover, Grande's martyrdom seems to have been the event through which the grace of conversion advanced Romero's prayer and praxis further away from obsessive self-preoccupation to a focus outside himself. Romero respected Grande for his total dedication to serving the suffering Christ in the poor. Romero had already made an option for the poor; Grande's death crystallized this commitment. His martyrdom inspired Romero to ground his prayer in the human reality of his time and place in history. This murder jolted Romero out of his illusion of "dressing and undressing dolls." Confronted with the reality of Salvadorans being killed, his friend being murdered for the Gospel, and the Church being persecuted on his watch, Romero was challenged beyond his expectations.

One key change was apparent two months after Grande's death. This shift would later predominate Romero's theological thinking. He had gone to Aguilares to celebrate Mass to mark the end of the month-long military occupation of the town and church. Preaching on Galatians 3:26–29 and Luke 9:18–24, his homily exposed a different Christology and displayed a radical shift in his discernment of a new direction in God's desire for him. James Brockman chronicled the history of the church in Aguilares:

> The parish in Aguilares, twenty miles north of San Salvador, was a model parish of the archdiocese of San Salvador. Covering a wide rural area besides the town, the parish included some 30,000 campesinos, poor farm workers often existing on tiny plots of rocky ground or none at all and dependent for a living on seasonal work on the thirty-five haciendas that monopolized most of the flat land for sugar cane. Beginning in 1972, a team of Jesuit priests and scholastics took over the parish and began training "delegates of the Word" and catechists, while organizing the grass-roots communities encouraged by the 1968 Medellín Conference of the Latin American Bishops.
>
> The work soon met with opposition from wealthy landowners and governmental authorities, who feared the awakening they saw occurring in the campesinos and the growth in peasant organizations that occurred in the area at the time. Rumors and newspaper articles called the Jesuits

Communists and the lay leaders subversives and terrorists. On March 12, 1977, less than three weeks after Oscar Romero became archbishop, assassins ambushed the pastor, Rutilio Grande, S.J. and two campesinos while driving his jeep to Mass in a nearby village. He was the first priest killed in the persecution in El Salvador.

Two months later, troops surrounded the town of Aguilares and moved through the town, killing dozens of persons and capturing hundreds. The three remaining Jesuits were summarily deported from El Salvador, the church was turned into a barracks, the tabernacle was shot open, and the hosts were strewn on the floor. Archbishop Romero tried to visit the town and the church and was turned back. He sent the chaplain of the Guardia National, one of the components of the occupying force, to remove the Blessed Sacrament, but soldiers arrested the chaplain.

A month later, the church and parish house were once more in Church hands. Archbishop Romero and a large crowd that overflowed the church and churchyard gathered to install a new pastor, a priest of the archdiocese, and three nuns, who would continue the pastoral work of the parish. The crowd applauded the archbishop as he made his way through to begin the Mass with two concelebrants.[37]

With a boldness heretofore unseen, Romero interpreted Scriptures within an historical hermeneutic. Making a link between Christ and the people, he courageously affirmed with the authority of his pastoral office, "We suffer with you who have suffered so much. We are truly with you. And brothers, we wish to tell you that your suffering is the suffering of the Church." He continued,

> The example of Aguilares is wonderful. It is a forward movement of the Church; it is a commitment of Church members to carry out the most dangerous part of its teaching. This is necessary, because I believe that we have mutilated the gospel. We have tried to live a very comfortable gospel, without surrendering our lives. We have tried to live a gospel of mere piety, a gospel that just makes us feel content with ourselves. But now in Aguilares begins a daring movement of a more committed Gospel . . . a gospel that means a very seri-

ous commitment to Christ crucified and the renunciation of many fine things that cannot coexist with one who embraces our Lord's cross.[38]

Romero went on to say that this commitment might engender persecution, crucifixion, and death. He also cautioned the people not to confuse false liberation with the true liberation of Christ. Liberation must have its starting point in Christ and cannot be separated from Christ. For as much as Christians are united to Christ in baptism, all participate in the Body of Christ. Romero affirmed an actual relationship between Christ and the Salvadoran people as the Body of Christ in history. He insisted that, as the Body of Christ, their share in Christ's crucifixion would allow them, personally and communally, to share in Christ's resurrection as well.

Grande's murder thrust Romero toward a new horizon. As Archbishop, he was now in a position of greater responsibility. He was a high-profile public figure who could no longer take the road of least resistance. Previous explanations to his questions no longer sufficed. The vision of Vatican II applied to the Latin American context at Medellín had already affected his ecclesiology and theology. Prior to his appointment as Archbishop, personal experience of the reality of the oligarchy's violent assault on the campesinos and the church in Santiago de María helped him see the Salvadoran reality more clearly. People like Grande, as well as Diez and Macho in Santiago, challenged Romero to see the truth of the Salvadoran situation, and to recognize that the Church was implicated in the repression by its alignment with powerful Salvadoran institutions.

Romero was now successful in cultivating personal and pastoral relationships with his priests in Santiago, and with friends like Angela Morales and Salvador Barraza. These relationships engaged Romero at deeper levels of personal investment and emotional vulnerability. Although we do not know if he was in therapy with Drs. Dárdano or Semsch at the time of Grande's death, from his previous patterns of consultation during critical times in his life, it is likely that Romero sought their professional expertise. And, there were shifts in his prayer. Conventional practices of prayer gradually gave way to a more relational style. All of these contributed to diminishing his illusions and defenses. Combined, these contributed to a radical change in Romero's personal and pastoral attitudes and behaviors.

It is clear that Romero's reshaped Christocentrism was related to his shifting personal experience of the paschal mystery. Anne Mary Dooley observed that "the religiously oriented, somewhat liberated obsessive can work effectively for human rights and Christian liberation because they have confronted slavery in their own flesh and have passed from bondage to freedom."[39]

Romero's diligence in assuming responsibility for the growth and development of his spiritual and psychological odyssey is only one aspect of his complex story. Responding to grace mediated through the witness of Grande and so many others, the encouragement and challenge from some Jesuits, and the renewal of Vatican II, Romero moved toward greater authenticity. This inspired growth beyond a rigid fall-and-redemption model of salvation to a soteriology rooted in his personal and communal struggle for spiritual and psychological liberation, growth, and integration. And what of these struggles? Dean Brackley said, "In his last three years, he seemed to be operating with extraordinary internal freedom and energy and very in touch with a complex reality, both interpersonal and sociopolitical."[40]

Romero's burgeoning shifts in Christology and fuller sense of his human integration are evident in a homily he gave six months after his installation as Archbishop. He said, "How I would like to engrave this great idea on each one's heart: Christianity is not a collection of truths to be believed, of laws to be obeyed, of prohibitions. That would be distasteful. Christianity is a person, one who loved us so much, one who calls for our love. Christianity is Christ."[41]

There is little question that the emerging liberation theology of Latin American countries influenced his Christology. The political, social, economic, and human dimensions of the Church's mission expressed in the documents, *On Evangelization in the Modern World* and *Gaudium et Spes*, and at Medellín and Puebla, contributed to a shift in his Christology. While these developments were being widely debated in the Church, others were moving in similar directions. As these changes were underway, Romero received support at crucial junctures from Pope Paul VI and the Jesuit Superior General, Pedro Arrupe, both of whom encouraged him to move along this path.

Romero's Christological thinking underwent profound reformations. He required a Christology that made sense to him in his historical context. Where is Christ in the midst of the oligarchy's greed, the military's absolute disrespect for human life, and the senseless repression and killing of innocent civilians? Why is this happening in El Salvador? Where is Christ among all this suffering? From these, pastoral questions emerged. What is the role of the Church in this situation? What is the response of the committed Christian? And, more personally, what is the role of the Archbishop?

As a pastor, Romero saw Jesus in a new light. His reformulated Christology provided solid and reasonable hope to his people in the midst of their terrible sojourn. Some of the Salvadoran Jesuits at the UCA (University of Central America), Jon Sobrino, Ignacio Ellacuría, Ignacio Martín-Baró, and Segundo Montes, along with their provincial, César Jerez, were also wrestling with these same pastoral questions, searching for hope, and for ways of reframing the mission of the Church in these terms. Trained and skilled in theories and analysis of political science, social psychology, economics, and theology, they were committed to viewing the world through the eyes of the poor. They came to see the plight of the poor not as natural, but as the result of the normal operations of capitalism exploiting the poor economically. These academicians and leaders encouraged Romero to see the realities of El Salvador in this new light.

This raises the much debated question of just how influenced or manipulated was Romero by his Jesuit consulters. Monseñor Urioste sets the record straight: "You know well that it has been said that Monseñor Romero was manipulated—by the Left, by a small group of priests, by the Jesuits. When delegations come to El Salvador or when I meet them outside the country and they ask me, 'Look, is it true that Monseñor Romero was manipulated?' I always answer that, yes, Monseñor Romero was manipulated; he was manipulated by God, who made him do and say whatever God wanted!"[42] Urioste's statement affirms Romero's gradual development through multiple stages in fidelity to whatever God asked of him; it affirms the measure of his self-transcendence.

Urioste also describes the connection between Romero's prayer and his teaching ministry in the pulpit: "He prepared his homilies with great dedication. . . . [In the pulpit] Romero was transformed. He was, I think, captured by the Spirit. Monseñor was a bit timid. In conversations in informal groups he hardly said anything at all. . . . But when he got into the pulpit, he was another man, completely different. He didn't hold back but said whatever he believed God wanted him to say, whatever he found by consulting God."[43]

Romero's prayer, at this stage, demonstrated two significant and related developments. First, he grew beyond having a relationship with God to someone who came *to know* God intimately. Second, there is a correspondence between his growing depth of prayer and the emergence of his prophetic charism. Previously, when confronted by an injustice, Romero constrained himself, modified his tone, and hesitated to denounce or condemn the crime publicly. That timidity dissipated. As Archbishop, Romero, knowledgeable of the Church's social theology, framed his role and responsibilities in new terms. Because he was convinced that Christ dwelled in his suffering and persecuted people, he advocated in a bold, clear, and straightforward manner for the human rights of the citizens of El Salvador.

Yet, along with these profound shifts, there remained signs of continued preoccupation with his former Rule of Life. An entry from his weeklong 1978 retreat indicates both his advancement and his constraint:

> It has been a very different experience. I wonder if it is the result of my habitual dissipation on account of the special circumstances I have experienced since I became archbishop. I have the feeling that I have lost some ability to turn inward. I also attribute this difficulty in turning inward to not having found a place for my retreat different from my workplace. [His offices were in the seminary building.] Although, thank God, I find that when I go at it seriously I am able to concentrate and to rise to prayer. God is good and I find him easily. But I must again do my part, more than I do; I too easily excuse myself from explicit times for prayer. I have neglected my systematic confession. I realize I must be more demanding and more organized. I will see to it that I withdraw in a more serious and full-time manner to reflect methodically. Although I can't say that these days have been wasted: there have been great values, like spending time with a group of young clergy, some of whom are held suspect, but whom I have gotten to know more deeply, with their goodwill, their

> concern for their priestly identity, and so forth. Also, the same
> surroundings have taught me that the Spirit does not need our
> methods, but brings about transformation in one single mo-
> ment of goodwill.[44]

Here, the coexistence and perhaps the tension of his ability to recognize
God anew in unconventional places and persons, and his own need to
"do his part," to predispose himself to grace, are obvious.

Ignatian spirituality continued to inspire development in
Romero's prayer. In 1979, during the Latin American Bishops' Confer-
ence in Puebla, Romero gave an important interview to the Jesuit José
Magaña. During the course of this interview, Magaña asked Romero
whether the *Spiritual Exercises* had any value in Latin America.
Romero's responses reveal the evolution of his prayer into the Fourth
Week of the *Exercises*, "Contemplation in Action."

Romero acknowledged that the *Exercises* have as their goal a
renewal of each person. (While the translator used the term *renewal*, I
believe *conversion* is closer to the meaning intended by Romero.) Once
converted, each person would, in turn and according to her or his gifts,
effect a renewal of Latin America. He explained that the conversion was
not to mean a mere regeneration of individual piety, or the good feelings
that come from having a tranquil conscience from sins forgiven, or of
intention or goodwill. Romero knew Ignatius was more realistic, practical, and psychologically astute than that. The *Exercises* challenge us
toward self-transcendence generated by a sincere love for neighbor and
flowing from a deep awareness of God's lavish love and generosity,
from a heart of gratitude. Romero maintained that Latin Americans
"must move from an individualist piety to a communitarian piety, to a
social awareness coming out of a piety and experience of God."[45]

Romero affirmed that the *Exercises* were a wonderful school of
discernment, which conditioned a person to seek God's will in the circumstances of one's own life, particularly in the sociopolitical and economic settings in which one lives.[46] Moreover, each Christian must
assume responsibility for doing something to change any unjust structure which denies other persons their basic human rights. He identified
no distinction between serving God and serving people. Based on his
broadened anthropology, Romero said, "The theocentrism St. Ignatius
teaches us in the *Exercises* would be seen from the human angle, and in

the human person we would see the image of God. Thus we would translate, 'for the greater glory of God,' as 'human beings who are God's glory,' in so far as they realize themselves, free themselves and develop themselves."[47]

For Romero, it was the Church's responsibility to assist people to realize, free, and inspire growth as individuals and as a community in history, and to participate in bringing about the reign of God. In his Second Pastoral Letter, Romero was clear that "it is the Church's duty in history to lend its voice to Christ so that it may speak, its feet so that he may walk today's world, its hands to build the kingdom, and to offer all its members 'to make up all that has still to be undergone by Christ' (quoting Col. 1:24)."[48]

Perhaps the most convincing demonstration of his evolution is in reference to his episcopal motto. Quoting St. Ignatius's "to be of one mind with the Church," Romero articulated a revision: "to be of one mind with the Church incarnated in this people who stand in need of liberation."[49] The liberation Romero was concerned about was twofold: "Integral liberation begins with freedom from sin and ascends to the progress that consists in being God's children, to holiness, to the transcendence of eternity. We need messengers of that integral liberation who can give to earthly liberation movements their true horizons, their true power, their originality, and their highest achievement."[50] This demonstrates that Romero's prayer had become more personal and contemplative in the Ignatian sense of finding God in the world. In doing so, his steady reliance on grace, inch by inch, transformed him beyond his imagination. This is, after all, the nature of the *Exercises*: conversion to greater love, by means of love.

Throughout his life, Romero had a sustained desire for God and responded generously to whatever God asked of him. Shortly after he took his stand on the side of the poor, his fate was sealed. He knew he was marked for assassination. He told Robert White, "I only wish that when they do it they do not take a lot of other people out with me."[51] With knowledge of an impending assassination, Romero went into his last retreat. His journal entries from that retreat reflect the essence of the *Exercises*, finding and responding to God in the reality of one's life. A month before his martyrdom, Romero wrote this:

We have come to the meditation on the Reign of God and on
the Following of Christ. Even 'against my sensuality and
against my carnal and human love,' I make my oblation:

> Eternal Lord of all things, I make my offering
> with your favor and help, before your infinite
> goodness, and before your glorious Mother and
> all the holy men and women of the heavenly
> court, that I wish and desire and that it is my de-
> liberate decision, if only it be for your greater
> service and praise, to imitate you in suffering all
> injuries and all affronts and all poverty, both ac-
> tual and spiritual, if your most holy Majesty de-
> sires to choose and receive me in such a life and
> state.

> Thus I make my consecration to the Heart of Jesus, who
> was always the source of inspiration and Christian joy in my
> life. I entrust to his loving providence all my life and I accept
> with faith in him my death, no matter how difficult it be. . . .
> To be happy and unafraid, it is enough to know surely that in
> him are my life and my death, that, in spite of my sins, in him
> I have put my trust and I shall not be put to shame, and others
> will carry on with greater wisdom and holiness the works of
> the Church and of the nation.[52]

This reflection is profoundly touching. I detect in it a disciple prepared
to cross the threshold into the Irenaean *paternal seeing of God*.

As *Archbishop* Romero, his prayer is consistent with previous
patterns of long, sustained times of prayer, particularly in chapels and
churches. While we might suspect that his heavy schedule and involvement in ecclesial and political matters would distract him, the opposite
is apparent. In moments of prayer, he became absorbed and capable of
deep concentration. A couple of moving testimonies bear witness to this
evolution.

As a consequence of the decision to hold a single Mass to celebrate Fr. Grande's funeral, Romero went to Rome with Monseñor
Urioste, his Vicar General, to explain the situation in El Salvador and
clarify his reasons for celebrating one Mass. Upon their arrival, the
two settled into their rooms, and immediately Romero wanted to go to

St. Peter's Basilica. Urioste describes Romero's prayer at the tomb of Peter: "When we arrived, he went straight to one of the altars. We knelt, and soon I could see that Monseñor Romero had entered into a deep state of prayer. It was as if he was laying all the worries of his recent work as Archbishop before the tomb of Peter, the first pope. After kneeling for ten minutes, I had to stand up, but he stayed there in the same position, without moving, in complete concentration. He remained like that for another quarter of an hour."[53]

Monseñor Rafael Urrutia recalled the role of sustained prayer during Romero's homily preparations. Customarily, the Archbishop met weekly with clergy and lay catechists to discuss the upcoming Sunday homily. He then continued the homily preparations on his own. Monseñor Urrutia recalled Romero's process: "The meeting would end, he'd say good-bye to the group, and then he'd sit down to organize his ideas and prepare himself. I'm a witness, having seen him on more than one occasion in his room, on his knees from 10:00 on Saturday night to 4:00 in the morning on Sunday, preparing his homily. He would sleep a little while and then be at the cathedral by 8:00."[54]

Finally, with an appreciable amount of humor, the young Juan José Ramírez, a seminarian at the time Romero was Archbishop, reported his observation of Romero's unwavering concentration in prayer in the early morning before his demanding day began:

> In the morning, we had to sweep and clean the whole building. . . . One day I was going with that monster of a mop—
> whoosh! here and whoosh! there—shining up the hall in front of the chapel on the top floor. As I went by, I saw that at that early hour in the morning, there was a priest praying in one of the front pews. He was all alone, kneeling.
>
> I kept going down the hall. . . . After awhile, I had practically polished the whole floor, and he was still in there praying. The fool didn't even move! I went down another hall and got it all shiny, and then went back and peeked in the chapel. There he was, still kneeling! "What is he doing there, praying so much?" Another fifteen minutes went by and he was still there. "Why so much prayer? With so much happening in the country, all he can do is pray? He should learn a few things from Monseñor Romero, a man with fire in his heart and in

his words, a man who doesn't waste his time! He ought to listen to some of those homilies."

Finally, I went in—making it [the floor] shine with the mop. I wanted to get a good look at the man so I could tell the rest of the guys at breakfast.

I went up and down with the mop, getting closer and closer to that motionless lump of a man, and I looked at him from head to toe . . . it was Monseñor Romero.

He didn't even move. When I left the chapel, he was still there, kneeling and praying.[55]

Even though Romero's prayer took on a deeper quality, he continued to struggle to be faithful to his Rule of Life amidst the extraordinary pressures of the time and threats against his life. A month prior to his assassination, he indicated in his last journal entry a need for more dedication to his spiritual exercises, particularly because of the many responsibilities of his office: "I'll therefore give priority to my spiritual life, being careful to live united to God. My principal concern will be to become more identified with Jesus each day, accepting the Gospel more radically. Toward this interior knowledge and following of Jesus, I will direct my devotion to the Blessed Virgin and my specific moments of prayer: meditation, Mass, breviary, rosary, reading, examination of conscience, spiritual retreat."[56]

While Romero's prayer changed and matured, indicating further evolution toward interior freedom, he nonetheless remained committed to a style of common prayer valued as part of his presbyteral responsibilities. This aptly demonstrates one of my basic claims about conversion—that patterns developed early in life continued to promise him comfort and peace in the midst of great turmoil, deep personal changes, and immanent assassination. This *change within constancy* is a key feature characterizing Romero's struggles to be obedient to the grace of conversion.

Scrupulosity remained a feature of Romero's psychological constitution until the end of his life. During that last February 1980 retreat, Romero discussed with his Jesuit spiritual director, Fr. Azcue, his fear of being lax and negligent regarding prayer. Azcue assuaged Romero's concerns, reminding him of his history with scrupulosity, and insisted the more important thing was the *desire* for prayer, affirming, "It is good to have a plan for prayer and the spiritual life, but without becoming a slave to it, because the most important matter should be life and spirit as the soul of activity."[57]

Two goals in helping people with scrupulosity are to alleviate their symptoms and assist in creating a life with healthy spiritual practices. Fr. Azcue seems to have understood Romero's internal suffering and counseled him toward a healthy spiritual life. Perhaps he was able to help Romero develop a new understanding of his practices. At the end of his life, Romero still exhibited scrupulous tendencies. How can I then justify my claims concerning conversion? As Archbishop, Romero's scrupulosity seemed contained and void of depression. It did not disable his personal or professional life as was the case previously. The grace of conversion did not eradicate his scrupulosity, but his struggle to be faithful to grace within this human condition freed him to make responsible choices regarding its control over his life.

Regarding Romero's asceticism, Bishop Sáenz Lacalle said that Romero was always an ascetic, recalling the Archbishop's practices of fasting, wearing a hair shirt, taking the discipline, and rising for Matins at midnight.[58] Monseñor Urioste noted that, after Romero's death, a discipline was found in the nightstand next to his bed.[59] This demonstrates, once again, *change within constancy*. Romero still practiced a physical asceticism.

Perhaps his physical asceticism was motivated by a sustained sense of guilt or shame for sins committed or opportunities for charity omitted, or the lingering effects of seminary training that insisted on a notion of holiness connected to self-domination and control. Or perhaps it was animated by the extraordinary demands of remaining faithful, counseling victims' families and loved ones, encouraging resistance to oppression, and speaking out in the face of certain martyrdom. While we may never know the reasons for his continued physical asceticism, a new, interior asceticism, an *ascesis of risk* emerged.

An ascesis of risk, as I use the term here, is the intentional spiritual discipline that dilates and channels one's attentiveness and availability to God. Romero's repeated response to the grace of conversion bore the fruits of greater freedom, deeper joy and love, and a more generous availability to what God desired of him. It was an ascesis of risk that eventually reframed the former attitudes and behaviors associated with OCPD. Herein is evidence that within the constraints of Romero's woundedness, grace was operative in his healing and interior liberation.

A central therapeutic strategy effectively used with persons with OCPD is risk taking, specifically introducing new assumptions and encouraging new behaviors.[60] Even though Romero feared personal and public risks, he now took them on. Why now? Something had happened to Romero that allowed him to relinquish previous securities and defenses and risk his life, the lives of others, the Salvadoran Church, and his ecclesial position.

While the risks Romero took during these three years of his life are more pronounced, his risk-taking asceticism was a continuation of a series of responses to grace he practiced during his life in various forms. The difference as Archbishop was that the stakes were considerably higher because he wielded greater authority, responsibility, and power. As previously, this last phase of his conversion engaged the same process. He recognized the invitation to grace and a desire to surrender himself to that grace. Then he engaged the struggle and effort to risk new assumptions and implement new behaviors and critical thinking regarding the consequences of his choices within his given theological and social contexts.

From the 1966 diagnosis of OCPD, Romero's risks were many. One significant risk was the movement from behavioral isolation to cultivating friendships and a collaborative style of ministry. This development was key to his conversion. It was a prelude to his capacity to see from the perspective of the suffering poor in El Salvador and to exercise prophetic leadership in the Church. Implied herein is his movement beyond some of his obsessive-compulsive defenses to the cultivation of a vulnerability that enabled him to accept and trust the love of others. Reflecting on his development during those years, María López Vigil identifies love as the essential quality that sustained him through his archepiscopacy:

> More than anything, I consider what sustained him was the support, the caring, the loyalty, and the unconditional love of so many men and women who worked in the Salvadoran Church. They were priests, religious, laity that accompanied him during those three years. Never had he felt so deeply the accompaniment of others. He had been a traditional priest,

and had a hierarchical relationship with the people. In these three years, he experienced solidarity and an ability to share with others their problems, their strengths, their fears and achievements, as he had never done before in his life.[61]

One has to wonder if Romero's evolving capacity for personal friendship was critical in his response to Grande's murder. Others had been assassinated; why did this particular death have such a profound effect on him? Up to the time of Grande's death, we know that Romero named two friends, Salvador Barraza and Rutilio Grande. I suspect that, due to their mutual intimacy, trust and respect, Romero came to treasure the love he experienced in their friendship. Because of his growing vulnerability to let himself be loved and to love, Grande's death touched him more deeply. The agonizing grief caused by Grande's violent murder may have been the final shock to dismantle earlier patterns of emotional defense and excessive deference to outside authorities. In grieving Grande's death, Romero confronted his fear of experiencing deep emotional pain which theretofore he had kept at a distance. Romero's love for Rutilio Grande and Grande's love for Romero played a significant role in Romero's conversion.

William Van Ornum states, "People with scrupulosity are compassionate and worry about others. They worry about the feelings of others, and they feel the pain of others. They make allowances for the suffering of others because they know how hard life can be."[62] Romero's compassion toward the poor was evident throughout his ministry. After Grande's death, however, there was a noticeable shift in the quality of his presence to the campesinos and his priests in Santiago, perhaps because Romero became increasingly comfortable with his own human struggle and limitations. Having reframed his notion of perfection as a condition for holiness, Romero became more comfortable with the weakness of the human condition and the raw pain of the tragedies and sorrow of others. Romero internalized more deeply his image as a pastoral bishop, a bishop with the heart of Jesus. He, too, risked his own comfort and exposed himself—his heart—to his people and their suffering. In this act of great love, Romero let his heart be broken. It is this particular ascesis of risk that advanced him toward greater interior freedom, which in turn, motivated his courageous and sincere efforts toward forming loving, mutual relationships.

Romero's internal ascesis was a unique, custom-designed struggle toward a healthier, more integrated personality and a more authentic Christian spirituality. Freud and psychoanalysts believe that a healthy personality consists of an ability to love and do productive work. It is an outcome of the harmony that comes to exist among the id, ego, and the superego.[63] Having integrated more realistic assumptions and behavior patterns, Romero experienced an increased ego-integration, resulting in a more spontaneous freedom and increased ability to relate and love.

Romero's radical change leads me to believe that he experienced being loved by God during his years in Santiago. St. Bernard of Clairvaux is credited for teaching that action naturally flows from the union a person experiences with God in contemplation. For him, as one begins to love God with all one's mind, heart, and soul, one begins to see and love oneself and others as God does, and begins to act out that loving vision. Romero's experiences of being loved by God and others—particularly Grande—together with a shift in his Christology, empowered his charismatic ministry.

Examining Romero's contemplative prayer and his interior ascesis enables further reflection on a few prominent dimensions of his archepiscopal ministry. His risk-taking ascesis can be observed in his prophetic leadership and collaborative administrative style. As Archbishop, Romero's thinking and behavior demonstrated the principles of episcopal leadership articulated in the Second Vatican Council document, *The Decree on the Pastoral Office of the Bishops in the Church* (*Christus Dominus*). Above all else, he was a committed pastor of souls. The integrity of his struggle to live the Christian paradigm to the point of martyrdom bore witness to Christ. In executing the responsibilities of his office he untiringly proclaimed the Gospel of Christ, be it welcome or not. Archbishop Romero's prayer and apostolate were rooted in his *cathedra*, the seat of ecclesial authority where he exercised his ministry as pastor and teacher.

Pastorally speaking, Romero seriously embraced his obligation to shepherd his people toward holiness. His efforts were directed toward motivating people beyond emotional piety to a religion of integrity that blended prayer and action. He called his people to live a radical Gospel and insisted on demythologizing Christianity. Recognizing Christ and the Reign of God in El Salvador, he exhorted the people to fuse prayer with life and to struggle toward a liberation from personal sin and social, economic, political, and human injustices. In his 1979 Christmas homily, he said, "We must not seek the child Jesus in the pretty figures of our Christmas cribs. We must seek him among the undernourished children who have gone to bed tonight with nothing to eat, among the poor newsboys who will sleep covered with newspapers in doorways."[64]

At every opportunity, he tried to point to Christ present, suffering, and crucified in the poor, persecuted Salvadorans: "The face of Christ is among the sacks and baskets of the farmworkers; the face of Christ is among those who are tortured and mistreated in the prisons; the face of Christ is dying of hunger in the children who have nothing to eat; the face of Christ is in the poor who ask the Church for their voice to be heard. How can the Church deny this request when it is Christ who is telling us to speak for him?"[65] Romero boldly insisted on the twofold integrity of the Gospel, recognizing and responding to Christ present in his sisters and brothers. In his lengthy letter to Cardinal Baggio, Romero justified his responsibility to connect theology with the reality of Salvadoran life:

> From March 1977 until now, the 8:00 AM Sunday Mass in the cathedral has given me occasion to bring the Gospel close to the life of the people in my diocese. With the cathedral filled Sunday after Sunday, and the Mass also broadcast by the cathedral radio, I have explained the Gospel, working so that the Word of God might never be chained (2 Tim. 2:9) and so that this Sunday encounter with the archdiocese might be a breath of hope for those who suffer in their material circumstances and in their spiritual dignity as human beings and children of God. I have maintained a continuous call to conversion and testified that there is nothing truly human that fails to find an echo in the heart of the Church.[66]

Romero's question, "How can the Church deny this request when it is Christ who is telling us to speak for him?" confirmed his conviction that, if the Church was to participate in the salvific event in Salvadoran history, it had to intentionally choose Christ and stand with Christ in the poor and humble in their struggle for liberation. Romero's

single-hearted love for God, his responsibility to witness to hope for the
liberation of the poor, his scrupulous conscience, and his unwillingness
to compromise the integrity of the Church prohibited him from acting
otherwise. López Vigil recalled,

> During his first visit (of four) to Rome during his archepis-
> copacy, Romero confided to César Jerez that he had been
> worried that he might be replaced as archbishop. He asked
> Jerez, "Do you think they'll take the archdiocese away from
> me?" Jerez responded playfully that they'd probably not
> make him a cardinal! Romero responded with all seriousness,
> "I would rather be removed as archbishop and go with head
> held high than turn the Church over to the powers of this
> world." Jerez commented further, "The sentence he (Romero)
> had just spoken was a very revealing one, because the 'pow-
> ers of the world' he was talking about were not the powers
> of the Salvadoran government. He was speaking about the
> Church government, the world of Cardinal Sebastiano Bag-
> gio. It seemed that he'd decided not to be intimidated by
> them."[67]

Recognizing Christ before him, Romero embraced the risk. "My
position as pastor obliges me to be in solidarity with all who suffer, and
to make every effort for the sake of peoples' dignity."[68]

In his address given at Louvain, Romero articulated his pastoral
charism:

> "I am going to speak to you simply as a pastor who, as one
> who, together with his people, has been learning a beautiful
> and harsh truth that the Christian faith does not separate us
> from the world but immerses us in it, that the Church is not
> a fortress set apart from the city. The Church follows Jesus
> who lived, worked, battled, and died in the midst of the city,
> the polis."[69]

After enumerating many instances of human rights violations,
Romero proceeded and, in doing so, articulated his evolving incarnational ecclesiology:

It is within this world devoid of a human face, this contemporary sacrament of the suffering servant of Yahweh, that the Church of my archdiocese has undertaken to incarnate itself. I do not say this in a triumphalistic spirit, for I am well aware of how much needs to be done in this regard. But I say it with immense joy, for we have made the effort to not pass by afar off, not to circle around the one lying wounded on the roadway, but to approach him or her as did the Good Samaritan.

This coming closer to the world of the poor is what we understand both by the incarnation and by conversion. The changes that were needed within the Church and in its apostolate, in education, in religious and priestly life, in lay movements, which we had not brought about simply by looking inward upon the Church, we are now carrying out by turning ourselves outward toward the world of the poor.[70]

Pastoring the Church in El Salvador was not easy for him. After all, he was under constant scrutiny and attacks by Bishops Alvarez, Aparicio y Quintanilla, Barrera, Revelo, Gerada, and Cardinal Baggio who went directly to Romero's Achilles' heel—his love for and loyalty to the Church. They accused him of betrayal, of endorsing Marxist ideologies, of perverting the Church's teaching, of an inability to successfully administer the archdiocese, of interfering in political matters, of being a pawn in the hands of Jesuits and politicized priests, and of mental incompetence. Though they misconstrued Romero's intentions and pastoral plans, he stood firm in his decisions and carefully insisted that the appropriate mission of the Church is to denounce injustice.[71] "Let this be clear," he said, "when the Church preaches social justice, equality, and the dignity of people, defending those who suffer and those who are assaulted, this is not subversion; this is not Marxism. This is the authentic teaching of the Church."[72]

Despite these and other struggles, Romero, together with other leaders who shared his vision and commitment, kept steady the course and navigated the Church in El Salvador through tumultuous times. With confidence, we can say that his pastoral mandate was consummated by his martyrdom.

As a pastor, I am obliged by divine commandment to give my life for those I love . . . even for those who would assassinate me. For that reason, I offer God my blood for the redemption and resurrection of El Salvador. . . . Martyrdom is a grace I don't believe I merit. But if God accepts the sacrifice of my life, may my blood be the seed of liberty and a sign that this hope will soon become a reality. May my death, if it is accepted by God, be for the liberation of my people and a testimony of hope for the future.[73]

Romero's preaching was long (sometimes an hour and three-quarters) and explicit. In preparing his weekly homily, Romero sat or knelt before an open lectionary and the newspapers from the previous week to pray for and include the names of victims so as to dignify their martyrdom, lest they be reduced to mere statistics. He did this "to incarnate in the people the Word of God," and he was clear that "it is not politics when a homily points to political, social, and economic sins. It is the Word of God taking flesh in our reality, a reality that many times reflects sin rather than the reign of God, to show people the path of redemption."[74]

Archbishop Romero's homilies exposed and denounced the sins of the country, particularly the economic inequality at the root of social sin in El Salvador. He protested, "Above all I denounce the absolutization of wealth. This is the great evil of El Salvador: wealth—private property as an untouchable absolute."[75] He condemned the widening gap between the wealthy and poor. He exposed the system which caused the gap—the oligarchy's greed that produced a monopoly over the land and its products, depriving the campesinos of the land they needed for survival.

As ardently as he denounced the sin of economic injustice, he condemned the oligarchs who were responsible. He called the obstinate oligarchs "Christless Cains," despised by God because they place more trust in money than in the value of humanity. Romero denounced the illusion of peace and prosperity maintained by some Salvadoran oligarchs. He decried the social disorder of the country and Church, and the lack of respect for the human person.

His pastoral letters and homilies increasingly defended the dignity and the value of human life and condemned the numerous human rights violations left unpunished throughout the country. On the agonizing dimension of his ministry, the Archbishop reflected, "I have the job of picking up the trampled, the corpses, and all that persecution of the Church dumps along the road on its way through."[76] Of these assaults against humanity, Romero proclaimed with certainty, "This blood, these deaths, touch the very heart of God."[77]

The Archbishop condemned the idolization of military power, an instrument in the hands of the oligarchy to preserve their interests. And he challenged the conscience of the military and went so far as to insist that the rank and file should defy military orders when they went contrary to the law of God.

The month prior to his assassination, during his February 17, 1980 homily, Romero read a draft of his letter to U.S. President Carter. While its delivery met with thunderous applause (interspersed five times throughout its reading, with a standing ovation at the end), it provoked great displeasure from the Vatican Secretariat of State. It also prompted Ambassador White to accompany Secretary of State Cyrus Vance to Romero's office for a diplomatic intervention on March 14.[78]

Following that homily, civil war escalated, retaliatory political murders increased and a suitcase with dynamite was found in the basilica where Romero presided. Further, two refugee centers that Romero had founded were invaded by the National Guard and ORDEN. They burned the houses and crops of the refugees and killed men, women, and children. Rectories, parish cooperatives, the Human Rights Commission offices and the headquarters of the Mothers of Disappeared Persons were bombed. This prompted Romero, in his March 16th homily to preach on reconciliation, targeting the oligarchy, government, and guerrilla groups. Despite his pleas, the killing increased, which caused Romero to preach one of his most fiery denunciations directly to the military on March 23, 1980:

> I should like to make a special appeal to the men of the army, in particular to the soldiers of the National Guard, the police, and the constabulary. Brothers! We are the same people! You are slaying your campesino brothers and sisters! When a human being orders you to kill, the law of God must prevail: "You shall not kill!" No soldier is obliged to obey an order in violation of the law of God. No one is bound to obey an immoral law. It is time you recovered your conscience, and obeyed your conscience instead of orders to commit sin. The

Church is the defender of God's rights, God's law, human dignity, and the worth of persons. It cannot remain silent before such an abomination. We ask the government to consider seriously the fact that reforms are of no use when they are steeped in all this blood.

In the name of God, then, and in the name of this suffering people, those whose screams and cries mount to heaven and daily grow louder, I beg you, I entreat you, I order you in the name of God: Stop the repression![79]

In his homilies, he exposed and denounced hypocritical and self-serving politicians. Upholding Puebla's commitment to the people's right to self-determination, he condemned the intervention of the United States. Romero censured the fraudulent media that sided with the powerful. He accused journalists of withholding significant facts, falsifying information, and manipulating the truth to the advantage of the wealthy. The media's refusal to accept the obligation to report the truth, to expose the oligarchy's greed and the military's abuse of power, betrayed its ethical responsibilities.

Implicitly criticizing his own previous stance, Romero reproached those who distorted the Church's mission or manipulated the Church to further their own agendas. He saw the mission of the Church through the eyes of Medellín and Puebla, Archbishop Chávez, and Bishop Rivera y Damas. This was a mission dedicated to justice and the integrity of the Church in El Salvador, persecuted by those responsible for the repression. He intentionally opted for the poor and would not close his eyes to the injustices committed. Again, in his letter to Cardinal Baggio, Romero wrote,

In my first months as pastor of this archdiocese, it fell to me to witness impotently the assassination of two priests, the expulsion and/or exile of nearly twenty more, the profanation of the Blessed Sacrament in the military occupation of the entire rural zone of Aguilares–El Paisnal, including its church and parish house, and above all, the harassment, jailing, torture, disappearance, and murder of poor Salvadoran peasants from my archdiocese, in whom the Lord Jesus Christ was repeatedly crucified [*Lumen Gentium*, no. 8]. Confronted with this inequity, all the more scandalous for occurring in a country whose governors are proudly Catholic, I could not be silent.[80]

In addition, Romero disavowed Church leaders like Bishops Eduardo Alvarez, Chaplain-in-Chief to the Salvadoran Army, who could not see beyond their own political biases and security interests. The Archbishop believed that if it was to have any moral integrity, the Church had to be about the work of its own conversion. He said, "We need someone to serve as our prophet, too, today, someone to call us to conversion, lest we become comfortable with our religion, as if it were untouchable. Religion needs prophets, and thank God we have them. It would be a sad Church indeed that would regard itself as sovereign over truth to the extent of rejecting all other claims to that truth."[81]

Romero reminded his people that, since God desired the fullness of life for all creation, those who presented obstacles toward this end were in violation of God's salvific work. In a remarkably similar spirit reflecting Irenaeus's developmental soteriology, Romero said,

> The human progress that Christ wants to promote is that of whole persons in their transcendent dimension and their historical dimension, in their spiritual dimension and their bodily dimension. Whole persons must be saved, persons in their social relationships, who won't consider some people more human than others, but will view all as brothers and sisters and give preference to the weakest and neediest. This is the integral human salvation that the Church wants to bring about—a hard mission! Often the Church will be catalogued with communistic or revolutionary subversives. But the Church knows what its revolution is: *the revolution of Christ's love.*[82]

Romero called not only for social and economic changes but a radical change of heart. Since he identified the oligarchs as obstacles to El Salvador's transformation, their conversion was the first order of business. Furthermore, he insisted that, by their rights as citizens, the poor be involved in El Salvador's conversion, healing, and reconstruction.

Romero's teaching charism was fortified by the conviction that, although the sins of El Salvador and the Church were great, God's mercy and compassion were greater still. This was the source of his joy, a grace he attributed to the intimacy and union he experienced with God: "Christians must always nourish in their hearts the fullness of joy. . . . I have tried it many times and in the darkest moments. . . . When slander and persecution were strongest, I tried to unite myself intimately with Christ, my friend, to feel more comfort than all the joys of earth can give—the joy of feeling close to God, even when humans do not understand you. It is the deepest joy the heart can have."[83]

Archbishop Romero's pastoral messages were meticulously prepared using the best academic resources available to him and contributions from people in the base communities. His delivery was matter-of-fact and confident, in a manner that conveyed an assurance that he was being faithful to what God asked of him.

The appearance of his earlier obsessive drives seemed to have somewhat dissipated. From a letter to Cardinal Baggio, in which Romero gives an account of his archepiscopal apostolate, we get a sense of this abated compulsivity.

> I have tried to proclaim the true Faith without divorcing it from life, to offer the rich treasury of the magisterium in its totality to all people, and to keep strong the unity of the Church, represented in the Roman Pontiff. For many years my motto has been, "Sentir con la Iglesia." It always will be. Many times I have said to myself: How hard it is to want to be completely faithful to what the Church proclaims in its magisterium, and how easy, on the other hand, to forget or leave aside certain aspects. The first brings with it much suffering; the second brings security and tranquility and eliminates problems. The former provokes accusations and scorn; the latter praise and flattery. But I have been confirmed by what the magisterium, through the Council, says to the bishops: "Bishops should present the doctrine of Christ in a manner suited to the needs of the times, that is, so it may respond to the needs and problems that people find especially worrying and burdensome. They should also care for this doctrine, teaching the faithful themselves to defend it and propagate it. In presenting this doctrine, bishops should proclaim the maternal solicitude of the Church for all people, whether they be among the faithful or not, and should devote special care

to the poor, to whom they have been sent by the Lord to give the good news."[84]

Archbishop Romero was a pastor entrusted with the responsibility of preaching the Gospel of Christ. He warned political organizations to bring their ideologies in line with Christian values, called the wealthy and those responsible for the repression to repentance and conversion, and exhorted rebel groups to work for peace through nonviolent means. Aware that the Church was one place, besides the revolutionary movements, where the poor could exercise their human dignity, he did all he could to encourage and empower them to grow to the fullness of their divine and human potential. Romero counseled his priests, with whom he now experienced a deep affection and collegiality, to balance their work for justice with the dignity of their vocation as men committed to the radical Gospel of Jesus.

Romero never lost focus. He maintained a deep love and respect for the Tradition, the Pope, and most bishops. True to the promises he made at his episcopal consecration, he shepherded his people and preached the Gospel. Romero transcended his fears as best he could, and courageously and cautiously applied the Council's new theology and ecclesiology to the Church in El Salvador, a daunting task for a Third World bishop of a Church undergoing repression.

Toward the end of his life, Romero reflected on the profound changes that characterized his episcopal ministry. As noted earlier in his letter to Cardinal Baggio, Romero said that his demeanor and ministry were the products of a natural evolution of his initial desire to be faithful to what God asked of him. That singular desire led him through significant though progressive changes in his spirituality and his ministerial life. It was that same desire that led him to discover and respond to grace within his constrained human condition.

It seems an accurate assessment that, up until his archepiscopal appointment, Romero endeavored to emulate a spirituality of priesthood modeled upon Blessed Luis de la Puente, and that, during his three years as Archbishop, his spirituality mirrored the fundamental aspects of what Rutilio Grande lived and died for. As I see it, these two men were icons who aptly represented the alpha and omega of Romero's process of conversion into an authentic human person and spiritually free Christian.

Romero's earlier prayer was mostly active and pious, motivated by a sincere desire to know and do God's will, and driven by his anxiety around perfection regarding the norms and prescriptions of prayer. Over time, his prayer became more relational and intimate, no doubt having a direct influence on his incarnational anthropology, Christology, pastoral theology, and ecclesiology.

Whether motivated by a desire to share the sufferings of Christ crucified or feelings of shame or guilt, or to exercise control and dominion over his human impulses, Romero practiced a severe physical asceticism. With the assistance of psychotherapy to aid self-discovery and integration, Romero's asceticism grew toward an interior ascesis of risk. This was a course of learning new ways of thinking and applying new behaviors that eventually freed him to love and be loved.

Perhaps overly committed to his pastoral obligations, or obsessed by a need for recognition, affirmation, and adulation, or fear of making a mistake, Romero's early ministerial life was successful. It was also detached, task-oriented, and compulsive. Whether motivated by a commitment to a radical gospel, or his compulsivity, or because he could no longer take the path of least resistance, Romero still confronted the sociopolitical situation in which his ministry as Archbishop was exercised. His ministry was no longer detached; it was deeply relational. It was a ministry of love sustained and energized by those who surrounded and supported his campaign for human rights and social justice which won him global respect and a Nobel Peace Prize nomination.

While his life and death stand as testimony to his transformation, Romero lived and died an obsessive-compulsive scrupulous person. As an active participant in his conversion process, Romero appears to have reconciled the constrained dimensions of his wounded human nature with the endless possibilities of grace. These transformed him beyond his expectations. Slowly, as he progressed, struggling to be obedient to the grace of conversion, and in the matrix of the struggle, he was transformed. Indeed, I would distinguish Romero as a "master," a fine example of Christian discipleship.

I have labored to make the case that, since the Triune God is present and active in created reality, human nature is subject to the transforming grace of conversion. In the dialogue between Oscar Romero and psychology, we note observable changes within the constraints of his personality disorder that occurred because Romero responded to grace. Had he ignored grace and left his OCPD unattended, we could well imagine the outcome. No doubt it would have had a detrimental effect on God's salvific plan for him, El Salvador, and us.

What happened to Oscar Romero was not random, unintentional, or isolated. It arose within a man's simple and sincere desire to do all that God asked of him—even if that meant doing the hard work of reframing the features of a personality disorder. Interpreting Romero's conversion through Irenaean theology, as in the following chapter, opens another dimension to my interdisciplinary dialogue to more fully understand Oscar Romero's conversion.

CHAPTER 4

AN IRENAEAN THEOLOGY OF CONVERSION
AS SEEN IN THE LIFE OF OSCAR ROMERO

All spiritualities are in some way implicitly conversion-oriented. The perspective of Irenaeus of Lyons is no different. He suggests an explicit focus on conversion as an essential dimension of the repeated challenges of spiritual development over a lifetime. Without losing sight of the reality of sin and its effects, Irenaeus pictures spiritual development in more positive terms. He offers an alternative to the sin-based traditional model of progress toward God as purgative, illuminative, and unitive movements by positioning purgation in the light of grace. In this sense, purgation is understood in terms of the struggle to respond to grace manifested in our human situation. While we enter into a world that is wounded yet graced—in Romero's case, a world that was wounded by exploitation and oppression as well as the limitations of his own family and seminary training and his responses to these—grace lures us into the struggle which heals our woundedness and also reveals the wonder of our being and the gifts we have yet to realize.

Inspired by Irenaeus's pastoral theology, we now explore Romero's spiritual journey not so much as a journey structured by sin and its constraints, but rather as a journey of faithful discipleship motivated by love of God, self, and neighbor and by the increasing freedom gained on such a journey. This developmental approach rests on three key Irenaean themes: his "divinely appointed environment" (the context of Romero's conversion, his progressive movement into the "vision of God"), Romero's growth toward human authenticity and spiritual maturity, and his "recapitulation in Christ" (a look at the transformed man).

From this theological foundation, I propose a spirituality of conversion in the following chapter. Now, on to exploring Romero's "divinely appointed environment."

Irenaeus's doctrine of God acknowledges that the Triune God relates to creation in love, absolute goodness, and a desire for human beings to share in the life of God. As Creator, God is immediately present to creation. And creation gradually mediates Godself to humans. Human beings, sharing in the image of God, are created with a remarkable capacity to receive God and become accustomed to God. Created by Absolute Beauty, we are endowed with gifts of beauty which, when painstakingly developed and brought to full growth, reflect God's glory—though not always, since human beings are constrained by the limitations of the human condition.

Irenaeus maintained that Adam and Eve were duped by Satan and deprived of original righteousness. As a result, their choice bequeathed a fundamental woundedness to humanity. Yet, ever focused on God's great mercy and kindness, Irenaeus interpreted their choice as an understandable lapse that occurred in the childhood of the race, due to their immaturity and lack of knowledge and experience of God. So, in this view, graced though wounded, humanity became partners with God in the work of personal and communal salvation.

Accordingly, redemption is not a sin-centered but a grace-based journey. Grace initiates, sustains, and leads us to salvation, engaging the struggling to become authentic human beings growing in an ever deepening relationship with God. Irenaeus is clear, however, that the soteriological journey of discipleship is one of balance. While we struggle from the woundedness imposed on us by sin, becoming converted into the likeness of the Son of God is integrally related to the struggle to discover and develop our unrealized gifts.

Irenaeus relies on grace as the only power and presence on which we can depend to grow into Christ's likeness. The decision to respond to grace is a matter of freedom. Where is this grace found? It is to be found in our "divinely appointed environments." This environment includes our personal and historical condition. Grace is found in discovering our fundamental wound and God's desires for us to be healed and freed from the constraints the wound inflicts. In light of Irenaeus's theology, I interpret Romero's conversion in terms of the discovery of his fundamental woundedness manifested in the features of his OCPD—the context of his conversion.

Rigidity, perfectionism, scrupulosity, living controlled by rules and regulations, and workaholism are symptoms of a fundamental woundedness. Within a psychological framework, such behaviors suggest that Romero may have, deep in the core of his being, believed himself to be unloved, unlovable, and incapable of love. His family of origin, particularly his relationship with his father, contributed early on to what was later identified as OCPD.

Santos Romero was a peaceful man. Yet he was tense, had a bad temper, and insisted on a quiet house when he wanted to read. Living with seven children in a limited space, his temperament and the demands he made were the source of (and aggravated) many tensions. These tensions contributed to Romero's personality disorder. This most essential relationship, charged with patterns of rigidity, distance, and lack of intimacy and nurture, proved emotionally challenging for Oscar.

As Santos Romero contributed to Oscar's early life, the seminary system of the day (which he entered as a child) reinforced his austerity and rigidity by encouraging affective detachment from family and friends as an ascetic norm for seminary and priestly life. Living in this milieu intensified the ambivalence of his childhood and reinforced his belief that obedience to his superiors is equivalent to obedience to God. Obedience, particularly in the seminary, which required unquestioning submission to authority and did not tolerate any semblance of autonomy, contributed to Romero's truncated development. For Romero and his contemporaries, unquestioning obedience to the wishes of superiors and the expectations of Church officials was esteemed as virtuous.

We cannot forget the common practice of dismissing seminarians for reasons few would consider legitimate today. Given the religious climate of the day, being sent home engendered shame, guilt, and a sense of failure. Since Romero's religious and cultural context conceptualized the self in fundamentally different terms, discouraging self-discovery and autonomy, fear of growth and development were important factors in determining his personality. As a result, the compensatory behaviors he developed in the seminary and early ministry, behaviors which contributed to his success, became self-limiting in the context of subsequent challenges and possibilities.

In this perspective, "pathological personality traits are traps, self-made prisons that are perniciously self-defeating in that they promote their own continuation."[1] For the most part, until his diagnosis, Romero showed little evidence of awareness of the limiting dimensions of the features of his personality disorder. Unfortunately, the theology of the day encouraged him and his contemporaries to accept as normative a body-denying spirituality. The notion of sanctity Romero internalized encouraged withdrawal from the world, aloofness, severe self-criticism, preoccupation with rules, norms, numbers, and rituals. These reinforced his already distorted cognitive attitudes and justified his self-deflating behaviors.

Romero's early pastoral life demonstrated a pervasive rigidity in some areas. In the eyes of some, he feared making mistakes. It stands to reason then that risk taking for Romero was anxiety provoking. Change was threatening. He was not yet able to consider matters from different perspectives because the unknown future represented danger, causing him to preserve established patterns. As a young man, Romero's demeanor was overly serious, joyless, and grim. He was careful to keep most emotions under tight control, a habit that required substantial psychic energy. He demonstrated socially commendable behaviors such as politeness, behaviors that, in the framework of OCPD, were the diametrical opposite of deeper, contrary, and forbidden feelings.[2] The young Romero's tendencies toward rigidity were expressed by his inability to negotiate, alleviate, or integrate his internal ambivalence, a demeanor somewhat mitigated later in life.

Romero's self-criticism nourished his scrupulosity. In psychoanalytic terms, this tendency was driven by guilt, shame, and a yet unintegrated superego. As an adult, he developed a cruel internal gauge that mercilessly evaluated and controlled him. We have only to recall his self-rebuke for being distracted and lacking reverence while celebrating Mass. This mechanism, according to some psychologists, would have intruded relentlessly, creating doubts which would have compounded his hesitancy toward action in some arenas. Romero was all too ready to condemn himself for his thoughts, feelings, and behaviors. Framed by an Augustinian emphasis on sin, he interpreted his thoughts and feelings in terms of sin and moral failure.

His regimen of self-inflicted punishments was a device to alleviate shame or guilt or to discipline the soul. In psychoanalytic terms, his controlling superego prevented him from exploring new ways of behavior. This perpetuated toxic habits and sustained his misery. His scrupulosity was linked to the development of a relentless superego that held him and others accountable for unattainable ideals. Romero's fear of making mistakes contributed to his perfectionist behaviors as he sought to avoid the tormenting pain of external criticism.

In this framework, in order to distract from the anxiety prompted by a fear of the unknown, Romero created rules and regulations to provide a semblance of order and security, a defense mechanism he employed to evade the discomfort of the natural ambiguities and insecurities of life. He not only lived by rules and regulations, he went out of his way to uncover legalities, moral presumptions, and ethical standards to judge others. Those who exhibited autonomy or resistance to the ecclesial status quo, like the Jesuits who became involved in social justice, violated his standards and met his condemnation and disapproval. Since rules, regulations, and social and religious hierarchies provided structure, restrictive injunctions, and external authority, Romero masked and avoided dealing with his contrary urges. His penchant for rules and regulations stemmed from deep insecurity and fear of vulnerability.

Through a psychoanalytic perspective, Romero, conscious of his self-image, terrified of failure, and unable to enjoy reasonable self-affirmation, derived his identity and value from external authority, his performance record, and his accomplishments. Seeing himself in traditional terms as generous, dedicated, industrious, reliable, meticulous, and efficient, he overvalued those aspects of his character that exhibited discipline, perfectionism, and loyalty. The combination of needing to be valued and accepted from sources outside himself, the sheer volume of his work load, and the energy needed to control his inner urges conspired against Romero and drove him to the point of mental and physical exhaustion. Although the spiritual frameworks of the day interpreted such behavior as meritorious, Romero's workaholism was, in psychoanalytic terms, partly a means of escaping the dreadful feelings of threatening failure. It was the means by which his desperate need to be valued was satisfied.

Oscar Romero's personal and historical condition together comprised his "divinely appointed environment." His humanity, while graced with a capacity to receive and become accustomed to God, was also endowed with wonderful gifts yet undiscovered. Though graced in his youth, Romero had been fundamentally wounded, most probably believing himself to be unloved, unlovable, and incapable of loving others. God, motivated by love and a desire for our companionship, fullness, and freedom, mediated grace through Romero's "divinely appointed environment." Irenaeus inspires us to pay attention to the stirrings of grace in our human condition because grace alone invites us out of darkness and bondage into God's light and freedom. As Romero demonstrated, response is a matter of desire for God and freedom. Interpreted through the prism of Irenaeus's theology, Romero's struggles to respond to the grace of conversion within his "divinely appointed environment" gradually accustomed him to the vision of God. Each response transformed him, little by little, into the likeness of the Son of God.

One of the basic assumptions I make about conversion is that grace stimulates spiritual and psychological change in the midst of continuity. Spiritual change results when the grace of conversion inspires a gradual shift from a narrow notion of holiness focused on self to a broad notion of holiness, refocused on the Trinity and our participation and role in the divine community. Psychological change results when the grace of conversion animates the discovery and development of God's gracious gifts. It is a progressive movement from entrapment in the constraints of our woundedness to a freedom appropriate to mature adulthood. This interdisciplinary dialogue is necessary to see how psychological and spiritual developments are two dimensions of a single growth process.

In Irenaeus's perspective, spiritual growth is gradual, purifying, and salvific. In his reading of the temptations of Jesus in the wilderness, Irenaeus noted that the human Christ struggled to discover and define his own humanity and his relationship to God. And he left an example for disciples. Contemporary disciples are no different. We too need to discover and accept for ourselves the ever revealing wonder of God and of our human reality. This reality includes accepting that God desires an intimate relationship with us, that we are endowed with gifts intended to be brought to fullness, and that our unique fundamental wound and its manifesting behaviors are the vehicle through which valuable growth occurs. This search for our gifts in the limitations of our woundedness comes about only by becoming accustomed to God, through our progress into the vision of God.

For Irenaeus, since we are endowed with a capacity for increase, we can receive God, but only gradually. Growth in knowledge of God involves growth in self-knowledge. God reveals Godself and, in the process, God gradually reveals us to ourselves. This process of increase in knowledge of God and self is captured in Irenaeus's three-movement schema for progress in the vision of God. This increase moves from a prophetic, to an adoptive, to a paternal seeing of God.

Central to his schema is the affirmation that the more we come to know God's beauty and gracious intentions, the more we respond by an ever increasing love. Further, as God reveals areas of our personalities and souls that are yet unhealed or unfree, grace beckons us toward deeper healing and greater freedom. The intersection of the call to conversion with the desire to respond forms a dynamic human struggle to be obedient to the grace of conversion. In these struggles, disciples are transformed, little by little into the likeness of the Son of God. The more advanced our transformation, the more we come alive. The more we come alive, the more clearly the glory of God is revealed. For Irenaeus, this is the purpose and destiny of each person created in the image of God and intended for likeness to the Son of God.

Receiving the vision of God is in itself a magnificent grace given to those who desire God. It is a gift given at God's discretion. Since grace is prevenient, the Creator initiates our movement into God, and mysteriously and slowly the Word and the Spirit direct this progress. As we will now see, this perspective is useful in recasting Romero's development in terms of becoming more accustomed to God as he struggled to be faithful to grace revealed.

God begins to re-create disciples in the vision first through a *prophetic* seeing of God, that is, the awakening of our call to deification. It is the beginning of God's gradual self-disclosure when grace either gently touches the soul or seizes it with disquieting force. In whichever manner it occurs, grace arouses a longing for God. The prophetic seeing is vague. There is a heightened perception that God is obscurely, mysteriously wrapped up in life. The disciple knows something of God but, as yet, has not personally encountered the Word.

El Salvador's deeply religious culture and a mysterious illness Romero sustained at age seven contributed to awakening his spiritual sensitivities.[3] Romero was a deeply pious child and demonstrated an inclination toward God and matters religious. The boy's frequent visits to his village church to pray in solitude, his resistance to his father's plans for him to be a carpenter, and his desire to be a priest—all are initial responses to grace. While still unaware of the dynamic movements of grace, his simple devotional practices, desire for prayer, and entry into the seminary were responses to this grace. Romero experienced his first struggle to respond to grace around the age of thirteen when he left his family for the seminary in San Miguel, seven hours away from home.

While in formation, Romero, though always dedicated to prayer, went the additional distance of getting up at midnight. Once ordained, prayer continued to be a priority in his busy life. His stubborn adherence to fulfilling his obligation of common prayer may have been compulsive behavior or his incessant desire to seek God's will. Already in his childhood and adolescence, Romero responded to a prophetic seeing of God.

As a young seminarian, Romero's desire for God was undoubtedly shaped by a theological system that promoted a body-denying spirituality. This perspective lacked a positive view of our embodied existence and failed to integrate human sexuality and emotions. Accordingly, influenced by the widely read Tanquerey, Romero considered human nature sinful, to be denied and dominated if he was to achieve his goal, perfection.

Desiring priesthood and leaving his family created an internal struggle. Uncompromising fidelity to numerous prayers and the demanding norms of seminary life created struggle. And corporal asceticism created struggle. In each, Romero made a choice to respond to his longing for God. Inspired by the theological context he was being formed in, he interpreted conversion as a movement from sin toward God. He was obedient to the grace of conversion as he then understood it. In the framework I am developing here, Romero's physical, emotional, and spiritual struggles were the result of his responding to grace within a prophetic seeing of God.

Progression into the vision of God builds upon the experience of the prophetic seeing to an *adoptive* seeing of God. In this phase, disciples experience a more comprehensive, personal encounter with God revealed in the Word. As a process of deification, the Word and the Spirit reveal God as God is, which challenges our earlier images. Through personally encountering the Word in our lived reality, we come to know more convincingly God's love and desires for us. We begin to see more clearly the actuality of our blessings and promise as well as our wound-edness and its consequences. In the choice to follow Christ more closely, we become more engaged in the struggle to become accustomed to God. The adoptive seeing initiates a new and deeper quality of turning inward toward God in prayer and a simultaneous reaching out in justice.

Romero's adoptive seeing of God originated during his thirty-day retreat, where he was led through a method of contemplation that nurtured a more graced personal encounter with Jesus. In the second week of the *Exercises*, Romero made an election to love and to follow Jesus more closely. Opting for a more intimate relationship with Jesus simultaneously touches a need for human intimacy. At this stage, the Irenaean framework suggests a twofold response to grace.

First, an encounter with the Word leaves disciples wanting more of God. This relational style of prayer moved Romero to reevaluate his task-oriented, rote style of prayer so neatly laid out in his Rule of Life, a style of prayer that placed him at center and God at a distance. Even as Romero remained attached to some forms of prayer from his early life, this new style of prayer initiated a movement toward a deeper, more personal relationship with God. This required him to relinquish some control and have greater trust in God. Obedience to the grace of con-version initiated a struggle in him to leave self-absorption. It required him to relinquish a false sense of security to enter more fully into the mystery of the Word and the Spirit. These Two Hands of God would then refocus and guide his conversion process.

Second, almost a decade after this retreat, two of Romero's pre-senting problems with Dr. Dárdano, a deepening depression and an in-creased misery of loneliness, were still causing him anguish. Notable is Romero's capacity to articulate these painful emotions when he con-sulted with the psychiatrist, which in the framework of OCPD is no small thing. His ability to articulate these feelings indicates that his hard, seemingly unemotional shell was pierced previously, perhaps even by a heartfelt experience of being loved by God. His depression and lone-liness were the raw indicators of his heretofore unspoken desire to be loved and to love, and his frustration at being unable to meet those needs.

If my suspicions are correct, Romero was overwhelmed by the invitation to believe himself truly loved by God. This powerful and profound grace challenged his deepest, most fundamental assumptions about himself. If he believed himself to be unlovable and, moreover, was encouraged to refrain from intimacy, such a grace would be in direct contrast to his faulty self-limiting assumptions. This triggered internal dissonance. Here, his obedience to grace involved a struggle to accept himself as loved by God, a key conflict which involves loving others. Expressing vulnerability regarding his need for love was an important step in accessing his own cycle of self-perpetuating destructive thinking and behaviors.

Romero's 1966 diagnosis by and sustained affiliation with Dr. Dárdano occasioned another graced intervention in his life. Romero sought out Dr. Dárdano because of his inability to hold his ambivalence in tension, his impotence in managing the avalanche of painful emotions that provoked increased discomfort, distress and disability, and his anxiety over the changes inaugurated by the Second Vatican Council. That Romero stepped outside his comfortable frame of theological and spiritual reference to consult with a psychiatrist is another response to the grace of conversion.

Grace was mediated through Romero's agony. His intense internal pain drew his attention toward his yet unhealed and unintegrated emotional woundedness. The grace of hope was mediated through his relationship with Dr. Dárdano and the psychotherapeutic skills he used to help Romero understand his complex personality.[4] Mediated grace awakened him to the destructive features of his obsessive tendencies which prevented Romero from further growth and from more fully enjoying life. It also called him to pay closer attention to the widespread realities of suffering and repression in El Salvador.

The grace of conversion invited Romero beyond his myopic interpretation of human life in terms of sin and grace to accept that human nature is not predominantly sinful and to be dominated. Rather it is a dynamic part of a greater whole of humanity in need of understanding and integration. This conversion generated a struggle for Romero to reframe his former notion of the human condition, relinquish his notion of human perfection and, most especially challenging, accept his own human weakness and woundedness. By engaging in these graced struggles through psychoanalysis, he took greater personal responsibility for his own psychological growth and development. He also assumed greater moral responsibility for the effect his destructive attitudes and behaviors had on others, a catalyst that spurred him on to further transformation.

By his own admission, the psychoanalysis he underwent in 1971–72 provided another encounter with the grace of conversion. Through psychoanalysis, Romero probed the foundations of his personality disorder and learned therapeutic strategies to facilitate some psychological integration and human growth. In psychoanalysis, Romero came to understand the possible genesis of his obsessive-compulsive thinking and behaviors. It gave him deeper insight into how his rigid formation and ecclesial worldview reinforced the distorted assumptions that perpetuated his injurious behaviors.

The experience offered him a new set of assumptions about himself and the world. It provided behaviors he could gradually introduce into his life to further his personal emotional maturity, not least of which was the encouragement and permission to foster relationships. Knowledge of skills, however, was insufficient. Romero chose to implement these skills intentionally in his day-to-day life. From an Irenaean perspective, Romero, summoned by grace, stretched toward what he was not yet. It meant breaking with his past cognitive patterns and behaviors. It also meant reclaiming his personal power, which he had handed over very early in his life to a theological system that he now recognized as flawed and antiquated.

Following the psychoanalysis, Romero struggled to establish healthy relationships and friendships reflecting greater mutuality. By his own admission and the testimonies of colleagues and associates (later, in Santiago de María and San Salvador), he did form satisfying, productive, collaborative working and personal relationships with his priests and people. Romero struggled to counter his workaholism by scheduling days off, taking siestas after lunch, and intentionally discerning what he could or could not physically and psychologically undertake. To counterbalance his rigidity, Romero struggled to be more flexible in his expectations of himself and others and increasingly delegated responsibilities to his assistants.

As Archbishop, Romero encountered many circumstances and people who mediated the grace of conversion, further crystallizing his conversion. Each of these elicited a struggle, inviting Romero to go beyond himself, to act on his commitment to the gospel that demanded justice, to exercise his authority, and to use his office to fight the uncontrolled injustice and brutal murders in El Salvador.

Romero knew his appointment as Archbishop was endorsed by some of the oligarchs to protect their interests. He also knew the Vatican selected him because of his record of public conflict with politicized priests, the progressive Jesuits, liberation theology, and his affiliation with Opus Dei. Romero knew that he was not the people's candidate for the post. His previous experience in Santiago gave him firsthand knowledge of the terrorism and violence that now characterized his ministerial world. Yet, he accepted the appointment. Perhaps his acceptance was motivated by a profound sense of loyalty to the Church, or a growing commitment to Christ crucified in the people by the Salvadoran military, or his inability to refuse Pope Paul VI. Perhaps he accepted out of a need for affirmation and validation from his superiors in Rome. Or perhaps he accepted as an act of self-transcendence, inspired by a belief that the appointment was actually God's will for him and that God would work through him to resolve his own inner conflicts and to bring reconciliation and peace to the Church and El Salvador. Whatever motivated him, Romero accepted. And while we will never have full knowledge of his motives for accepting the appointment, what is certain is that he did accept, and the fruits of his prophetic leadership continue to inspire faithful discipleship today.

From an Irenaean perspective, Romero, having become increasingly accustomed to God in his previous struggles, was able to discern and respond to the grace of conversion mediated through Rutilio Grande's assassination. Romero deeply admired Grande for his total option for the poor and his dedicated priesthood. Jesuit Provincial César Jerez notes Romero's sentiments about Grande: "You know how I admired him. When I saw Rutilio dead, I thought, 'If they killed him for what he was doing, it's my job to go down the same road.'"[5] As Romero came to value Grande's pastoral theology, his death—the death of a martyr—intensified Romero's struggle to reframe his vocation as disciple and pastor. As Archbishop, Romero, entrusted with greater authority and responsibility, came to see himself as called, like Grande, to serve Christ whom he came to see incarnated in his suffering people.

Romero's previous struggles helped him mature. Former theological and spiritual explanations no longer sufficed. The Jesuits and his close advisors provided more compelling pictures and explanations of Salvadoran realities. They helped to articulate a theology more deeply rooted in the Bible and responsive to the suffering of the poor. This moved Romero and increasingly called him to conversion.

All of these converged to stimulate radical theological and ecclesiological shifts. Obedient to this grace, Romero struggled to break with the traditional image of the Church as an institution of power and, in opting for the poor, committed the Church in El Salvador and its resources to the service of the poor. It was a bold move. Romero, who previously had feared the disapproval of the powerful, now confidently sustained continuous public ridicule, blame, and criticism from his wealthy friends. Despite being personally disappointed by the opposition of the Salvadoran bishops and some powerful Vatican officials, Romero was able to keep steady on his course. New levels of serenity and confidence in God enabled him to withstand these public attacks with composure, indicating much personal growth.

From his homilies and talks, Romero, like Grande, came to understand himself as a poor, simple pastor. This is no small achievement for one who had previously relied on external sources to define his identity and validate his worth. Reflection on Grande's life and martyrdom piqued Romero's conscience, igniting his struggle to respond to another, more demonstrative conversion. This struggle moved him toward the authenticity of his identity as disciple, pastor, and prophet. Again, confiding in César Jerez, Romero tried to explain his struggle to discern and reclaim his identity.

> "Monseñor, you've changed. Everything about you has changed. . . . What's happened?"
>
> "You know, Father Jerez, I ask myself that same question when I'm in prayer . . ."
>
> "And do you find an answer, Monseñor?"
>
> "Some answers, yes. . . . It's just that we all have our roots, you know. . . . I was born in a poor family. I've suffered hunger. I know what it's like to work from the time you're a

little kid. . . . When I was sent to seminary and started my studies, and then they sent me to finish studying here in Rome, I spent years and years absorbed in my books, and I started to forget about where I came from. I started creating another world. When I went back to El Salvador, they made me the bishop's secretary in San Miguel. I was a parish priest for 23 years there, but I was still buried under paperwork. And when they sent me to San Salvador to be auxiliary bishop, I fell into the hands of Opus Dei, and there I remained . . . .

"They then sent me to Santiago de María, and I ran into extreme poverty again. Those children who were dying just because of the water they were drinking, those campesinos killing themselves in the harvests . . . . You know, Father, when a piece of charcoal has already been lit once, you just have to blow on it to get it to flame again. And everything that happened to us when I got to the archdiocese, what happened to Father Grande and all . . . ."[6]

Romero came to accept and somewhat appreciate his heritage, his human reality and his sense of growth and development. He moved toward recovering some of the defining features of his childhood, affirming the conversion in his later adult life as a return to his origins. Having embraced his own limitations, Romero became more understanding and more deeply compassionate. For me, there is no better story that proves Romero's process of conversion and his expanded capacity for compassion than the touching one offered by his personal secretary, Angela Morales:

When I started seeing a young man who had been a seminarian and who was working with the communities, I didn't say anything at home. Not because he'd been a seminarian, but because my parents were against everything—against my having a boyfriend, against my getting married, against my living with anyone. So I was silent. I was afraid of the scene it would cause.

When I got pregnant, the guy behaved badly and left me. I was afraid of an even bigger scene so I kept even quieter.

But Romero . . . I did have to tell him. And his was the scolding I was most afraid of.

I'd been working for him for about ten years as his secretary, and practically his housekeeper, since the time he'd
come to San Salvador as the auxiliary bishop, then later in
Santiago de María and now as Archbishop. I wrote letters for
him, I cleaned up his desk, his files, and his recording room
everyday. I made his bed. . . . I took care of his scheduling.
And I always brought him the boldo tea he liked to drink mid-
morning when he needed to calm his nerves. And the honey
for his throat which would get irritated from so much preaching. By now, Monseñor Romero was like my father, and the
anger I most feared for being pregnant and without a husband
was his.

But I had to tell him. Some people already suspected, and
they were going to go to him with the gossip anyway. Or he'd
figure it out himself since he saw me every day in the office.
But how?

How could I work up the courage to tell him, and what
could I say? What if I started shaking and got a frog in my
throat? How could I begin? I couldn't just deal with the problem myself either, because he was my father and also my confessor. But how could I survive a scolding from him? He
wouldn't just scold me, he'd fire me, and I'd be left without
work, and then what would I do? How could I earn enough?
It would be me and the baby on the streets without money,
without a soul we could count on. Dear God, what are we
going to do on the streets?

But I had to tell him. I went over it again and again in
my mind for I don't know how many days, and finally one
day I tiptoed into his office with that glass of orange juice
that he liked to drink at 10:00 in the morning. I was sick with
worry and fear. "Monseñor, your orange juice . . . ."

"Oh good. It's so hot today. . . . Sit down, Angelita. I
want to say a few things to you."

"I have something to say to you too, Monseñor. It's just
one thing . . . ."

"Well then, ladies first!"

My whole body was shaking from head to toe when I
started telling him. And I told him everything from the beginning—from the time I'd started seeing the seminarian to
the time of the swelling of my belly which was now beginning to show.

"And he's going to be born in five months." I was sobbing.

He looked at me and smiled. And he stayed like that for a minute or so, but it seemed like an hour to me.

"It's alright, Angelita; the first time is forgiven."

"What did you say, Monseñor?" I was so flustered that I didn't even understand him.

"Don't worry, *hija* [daughter]. The first time is forgiven. Right now you have to do what you can for the baby that's going to be born."

He kept smiling, and it was me that felt like I was being born again!

From that day on, he helped me out with everything like a worried father. He told Silvia Arriola to help me, and so the two of us went out to talk several times. He asked his sister Zaida to take care of me until the baby was born. He even spoke with my parents to tell them what was happening, and if they ended up forgiving me, it was only because of his intercession.

During the last month of my pregnancy, he said, "You have to go and rest, Angelita. I'm not running you off, mind you. When you feel better, you've always got your job here and I'll be waiting for you. Better yet, I'll be waiting for the both of you—you and the little guy!"

It was a little girl. Claudia Guadalupe. I named her after Monseñor's mother, so that her memory would be alive in my daughter.[7]

In this account, two particular gifts emerged from Romero's graced struggle. First, where before he was unable to engage deeply in personal relationships, here he demonstrated the heart of relationships, love, and an ability to receive and express love. Second, while rules previously played such a large role in his interactions with others, this anecdote demonstrates compassion and his ability to go beyond rules to understand human fragility.

When Romero assumed responsibility for the Archdiocese of San Salvador, he understood his primary role was to uphold the Tradition and appropriately implement the teachings of the magisterium. Supporting new interpretations of the Church's social teachings and mission of justice in defense of a persecuted and defenseless people in a Third

World country on the brink of civil war, however, provoked many questions and conflicts in him.

Romero gradually learned to put others before himself, to face his fears, and to exercise his prophetic leadership. Eventually, obedience to the grace of conversion led him to repeatedly risk assassination for passionately condemning the oligarchy's greed and obstinance, human and civil rights violations, U.S. political and military intervention, military terrorism, and a corrupt judicial system. His struggle transformed him into a prophetic pastor whose acceptance of martyrdom in the cause of liberation for his people brought him to the threshold of a *paternal vision* of God.

This final stage in Irenaeus's schema of progression into the vision of God is, in fact, the *paternal* seeing of God. Having been transformed in and by the adversities of life and the struggles to be obedient to the grace of conversion, one is rendered, in a sense, broken, purified by fire, and perfected for the royal banquet. It is the moment when God grants incorruptibility— a seeing of God face to face. For Irenaeus, this constitutes the fullness of the vision of God, which, without question, was at the heart of Romero's increasing longing for God.

Within the psychological and spiritual environments of his life, the grace of conversion was mediated through persons and situations. Each summoned Romero to a more mature humanity, deeper integrity, and fuller participation in the life of the Triune God. Each struggle called forth his gifts and challenged his faulty assumptions, motivations, behaviors, and beliefs. Each revealed a little more concretely the presence and reality of God and the demands of Christian discipleship.

Each time, Romero struggled to choose grace and to remain faithful to it. Although he was unsure and the process was untidy and unmapped, each response gradually advanced him toward a new horizon of becoming more human, and spiritually freer to respond to God. In an Irenaean sense, Romero became accustomed to God. At the end of his life, Oscar Romero entered into the fullness of union with God as one who shared in the recapitulation of Christ. That is, as one who advanced into the vision of God through a lifetime of struggles to be faithful to the grace of conversion. Romero's journey through a prophetic, adoptive, and paternal seeing of God transformed him more completely into the likeness of the Son of God.

The context of Romero's conversion was his "divinely appointed environment." His progress into the vision of God yielded enormous human growth and spiritual maturity. Finally, at the end of his life, Romero returned to God transformed. This soteriological transformation gained him a share in the recapitulation in Christ.

In these words, Paul frames the essence and purpose of the Christian life: "Before the world was made, God chose us, chose us in Christ, to be holy and spotless, and to live through love in God's presence, who determined that we should become God's adopted children through Jesus Christ for God's own kind purposes."[8] Vatican II confirms and supports this election and offers direction for discipleship: "It is therefore quite clear that all Christians in whatever state or walk in life are called to the fullness of Christian life and to the perfection of charity, and this holiness is conducive to a more human way of living even in society here on earth."[9]

Irenaeus's theology provides keys to mapping this path of discipleship. In his exegesis of Christ's temptation in the desert, Irenaeus emphasizes the critical importance of struggle in the salvation process. Called by grace toward human growth and union with God, we come to self-knowledge and knowledge of God by taking up the struggles to be faithful to grace in the context of the ordinary circumstances of life. Irenaeus draws our attention to Jesus, who followed the Spirit into the desert to be tempted away from his humanity and to denounce his divinity. Disciples, too, can be tempted to do the same.

For Irenaeus, Jesus clarified and discerned his human identity and mission in and by those struggles. Irenaeus is explicit. It is only through a series of human struggles that we discover the wonders of God and our created reality, that our errant assumptions and behaviors are rectified, that our character is strengthened, and that we become more confident—thus better able to recognize and withstand the cunning of the evil one. When in imitation of Jesus and his Spirit we are faithful to the struggle, Irenaeus affirms, we share in the recapitulation of Christ. We become more humanly authentic and more deeply united to God.

The Irenaean exegesis of Jesus' temptation in the wilderness provides a promising metaphor to help probe more fully Romero's conversion. When the Spirit led Romero into the "desert" of depression, misery, loneliness, and the injustice of the poverty of El Salvador, he had to confront the ideals provided by a theological and spiritual formation that tempted him to deny his humanity—and the humanity of the Salvadoran campesinos and workers suffering under the oligarchs. Romero struggled to discover, accept, and integrate his new affirmation that to be human is to be graced, yet wounded and limited, and that community, intimacy, and mutually loving relationships are good, healthy, and necessary.

Anne Mary Dooley, reflecting on the qualities that denote maturation in persons marked by obsessive-compulsive behavior, says that the mature religious sentiment is open to continuous reorganization on the basis of new data issuing from relevant experience. It becomes largely independent of its origins, which can be traced back to childhood. Likening it to a butterfly that has shed its cocoon, she observes that one's religious sentiment is developed by fresh motives and conceptualizations which arise from broadening interests, values, and experiences of the maturation process.[10] Romero's courageous confrontation with the oligarchs, the four opposing bishops, and the Vatican—and the sure sentence of death—indicate that his motives and values were reoriented. As he came to accept the broader spectrum of his human condition, he became a more effective, passionate, and compassionate minister.

When the Spirit led Romero into the "desert" and propelled him into psychotherapy, he had to confront his fears, anxieties, and faulty assumptions which promoted behaviors associated with using power to control and dominate himself and others. He also confronted his own soteriology, the belief that salvation is won through a rigid and blind obedience to the law, which colored his early styles of prayer and physical asceticism.

Maturity—for persons with obsessive tendencies—involves spiritual, somatic, cognitive, and affective growth. The more integrated Romero's ego and superego became, the more his personality structure became organized and stabilized, permitting him to take responsibility for his actions. Applying new cognitive patterns made it possible for him to make decisions to transcend the limiting effects of his behavior. Toward the end of his life, Romero was able to make new kinds of choices regarding social pressure to conformity, extreme stress, and his impulses. His new self-assurance allowed him to determine for himself the extent to which his fears and anxieties would constrain him. Romero's life demonstrated a significant development of what began as very traditional Christology and anthropology. This was so not because it made sense in his sociopolitical context, but because he came to believe himself loved by God, loveable, loving, and committed to the power of love.

When the Spirit led Romero into the "desert" of his own conflicts regarding his episcopal identity and ministry, he had to come to terms with his underdeveloped sense of personal authority, shown in his prior need for approval and acceptance of externally defined norms. As Archbishop, he was tempted to maintain his earlier patterns of supporting the agenda of Opus Dei and the status quo of the Church in El Salvador, perpetuating the Church's alliance with the country's elite. Romero's struggle to internalize and minister in concordance with his chosen episcopal image, "a bishop with a pastoral heart," brought many consequences. As a pastor and teacher, he proclaimed the Gospel, welcomed by the country's elites or not, and struggled to implement the Church's theology of social justice.

In psychoanalytic terms, one feature of a mature personality is an ability to take responsibility for forming one's conscience and taking responsibility for acting on it.[11] The integrated and healthy personality calls for an enlightened perspective upon the society in which one lives. It also calls for active engagement in providing social conditions suitable for humans to live and develop their potentialities. If a personal commitment to religion does not encourage a person to grow in understanding society and to protest unjust policies and practices, then it is no more than a tranquilizer.[12]

As Archbishop, Romero stood resolute in his own moral convictions and demonstrated a calm demeanor amid countless accusations from those who supported the oligarchs and their relationship to the official Church. Convinced that greed was the evil that threatened the people and country of El Salvador and the Church, Romero did not deviate from his pastoral identity and prophetic ministry. He was persecuted and his appointment as pastor of a persecuted Church meant an obligation to protect his people, to call those in error to conversion, and to participate personally in the people's struggle for freedom from dehumanizing systems.

Irenaeus would have said that Romero was, at the end of his life, recapitulated in the image of Christ through the crucible of graced struggles. Irenaeus's theology of recapitulation is applicable here. The purpose of human existence is the making of character by the mastery of difficulties and temptations throughout life. Through an interweaving of nature and grace, disciples, in a "divinely appointed environment" where good and evil coexist, participate in the struggle, like Christ in the desert. It is a struggle against the temptation to deny their humanity or divinity, or against the threat of death which has the power to hinder union with God or the fullness of human potentialities. Through the struggle, Christ recapitulates us. This means that our relationship with God is rectified. It is *only* through this graced struggle that disciples are healed and liberated. Romero was recapitulated by Christ through his struggles. As a result, he entered into union with God as a martyr, a man who revealed the glory of God because he himself was transformed into a living human being whose true life was found in the vision of God.

Irenaeus affirms that, having been created by God, we are able to receive God's ever revealing Self and grow toward union with God. To be human is to be created with a longing for God that is deeper than the woundedness that impedes our growth. Since personal growth and development for Irenaeus have soteriological significance, our inherent motivation toward becoming more human lies at the heart of becoming divinized. The divinization occurs within the internal "divinely appointed environments" of the human personality and soul, as well as the exterior communities in which the converted find themselves. Positive and sustained responses to the grace of conversion revealed in the circumstances of life produce struggle. This struggle is the matrix of conversion which refashions disciples into the likeness of the Son of God and makes it possible to participate in the recapitulation of Christ.

Though Romero continued to struggle with his limits, he responded to the grace of conversion and the features of his OCPD diminished to subclinical levels. Romero became reoriented and relational. Little by little, he came to enjoy an intimate relationship with the Triune God. His struggles helped clarify his episcopal identity and mission. They also helped to strengthen his resolve to bring forward God's reign of justice to the country and Church of El Salvador.

At the end of his life, we see a man who became more compassionate, freer, and comfortable in his identity and mission. He became more self-confident, happier, stronger physically and mentally, passionate, and focused. Romero's humility developed as he became more reliant on God and worked more collaboratively with his advisors. He was generally loved and gained the respect of many of his priests, the religious, and the campesinos. The support of some prestigious academic institutions and international humanitarian organizations helped sustain him in his prophetic leadership and his work for human rights. It was love that motivated Romero to live, to preach, and to die for the radical Gospel and the people it served. In this way, Romero's odyssey of conversion bears witness to and calls our attention to the need to treat the powerful psyche and spirit as a unity so as to better facilitate a model of discipleship that responds to the vision of renewal issued by *Lumen Gentium*.

Romero's transformation was the result of grace mediated through a community of disciples and good psychotherapy. Clinical therapy indeed engages the dynamics of spiritual conversion. Romero's psychotherapy was central to and in service of his conversion process. Therapeutic relationships offer a wide range of benefits, not least of which are further growth and integration of life's gifts and wounds. They also help to expand narrow visions and interpretations of life, and encourage growth from self-centeredness to other-centeredness. Further, clinical relationships hold us accountable for taking personal responsibility over the negative effects of our woundedness which we might otherwise, unconsciously inflict on others.

Oscar Romero possessed a longing for God that remained constant throughout his life—although its content and form shifted. How he understood that longing and the manner through which he encountered God, however, broadened, deepened, and widened as he grew in self-knowledge and matured in his relationship with God. Graced, yet wounded, he struggled against the temptation to deny his humanity and his divinity. In his graced struggles, Romero was recreated and reoriented more fully toward God and concerns outside himself. His sustained struggles advanced him farther into the vision of God, and in the process, Romero revealed God's glory.

I believe that Irenaeus would identify Romero as a master disciple. Although particular to the Salvadoran cultural and social context, with the inclusion of martyrdom, the conversion of Oscar Romero suggests the broader outlines of a spirituality of conversion. It points to a renewed paradigm for a spirituality of conversion based on Irenaean resources, honoring the powerful, multidimensional integration of psyche and spirit. Extracting insights and conclusions from what has been said, I will articulate a dynamic spirituality of conversion for the contemporary disciple in the following chapter.

CHAPTER 5

A SPIRITUALITY OF CONVERSION
INSPIRED BY IRENAEAN THEOLOGY,
THE LIFE OF OSCAR ROMERO,
AND DEVELOPMENTAL PSYCHOLOGY

"The story of Job tells us that conversion of the just person is not from evil to good, but from self-centeredness to God-centeredness: allowing God to take possession of one's very being through a free surrender of absolute autonomy."[1] Interpreting Romero's conversion through Irenaeus-inspired lenses, we note that growth into God-centeredness occurs through a series of lifelong struggles to be obedient to the grace of conversion operative in the particular circumstances of all life's dimensions, including the psychic and spiritual. Here, in the weaving together of Irenaean theology with the life of Oscar Romero and developmental psychology, I propose a contemporary spirituality of conversion.

This spirituality of conversion is grounded in the work of Bernard J. Lonergan's multidimensional notion of conversion, which drew on the discourses of philosophy, theology, psychology, and pastoral practice. Influenced by Ignatian spirituality, Lonergan articulated a sharp and distinct framework for the phenomenon of Christian transformation, which is important for the model of conversion I propose. To round out this dialogue, I blend in the contributions of two of Lonergan's heirs who developed his theory into the realms of psychology—namely, Bernard Tyrrell, who blends theology, psychotherapy, and spiritual direction, and Robert Doran, who weaves together depth psychology and theology. Since social conversion, implicit in Lonergan's schema, is vital to my proposed spirituality, I have included a section on social conversion. Drawing on these key insights, I offer a contemporary spirituality that honors personal development and spiritual maturity, and I recommend formative spiritual disciplines that can nurture and support a spirituality of conversion.

Bernard Lonergan went beyond the work of Thomas Aquinas, whose notion of conversion has been interpreted as a turning away from sin toward God, to conceive of conversion as a process of personal development.[2] His work recasts theological thought about conversion, arguing that conversion involves the entire person, promoting human authenticity and spiritual maturity. Walter Conn further developed these insights in dialogue with developmental theorists.[3] In this light, conversion can be understood simultaneously as a movement toward human authenticity[4] and a shifting of our orientation toward God.[5]

Conversion is a lifelong process. It is a series of interlocking radical changes and developments, some subtle, others dramatic. Explicitly, Lonergan identified conversion in three interconnecting categories: intellectual, moral, and religious. For him, transformation happens in two phases. First is an awareness of a radical interior shift, and second is the intentional decision to implement one's newly acquired knowledge toward a sustained self-transcendence into daily life. Experiencing and responding to the grace of conversion and integrating newly acquired awarenesses into life moves us from one horizon of consciousness to another.

Epistemologically, Lonergan was concerned with developing the norms of truth, showing how we attain the truth, and clarifying how the pure desire to know affects consciousness and choice. Intellectual conversion concerns clarifying experience, understanding the meaning attributed to the experience, and eliminating any myths that could obstruct that meaning. Making an important distinction, Michael Rende contends it is "a psychological fact that we desire to know; it is an epistemological fact that what we desire to know is being."[6] Thus, concerning self-appropriation, to know is, ontologically, the dynamic process of coming to greater self-awareness, self-discovery, and self-understanding, a prerequisite for informed, knowledgeable, and responsible judging and deciding.

Intellectual conversion challenges intuitive and inferential beliefs so we can arrive at the truth about the nature of reality. Lonergan advocates taking responsibility for the truth or falsity of our beliefs and for the adequacy or inadequacy of the frames of reference that we employ in trying to understand reality. When we take personal responsibility to cooperate with grace to confront ideologies, personal biases, intellectual sloth, and prejudices, we become free to transcend the horizon of conventional wisdom.

Intellectual self-transcendence seeks truth regardless of cost or discomfort. Attaining clarity, we are able to practice a more sustained self-transcendence, consciously opting for choices based on value. The fruit of intellectual conversion orients us toward responsible action, action informed and guided by truth and the pursuit of value.

Romero displayed tenacity for the truth. His own intellectual conversion included, early on, the difficult task of self-appropriation. With the help of his psychologist and spiritual director, he became able to accept and deal with the features of his OCPD and scrupulosity. Later, his pure desire to know the true realities of his afflicted country, the cause of the suffering of his people, and the authentic characteristics of true Christian discipleship within a changing Salvadoran and post–Vatican II context enabled him to see more clearly the truth of his national and ecclesial situations. His pure desire for truth led him to the door of a moral conversion.

Moral conversion begins with distinguishing the operations of one's conscience and taking conscience seriously. This leads to an awareness that the criterion for making decisions has evolved from self-satisfaction to the pursuit of value. One's choices are therefore governed by a movement toward morally deliberate ethical behaviors based on what is truly good. After opting for the good or the transcendental notion of value, putting the decision into practice commences the real moral self-transformation. This transformation moves from moral intentionality to moral performance, with each act of choice contributing to the ongoing creation of an authentic person.[7]

The criterion for moral living is the pure detached desire for freedom, which calls for discernment. "To exercise one's pure desire for freedom means dying to one's fears concerning the unknown and to one's cravings for security; it means breaking away from one's settled routines."[8] Freedom gradually compels us to live in a way that is detached from self-interests and inordinate attachments in the human community. It strives toward securing the common good for all people. Christian conversion is linked to concrete action which mirrors the changed internal reality. Responding to the gospel mandate to transcend self for the sake of the neighbor leads directly to greater participation in social responsibility and efforts toward obtaining human rights for all people.[9]

Romero's intellectual conversion paved the way for him to act in pursuit of value, and for him, Christ was his ultimate value. Transcending his fears, he acted in conscience which required that he challenge the unjust social and ecclesial systems responsible for perpetuating social sin. Aware that he was marked for assassination, Romero nonetheless accepted his fate—a martyrdom that enabled his full identification with Jesus Christ.

Religious conversion moves us from conventional faith and attachment to religious practices to a faith based on an ever deepening relationship with the Triune God. Lonergan insisted that religious conversion is a progression of horizon shifts which consists of two movements, falling in love with God after having been seized by grace, and responding to grace through acts of self-transcendence.

Being in love with God enables us to subordinate everything to an "undertow" of grace that floods the human heart. Convinced that we have been touched by grace, our focus alters from loving God for what God does to loving God for who God is. Such a transition evokes profound wonder and gratitude and gives rise to a natural sense of appreciation.[10] When we become confident of God's tremendous, unconditional, and incessant love, we more easily surrender to the Spirit, and are liberated from egocentrism. Egocentrism, according to Walter Conn, is the tacit assumption of the self as the center of reality. And since authentic development is a process of decentering, or moving beyond or transcending the self, religious conversion effects the most authentic, realistic self-transformation insofar as it is a radical decentering of self.[11] Relinquishing an assumed control over God and self is critical to religious conversion because it positions us to be in right relationship with the Creator.

Being grasped by the absolute love of God requires religious self-transcendence, the gradual movement toward a full and complete transformation of the whole of one's living and feeling. Responding is the intentional choice to transcend self for the sake of otherworldly love and the absolute good of the neighbor. Religious self-transcendence means abandoning the quest for absolute certainty, satisfied that it is enough to dwell in mystery, reliant on grace and one's community of faith. The religiously converted live with the joyful assurance of being loved by God and are freed interiorly to respond to the demands of the Spirit.

Romero's religious conversion can be interpreted as a movement from seeking to do God's will to being in intimate relationship with God. Grace mediated through the *Spiritual Exercises*, his relationships, the Salvadoran reality, the limitations of current Church practices, the biblically inspired vocation to witness to the coming of the reign of God, and his responsibilities as bishop all forced open his heart to new dimensions of God.

Within Lonergan's vast corpus, affective conversion is the least developed.[12] He acknowledged the important role emotions play in revealing truth and value, and the need to heal life's wounds, both of which are of consequence to conversion. Subsequent theologians, particularly Bernard Tyrrell and Robert Doran, have further developed a more comprehensive understanding of the vital function of psychological/affective conversion in the process of radical human transformation.[13]

Bernard Tyrrell, a Jesuit psychotherapist combined the discourses of psychotherapy and the *Spiritual Exercises* in the service of promoting spiritual and psychological conversion, especially conversion from addiction.[14] In Tyrrell's view, psychological conversion is a two-stage radical shifting from a neurotic to a healthy state.[15] This shift is brought about by healing one's deeply felt sense of being unloved and the self-destructive attitudes and strategies for living that people develop as a result of feeling unlovable and worthless.[16] This conversion involves the healing of feelings and self-image. It requires a reorienting of attitudes and behaviors so decisions can lead to a transformation of the sufferer on the levels of meaning, value, and behavior. Conversion from addiction is a radical and ongoing process of turning away from the addictive object and turning toward health, life, and freedom from the addiction.[17] To facilitate psychological conversion and the conversion from addictions, Tyrrell's *Christotherapy*, a form of spiritual direction, uses the *Spiritual Exercises* as a type of psychotherapy which incorporates prayer, the encounter with God, and the engagement with the Christ-event as central to the unfolding of one's unconscious unfreedoms, areas in need of conversion.[18] In the end, we move from a state of neurosis to health as we become convinced that we are lovable and worthwhile to God.

Robert Doran integrates Jungian depth psychology and Christian theology. He complements Lonergan by suggesting that for conversion to be complete we need to "descend into the valley" of the unconscious to access important data for self-appropriation. Because psychic conversion releases the capacity for the internal symbolic communication important for self-appropriation, Doran says, "the task of the philosopher or theologian educated by and indebted to Lonergan may be to descend the mountain of cognitive self-appropriation so as to attentively, intelligently, reasonably, and responsibly appropriate and articulate the rich psychic basis of human experience."[19]

Mature consciousness and psychological integration involve discovering and acknowledging submerged feelings together with the ability to articulate one's inner story with clarity and precision.[20] It is having a sense of one's psychic history: what has contributed to its woundedness; what has been healed and liberated; what still needs attention. Dreams, says Doran, play a crucial role in transmitting to our consciousness important information to better understand the inner story. Dreams have value because the images and content are not controlled by our waking consciousness, and the spontaneous responses they elicit can offer deeper insight into the complexity of our human psyche. Recognizing and distinguishing symbols can facilitate our orientation to truth, moving us in the direction of discernment by clarifying value. Through attention to the internal reality of dreams and the spontaneous feelings they elicit, we can see the connection between intentionality and psychic vitality.

Romero's psychic/affective conversion opened the censors of his experiencing, understanding, judging, and deciding, allowing him to receive the important data of his affective consciousness. This furthered his quest for human authenticity and spiritual transformation. Psychic/affective conversion within the particularities of his OCPD and scrupulosity revealed psychological complexes, which, once he engaged, freed him from the rigidity of their hold, healing and transforming the complexes into a source of energy he never imagined or realized he had at his disposal.[21]

Conversion is authentic when those who have been converted bridge humanity and God, influencing the communities in which they live. Having discovered and attended to their own woundedness and sin, they are better able to detect signs of woundedness and sin in society. Transformed by their own conversion, they possess the moral authority and integrity to call others to conversion.

As conversion causes a radical awakening and reprioritization of values facilitating a movement from selfishness toward God, it animates a greater concern for the common good. Internal conversion enables us to recognize more readily the ever revealing presence and salvific activity of the Triune God. It also awakens us to the reality of ontic and moral evils within human nature. It allows us to recognize the presence of God and evil within unjust systems and structures.

Social structures that deprive human beings of their dignity as persons created in the image of God or which impede human beings in fulfilling their fullest potentialities, or which promote individual acts of selfishness over the common good are sinful structures. Persons or groups that knowingly and willfully cooperate with these structures and resist efforts to change are guilty of the sin of complicity or worse.[22] Since these structures are antithetical to the Gospel tradition, social conversion involves conscientization and efforts toward social transformation to ensure human dignity and restore the common good.

Although Lonergan does not treat social conversion explicitly, he discusses the role of bias in relationship to social sin.[23] Subsequently, Donald Gelpi has developed the Lonerganian framework to include the prudential formation of conscience on both the personal–moral and the social–political levels. Personal–moral conversion is concerned with individual rights and duties particular to interpersonal relationships, taking into consideration those norms that form our conscience, guiding good moral interaction with others. The social–political dimension deals with prudential judgment with the common good as its goal. This has a twofold effect. First, social–political conversion leads to influencing the decisions of those who control larger social institutions. Using the criteria of justice, those who have experienced social–political conversion evaluate the norms by which governments, economists, church leaders, and politicians make decisions. Second, it seeks to influence the decisions of responsible policymakers so that the norms they use work for the common good.

Social sin is a structural phenomenon. Therefore, social conversion challenges our views about established structures and often shatters the images or mindsets by which we are accustomed to perceive reality. In the end, social conversion compels solidarity with the oppressed and growth toward responsible, autonomous, ethical behavior. It reorients life's direction with a new set of values.

Romero's social conversion forced him to look at and confront his biases, prejudices, and fears. It inaugurated a transvaluation and a reorientation of how he understood justice and his responsibilities toward truth. His social conversion, enlightened by new information and personally acquired truths, inclined him to use the authority of his office for those who had no power or authority.

Lonergan's work on intellectual, moral, and religious conversion broadened the conception of conversion beyond narrowly religious terms to the fullness of human experience that is addressed in the discourses of psychology and the social sciences. He pioneered a broader, more inclusive understanding of conversion as the process of awakening consciousness concerning multiple dimensions of humanity. This included opting for integrating that consciousness with daily life. In particular, Tyrrell and Doran have focused on affective conversion as a means of attaining valuable insights and accessing energy for growth and integration, both of which can influence future choices. These types of conversion are predominantly internal operations. But social conversion, with its emphasis on attentiveness to existing social sin, also compels us toward autonomous ethical behavior based on the value of justice. Each of these aspects of conversion influences the others, creating a dynamic movement together, advancing disciples concurrently toward fuller humanity and unity with God.

While these gifted theologians have broadened our understanding of the phenomenon of conversion, they do not directly address an integrative spirituality. To meet the challenges of contemporary discipleship, we need to complement our intellectual comprehension of a theology of conversion with the lived experience of a spirituality of conversion. For me, a spirituality of conversion based on the pastoral theology of Irenaeus is a compelling completion of that whole.

Irenaeus, although writing to refute heresy, focused primarily on pastoral concerns. Although we are living in an era significantly different from his, Irenaeus's insights can shed light on contemporary thinking about discipleship. Since we also seek a credible reason for following Christ in a way that respects the relationship between nature and grace, Irenaeus's faith vision, which is Gospel-oriented, Trinitarian, and transformative, inspires a spirituality of conversion for our times.

Firmly rooted in a dynamic and relational theology of grace, a spirituality of conversion can be healing and liberating. Transformed, disciples become active participants in the salvific work of the Triune God in the world today. As a spirituality of conversion is predicated on a theology of grace, I ground this next section in Irenaeus's notion of grace, then go on to describe the strands of his theology that weave a spirituality of conversion.

Grace is at the heart of discipleship. Discipleship originates in grace and is sustained by grace. A spirituality of conversion celebrates grace present in creation and in the human experience. Since creation is permeated by but distinct from God, it is in the process of being completed by participating with God. Therefore, nature—including human nature and history—is acknowledged as good and as a channel of divine love, revelation, and communication. Framed in this graced tradition, we will examine the fundamental characteristics of a spirituality of conversion that mediate grace. These are humanity's capacity to receive and grow in God, the divinely appointed environment as the context for conversion, the soteriological struggle that emerges when we respond to the call to conversion, and the community of disciples.

For Irenaeus, the immediate presence of God suffuses creation. Therefore, it stands to reason that the Triune God who is love and who desires to give Godself in love, would in some way create human beings with an ability to receive God. Karl Rahner echoes Irenaeus: "God wishes to communicate himself, to pour forth this Love which he himself is. And so God makes a creature whom he can love: he creates man. He creates him in such a way that he *can* receive this Love which is God himself, and that he can and must accept it for what it is: the ever astounding wonder, the unexpected, unexacted gift."[24]

Discipleship, guided by this spirituality, is a way of life lived in and empowered by the principles of love because God is love and the person who lives in love lives in God and God in her/him (1 Jn. 4:16). Experiencing God's love deeply ignites an insatiable longing for God—but only if we are made aware of it and are called to attend to it by those also on the journey. As though seduced, we are gradually led by the Word and the Spirit down into the usually unnoticed regions of our own lives and histories to discover that which may enhance or hinder us from fuller life with God and our own human flourishing. Here we come to know God as God is. Here we experience, firsthand, the tender embrace of God. Convinced of God's love through these graced experiences, it becomes easier to trust God. Trusting, we can more easily relinquish control and surrender our preoccupation with self-centeredness and advance toward union with God. Experiencing the love of God, then, leads to conversion.

Lonergan described this experience as being seized by grace and otherworldly falling-in-love. Tyrrell believes that when we are convinced we are loved by and worthwhile to God, healing begins. And many psychotherapists call attention to the therapeutic value of patients recognizing their need for love. Seen in this light, Romero's conversion was a process of coming to a realization of being loved by God and others, and his awareness that he too had the capacity to love. Such were the *kairos* moments in his conversion process. As grace began to call him out of his isolation and his focus on sin, grace enabled him to recognize his woundedness and its effects on himself and others.

Irenaeus's "capacity for increase" makes it possible to grow and develop as God's ongoing self-revelation is communicated through our human experience. Yet, because we are able to experience God's self-revelation and self-communication only incrementally, human growth, including spiritual growth, is often slow. Because human nature is so complex, there is always some new reality to be learned and integrated. We need not look any further than our immediate interior and exterior "divinely appointed environments"—the context of conversion.

Oscar Romero's longing for God was evident early on, in his seeking God in the presence of the Blessed Sacrament in his village church and in his desire to dedicate his life to God as a priest. As a constant presence and energy, this longing inspired multiple intellectual, moral, religious, affective, and social conversions throughout his earthly sojourn. His capacity for God enabled him to receive grace mediated through his graced and wounded human nature. So, too, grace was mediated through various styles of prayer, the example of master disciples like Luis de la Puente and Rutilio Grande, and a challenging and supportive community of faith. These converged and reoriented his gaze from self-preoccupation toward God present and active in the reality of his world.

In our "divinely appointed environment" good and evil coexist. Since grace is mediated through creation, nature, and history, the ecclesial image expands to the marketplace, base community, city, village, or world—indeed, to creation itself! Thus the locus of salvation is no longer the Church alone, but the Church *and* the world. Movement toward God is contingent upon encountering the mystery of grace revealed in Scripture, sacrament, creation, and human experience, with particular attention to the call of grace in our human nature and personal histories. However, while we may be animated by love to respond, evil impedes our movement toward God.

The grace of conversion, when mediated through the human personality, illuminates unrecognized blessings as well as psychic unfreedoms, areas in need of conversion. Jean-Marc Laporte appropriately captures this dimension of grace: "Grace deals with me as I am in my total personal history, my sin, my weakness, the obstacles that beset me and releases within me the authentic power of who I am as a human being. I am affirmed, confirmed, healed, and empowered to become my genuine self."[25] When responded to, grace heals the human personality, enabling it to flourish beyond our expectations. Oscar Romero remarkably demonstrates this, particularly in the last three years of his life.

Romero attended to his misery, depression, loneliness, inability to control his feelings, and exhaustion. Psychological therapy, psychoanalysis, spiritual direction, and his relationships led him to a deeper awareness of the intense personal dynamics diagnosed by his therapist as OCPD. These relationships enabled him to recognize his graced nature and his sin in the light of grace. They also provided him with vital information to differentiate between sin and the personality disorder, which he had confused, and insight into how one affects the other.

Romero's professional and personal relationships at times challenged and, at other times, supported his new attitudes and behaviors.

Reading his journals, we find evidence that knowledge of the psychological and spiritual made it possible for him to be clearer and more intentional about his choices. Each time he chose behaviors contrary to those of his OCPD, he chose for God. Choosing for God diminished the power his compulsivity had over him. Eventually, Romero came to accept the limitations of his humanity and worked to change what he could of his cognitive assumptions and behaviors. Throughout, Romero struggled to respond to grace operative in his woundedness. He also discovered wonders of God heretofore unobserved.

A spirituality of conversion attends primarily to recognizing and accepting God's gracious desires for us as well as personal healing, liberation, and the work of integrating the human personality. This contributes to the healing and liberation of the human community which suffers the effects of social sin. Regarding personal healing, recognizing God's love calling us out of the darkness and the bondage of unhealed psychic wounds and unhealthy cognitive assumptions, our response to grace is twofold. First, it is in submitting to the light that grace casts on our human nature, accepting the reality that we are desired by God and graciously endowed to receive God. Second, it is in attentiveness to the fundamental wound and its destructive tendencies in matters of ethical conduct. Vigilance engages intentionality, necessitating a choice of behaviors that will not cause or perpetuate suffering and harm to others. Once Romero became aware of how the features of his OCPD affected others, he worked to reframe his assumptions and to choose appropriate behaviors.

Discipleship begins with an awareness of God's presence and activity in our lives. Growth in this relationship and, later, intimacy with God requires a single-heartedness for God and the desire to appropriate a lifestyle reflective of the virtues and values of Christ. It requires docility to the Spirit whose work in the economic Trinity guides disciples further into the transforming mystery of God. Irenaeus knew that fullness of life with God is not automatically given. Each disciple, like Jesus, struggles to grow in knowledge and intimacy with God.

Spiritual direction—mediated through the examples of master disciples, the community of faith, responsible preaching, the RCIA process, or an individual mentor in the spiritual life—can help disciples recognize interior forces of good and evil and how these manifest in our lives. In the framework being developed here, Romero identified and discerned the particular manifestations of good and evil in his own life. This made it possible for him to *choose* to respond or not to the grace of conversion. The choice was not only for himself as Archbishop; it was for the lives of those entrusted to his care. Self-knowledge and reflection on one's personal experience and history provide the necessary data to discern the movements of grace and sin in daily living. These help disciples *be* whom God intends, then *do* what God asks—in that order.

Repeatedly responding to grace fine-tunes the ear of the heart to the call of grace. Then, recognizing God's invitation, we may, like Romero, selflessly serve at the pleasure of God. This ongoing surrender to grace continues the salvific paschal mystery of Christ in whose likeness we seek to be transformed. In the end, Romero never intended to be a prophetic figure, nor did he deem himself worthy of martyrdom. Yet, ironically, because he lived the paschal mystery of sustained intentional self-transcendence, his identity as a martyr was cast long before March 24, 1980.

Attentiveness and response to grace in our own lives awaken disciples to those areas in the human community in need of healing and liberation. The converted, convinced God and others love them, become refocused and look beyond themselves to the needs of the common good. A mature love prompts conscientization, illuminates biases and fears, gradually reorients our vision, reprioritizes our values, and engages new psychic energies. As a result, disciples become sensitized to the presence and operations of grace in the world and to the potential for enabling the progress of peoples and whole societies.[26]

Motivated by this recognition of God's action in the world, and inspired by the life and commitment of someone in the community who demonstrates discipleship, the converted become aware of and concerned with exposing unjust systems and structures that hinder people from realizing their endowments as human beings and children of God. A spirituality of conversion involves efforts to alleviate the suffering that social sin imposes on people in the communities in which disciples find themselves.

From his first assignment, Romero worked to meet the human needs of his congregations, insisting that a religion void of service is empty. As he grew in the spiritual life, that inclination flowered into the passionate campaign for human rights that caught international notice. Romero was familiar with his own woundedness and the power of his own conversion. Moreover, coming to terms with his own human constraints strengthened his solidarity with his oppressed people. This led him to place his authority and resources at the service of condemning human rights violations, and promoting the basic rights of Salvadorans then under repression and persecution. Influenced by his own personal conversion, by the powerful example of the discipleship and martyrdom of Rutilio Grande, and by the Church's mission to evangelize, Romero was not deterred from calling his people—the campesinos, the Salvadoran elites, and the military—to conversion.

Romero demonstrates what happens when disciples recognize and respond to the grace of conversion. In his struggle to respond, he discovered an astonishing freedom, a spontaneous joy, a new physical and psychological energy, and a deep interior peace—all fruits of conversion. Engaged in the struggle, he was transformed into a more authentic human being and a master disciple. The same awaits those who embrace a spirituality of conversion.

For Irenaeus, the struggle born of the tension between the call of grace and our human constraints induces human and spiritual development. Such maturity is brought about by responsibly exercising the gifts of personal freedom and choice. In the struggle, character is built and we come to value all the more that which we have achieved with God. Perhaps most importantly, when we struggle, we do not struggle alone. Rather, we are led to the struggle and accompanied in the struggle by the Triune God in a community of faith. Such a journey, Irenaeus believed, was salvific.

Becoming accustomed to God is vivifying yet difficult, even heroic. It was so for the human Christ, it was so for Romero, and it will be so for anyone who embraces a spirituality of conversion. Becoming accustomed to God is a struggle because, as we progress further into God, we are required to relinquish attachment to any untruths or pretenses that obstruct intimacy with God. Truth and falsehood cannot coexist. At its most fundamental level, this is the struggle with ego and the myth of self-sufficiency.

Through the struggle, our gaze will be reoriented to God, something only grace can do. Then, trust will increase, enabling a more generous surrender of self. Ultimately, this is gift. It is the invitation to relax into the Triune God and relinquish control of directing our own deification process, our assumptions about holiness, and our futile attempts to accustom ourselves to God.

This is apparent in Romero's life when, early on, his strategies toward achieving holiness led him to increased prayers, physical asceticism, and numerous pastoral projects. One does not *achieve* holiness! One is *made holy* by grace and participating in the human struggle! Despite Romero's sincerity and good intentions, his early efforts did little to transform him internally. It is easy to understand why. Imposing disciplines and pious practices can lead to a false humility and the illusion that one is, from external appearances, progressing in holiness. However, when prayer, asceticism, and good works flow from falling ever more deeply in love with God, resulting in an increase in compassion, then authentic holiness is in process.

Think about it. When Romero could no longer tolerate his misery and internal ambiguity, he reached out to psychological intervention. It was then that the work of transformation really began to intensify and changes in him became apparent. Perhaps aware of God's ever-present love and attentiveness to him, Romero confronted his wounded humanity and focused on reframing attitudes and implementing behaviors that were more like those of Christ.

Living a spirituality of conversion eventually leads to another set of struggles, equally as challenging if not more challenging than the first: knowing ourselves to be loved by God and others. Our relationships can draw out gifts and talents we never knew existed. Developing them acknowledges that we have, in some way, begun to accept God's vision for us. We have noted how Tyrrell and some psychiatrists affirm that humans begin to flourish when we experience love. Being obedient to the grace of conversion, which reveals and conveys God's precious personal love and desire for us to participate in the life of the Triune God, creates a struggle to *believe* ourselves loved and desired. This is *the key* that opens the door to ongoing conversion since we can move forward convinced of God's love and trusting God enough to surrender ourselves to a mysterious process not always comprehensible in human terms. The significant turning points in Romero's conversion came about when he discovered and accepted that he was loved deeply by God and that others loved him.

In Irenaeus's soteriological view, humanity is endowed with various potentials to continue God's work of salvation. We are intended to achieve the fullness for which we were created because, in this, God's glory is revealed. Misinterpretations of theology have, in the past, distorted our perceptions of God's desire for us, thus obstructing the development of latent human potentials. Fear has also prevented us from developing concealed gifts because of where the risks associated with the new horizon of self-development might take us. Obedience to the grace of conversion invites us to discover, accept with proper humility, and develop our God-given potentialities. Responding to this grace involves struggle because our wounded self-image tempts us to disregard the fact that other possibilities have yet to be discovered. As we have seen, while therapy gave Romero the needed permission to begin reaching out to establish relationships and friendships, Vatican II and Medellín provided him with a new, more relational theology and ecclesiology. This helped him better understand God, the mission of the Church, and his identity and role as bishop.

Becoming accustomed to God's love and desires for us requires openness to new paths and possibilities heretofore unimagined. Accepting the vision God has for us challenges the established vision we have for ourselves. Obedience to the grace of conversion evokes a conflict between joining the efforts of the economic Trinity in furthering salvation history on the one hand or, on the other hand, sinking into complacency, staying with the familiar. It also challenges disciples to discern their real motives for ministry.

Early on, Romero's fear of vulnerability, his need to be in control, and his need for affirmation unconsciously drove his task-oriented, compulsive ministry. Later, we observe that, while his motivation remained the same (to do whatever God asked), he was more composed, focused, and peaceful. These flowed from his deeper relationship with God and others. Although the behaviors of his OCPD continued, they were not as frenetic as before and were significantly redirected. Romero's pastoral identity, now aligned in a new way to the Sacred Heart of Jesus, impelled him to be a message of hope to a persecuted people, to reach out in compassion to victims of the Salvadoran military, and to genuinely do all he could to alleviate the suffering of an oppressed people. Irenaeus would suggest that Romero's powerful presence and prophetic ministry could not have been fully realized without the support of a community of disciples.

For Irenaeus, the *ekklesia*—the community of disciples—supports and encourages the progress of conversion. For those baptized into this community, the Eucharist and the Word bring us to the fullness of our Christian identity, ministry, and destiny. Through the kerygma of the *ekklesia*, Christ extends himself through master disciples, opening new life and offering a future filled with promise and hope. For Romero, the Vatican Documents and the post-conciliar documents, especially Pope Paul VI's *Evangelization in the Modern World* and Medellín, played a key role in forcing open his imagination and heart. While these challenged him to new ecclesial visions and pastoral practices, his human relationships powerfully inspired his development.

Once Romero addressed the issues of loneliness and isolation, his efforts toward the development of meaningful personal and professional relationships exposed him to further growth. Rutilio Grande's life, his option for the poor, his dedicated ministry, and his martyrdom called forth unprecedented growth in Romero. Grande was, for Romero, a new paradigm of discipleship. Romero's relationship with Pedro Arrupe, César Jerez, Segundo Azcue, and previously noted Jesuit scholars and advisors opened new horizons. Similar to Irenaeus, whose Church was persecuted and who found inspiration from master disciples and the community, Romero was supported and encouraged by his priests and people, many killed for living their faith. Finally, as beautifully illustrated by Angela Morales's testimony, people who loved, respected, and worked with him summoned forth and supported his strengths.

The Christian community is a community of disciples who challenge people to grow through love. Since the community of disciples gathers around love and aspires to love, love—not fear of sin—calls forth beauty, gifts, and fullness from disciples. Romero's life spanned pre– and post–Vatican II faith visions, making the differences tangible. He was formed in a sin-centered spirituality and was re-formed by love mediated through personal friendships and through the larger community of disciples who challenged him to minister in love and to be love. As bishop, he positioned himself close to the suffering of his people, which touched his vulnerability and changed his heart. Knowing first-hand the pain of his own struggle and the limits of his human condition,

Romero became more understanding and compassionate. The community of disciples, the poor ones, the ones who suffer, mediated the grace of conversion to Romero through their lives and stories, calling him to deeper authenticity and Christian integrity.

Among the community of disciples we find master disciples, Christians whose lives—and sometimes, deaths—are examples of true discipleship. While the Church has traditionally celebrated such persons, its official criteria for judging sanctity rests on extraordinary signs of uncommon relationship to God and places great stress on sinlessness. There are those, however, whose quiet, ordinary, single-hearted desire for God and commitment to their baptismal promises lead the community to identify and mark them as master disciples. In doing so, the community calls the Church to a new awareness of being in the world by recognizing a graced humanity dwelling in the midst of society. By the very presence of these master disciples, society and the Church are challenged to conversion.

Early on, Romero recognized Luis de la Puente as a model for discipleship. Later, he discovered a new paradigm in Rutilio Grande. As a master disciple, Grande's heroic discipleship and martyrdom inspired Romero to a courageous response to grace, and challenged Romero to love and serve in ways he had never imagined.

A community of disciples inspired by Irenaeus's vision is one of service. Irenaeus saw Jesus as a man of deep prayer who extended himself in humble and gracious service to those in need. A spirituality of conversion challenges disciples to be vigilant of the needs around them and, with free and generous hearts, to discern the best means of response. Too, a community that honors the place of humble service challenges nascent disciples' motives for service. As a community committed to the needs of the neighbor, it challenges and supports a healthy balance of prayer, leisure, and service. Further, service summons disciples to grow beyond self-interests, to go where they might rather not go, and to meet the needs of those in their company with graciousness and kindness. The young Romero served the needs of his people, but his service in that era was task-oriented, ego-driven, and compulsive. As Archbishop, his ministry still reflected some compulsive tendencies, but his service was motivated by a compassion heretofore unobserved.

Romero was converted by grace mediated through his human struggle, his relationships, and the community of disciples. Observing—

through an Irenaean lens—the person Romero became at the end of his life, we are positioned to see the benefits that living a spirituality of conversion yields.

A spirituality of conversion is a response to the vision of Vatican II. It is available to all people who are called and who take seriously the invitation to holiness. Above all else, Irenaeus inspires a shift in focus. He understands the value of the soul and is concerned with how disciples can live in relationship with God, others, and the world. Obedient to grace, Romero, re-created in the likeness of the Son of God, reflects Irenaeus's ringing vision: "The glory of God is the living human being and the human person has true life only in the vision of God." For anyone committed to a spirituality of conversion with an Irenaean flavor, the glory of God is the *only* reason for life because the glory of God *is* the fully authentic human person who has found life in the vision of God.

A spirituality of conversion provides a clear and positive purpose for discipleship: to become fully alive and in the process reveal God's glory. Irenaeus insisted that God is Love and is motivated solely by love. Moreover, love motivates our desire to respond to grace. In the simple act of responding we are formed in a community of support into the likeness of the One who is Love. The process of conversion is an odyssey from self-love to love of God manifested in love for others.

A spirituality of conversion is, in one sense, custom-designed. Although broad enough to suit every lifestyle, it is, nonetheless, uniquely personal. Conversion effects a radical, deep, and lasting transformation, primarily by recognizing both the wonder of God in our graced humanity and the wound that affects, but does not destroy, the deepest dimension of our human personality. As a way of life, it attunes disciples to be attentive to incessant grace which illumines and calls forth gifts not yet discovered. It also means paying attention to the grace that can transform, not take away, our human woundedness so we can live in a harmonious coexistence with the limitations of human nature, others' and our own.

Attending to the wound has a moral dimension. Self-appropriation gives us the experience needed to discern between good and evil as they get played out in the unique peculiarities of our lives. Recognizing the traps that might threaten mishap, we can be intentional and choose to respond more fully instead of being driven by unconscious and unbridled psychic impulses. In doing so, we take responsibility for not perpetuating evil and causing others to suffer. Such a way of living is intended toward the glory of God through human flourishing.

Irenaeus's faith vision animates a powerful and exciting new paradigm that is meaningful for contemporary discipleship. To remain faithful to such a way of life requires the practice of formative spiritual disciplines that will sustain the lifelong journey of transformation into the likeness of the Son of God. As mediators of grace, these disciplines are the vehicles through which individuals and the communities they affiliate with are transformed.

Irenaeus was aware that the essence and energy of God are found in a universe that originates in God and struggles toward unity with God. For a graced and wounded humanity engaged in the same dynamic, personal and communal prayer, an asceticism that is sensitive to a suffering humanity, and discernment are some spiritual exercises that nourish a spirituality of conversion.

Prayer predisposes us to grace, fosters relationship with God, nurtures participation in the larger sacramental and liturgical life of the Church and strengthens us for ministry. Disciples are formed by Christ and the Spirit through personal prayer and the prayer of the community—the Liturgies of the Word and Eucharist. While the prayer of the Church nourishes and shapes us, so too, our personal encounter with the Word is profoundly transformative. Both personal and communal prayer are vital to the formation of disciples.

Personal prayer is complex and is practiced in countless ways, depending upon one's personality type, experience, and level of maturity. To nurture a spirituality of conversion, however, a type of prayer that focuses on listening to God is requisite. Contemplative prayer in its various manifestations is the best suited for this spirituality because it mediates personal encounters with God, invites self-transcendence, and reorients and deepens our desires for God.[27]

Whether it takes the form of *Lectio Divina*, Centering Prayer, the practice of the Presence of God, or Ignatian Imaginative Contemplation, contemplative prayer arouses the emotions and the deepest desire of the human heart. It invites the whole person, not just the intellect, to participate in a relationship with God. A continuous practice of contemplative prayer fosters self-knowledge and true knowledge of God and helps us discern God's desires for us within the reality of our human condition. Since a desire for intimacy—not just relationship—with God impels contemplative prayer, contemplative prayer is hospitable and welcomes God as God is, enabling spiritual growth into an ever-deepening union with God.

Contemplative prayer is primarily focused on the Word. Since Jesus is the single-hearted, recapitulated human being who withdrew into solitude to be alone with God, who was faithful to the Spirit, and who struggled toward human authenticity and interior freedom, a steady diet of constant interaction with the resurrected Son of God is itself transformative. Contemplative prayer forms not only an inner attentiveness to the presence of Christ, it produces a sensitivity to the presence and activity of Christ in the world. As with Jesus, and as with Romero, personal encounters with the true nature of God, the God of love, inspires in the disciple the only appropriate response, love. In this, we imitate Christ more fully, co-laboring with him in the work entrusted to him by God.

For Irenaeus, the Spirit constantly animates the Church because the Spirit dwells in the Church. Communicating Christ in word and sacrament, the Spirit transforms the whole community according to the image of the Son; the community follows Jesus Christ's transformative path through passion and death to resurrection. The Christian community gathers in the presence of the risen Christ through the Spirit who proceeds from him and who gathers the assembled community to renew the covenant of grace embodied in the paschal mystery. Arguably, this is *the* central formative experience. First and foremost, communal worship forms disciples and the community into the likeness of the Son of God through the proclamation and preaching of the Word and partaking of the Body of Christ.[28]

Since the Word of God is living and active, it has the power to convert hearts and lives. God initiates the conversion process through the proclamation of the Word. God also discloses Godself in the narratives of Scripture and more immanently in the life and ministry of Jesus. Mary Catherine Hilkert beautifully articulates the dynamics of this formative process:

The word of God forms the assembly of believers into a community of forgiveness when they hear the story of the prodigal son, fashions them into a Eucharistic people dedicated to responding to the hungers of the world when they hear again of the multiplication of the loaves, shapes them into a people of compassion when they hear of the cure of the leper or the son of the widow of Naim. Believers become more deeply grateful for their heritage of freedom and more committed to the liberation of all peoples when they hear again the story of the Exodus. The word of God breaks down the limits the community would place on where God is to be found and who speaks God's word as the assembly listens to the testimonies of the shepherd Amos, the youth Jeremiah, the Samaritan woman, or Mary Magdalene. The word of God challenges limited understandings of ministry and social roles as Jesus' washing of feet is proclaimed as the gospel narrative on Holy Thursday.[29]

By its very nature, preaching is formative. Its goal is to trigger human consciousness and inspire a praxis toward personal and communal freedom, wholeness, reconciliation, and flourishing that overflows in joy and praise.[30] Carla Mae Streeter has this to say about preaching: "Preaching is the primary act of the self-constituting process that we call 'church.' The community called church is actually formed by this word. It is brought more and more into being every time that word is preached. More, the community enters into this formation by its choice to engage the word. Because preaching means or intends something beyond information, it is *formative*."[31]

Preaching inspires personal conversion and, by association, effects communal conversion. As it stands now, an ecclesial conversion would challenge the Church to be more teleological in its identity. This new way of being church would have at its center a dynamic and powerful way of preaching evident in the transformed *lives* of the preachers.

Hilkert notes that the mystery of preaching is at once the proclamation of God's word and the naming of grace in human experience. The preacher, first, by her/his personal experience with conversion, embodies the word, then interprets what has been operative in the depths of the community's human experience.[32] Francis of Assisi, who lived in an era where preaching was impoverished, demonstrated by his life an extraordinary way of preaching. Oscar Romero, a powerful biblical preacher, was formed by the Word and possessed the charisms of preaching.[33]

By its prophetic nature, preaching ought to reflect on social sin and challenge unjust systems and institutions. Inspired preaching holds out hope in the struggle toward union with God and liberation from personal and social sin, denouncing attitudes and behaviors incompatible with the Gospel and Christian lifestyle. Such preaching calls us to be church in a new way. While we know that the call to conversion is natural to us but is not normally noticed, effective preaching calls us to pay attention to the presence and power of God constantly recreating the hearts and lives of disciples and the community.

This theological premise, of course, puts enormous demands on the preacher of the Word. Lack of prayerful preparation or a lifestyle that fails to model the preached word is disingenuous and deprives the community of an opportunity to grow in grace and freedom. But even more so, the faithful who are the hearers of the preached word have an obligation. The objective quality of the preaching notwithstanding, theirs is the opportunity to find, in the preaching, their own personal occasion to grow in knowledge and love of the Word.

Since the basic structure of the Eucharistic celebration is word and response, it follows that the Eucharist, and our willingness to accept the Word proclaimed, are also formative.[34] Eucharist forms conscience so that individuals and communities can move toward more mature freedom to freely respond to the word of God as Jesus did.

Disciples, members of the body of Christ, are transformed by the *epiclesis*, the invocation of the Spirit on the offering of the gifts of bread and wine, and by a second, little commented on *epiclesis* on the communicants.[35] Concerning the former, in the second Eucharistic prayer, the presider prays, "Lord, you are holy indeed, the source of all holiness; grant that, by the power of your Holy Spirit, these gifts of bread and wine may become for us the body and blood of our Lord Jesus Christ." Later, he asks, "Grant that we, who are nourished by his body and blood, may be filled with his Holy Spirit, and become one body, one spirit, in Christ." The invocation of the Holy Spirit transforms the community into the Body of Christ through the unity of love of the Spirit.

In effect, the Eucharistic prayer opens us up to God and others. It calls us who are in the process of continuous transformation to embody the paschal mystery in daily life. As members of the Body of Christ, we strive to be in solidarity with Jesus in his death to sin on the cross and to participate in the risen life of Christ through the Spirit. To have died with Christ means that we consciously and intentionally commit ourselves, personally and as a community, to bring about God's plan for the world. Recall that a prominent theme in Romero's preaching, writing, and life was the reality of the paschal mystery being lived out in El Salvador. Romero's martyrdom certainly cast him in true likeness to the paschal event of Christ.

Cesare Giraudo grasps the formative nature of our common worship. "Liturgy and ethical commitment, or *lex orandi* and *lex agendi*, constitute the two sides of the one and selfsame reality; without liturgy it is difficult to have true ethical commitment; without ethical commitment, it is impossible to have true liturgy."[36] Listening to the Word proclaimed demands an ethical response, at once personal and communal. Nourished and strengthened by Word and Eucharist, both in the sacramental body and blood of Christ, and through the lives of master disciples who are/have been blessed, broken, and shared, disciples are sent to love and serve, to be Eucharist for others. The community to whom we are sent in this postmodern world provides yet another dimension of formation in a spirituality of conversion—namely, a deep, personal, and effective asceticism.[37]

A spirituality of conversion inspired by Irenaeus is based in and sustained by a community of love. Its integrity rests on the premise that the community of love needs to be immersed in the reality of the culture, local and global, in which we live. While the constraints of my work here prevent a thorough articulation of postmodern distinctions, suffice it to say that, for some writers, Auschwitz marked a key transition into the postmodern world. In our day, the image of the concentration camp continues to serve as a powerful symbol of the normalization of death in our global society where life is held cheap.[38] This reality takes on many forms: famine, genocide, homelessness, loneliness, and isolation. At the intersection between this grave devaluing of human life and this incarnational spirituality, God is present in God's seeming absence when disciples who have become accustomed to God share the suffering of others.

Our postmodern reality requires a new asceticism. That is, it requires an effective and intentional discipline and self-denial that immerses one in and serves a suffering world. This asceticism invites and places us, with Christ, in solidarity with a suffering humanity. Such praxis fosters reaching out beyond self in compassion for the other, irrespective of personal cost.[39]

As the locus for encountering God and co-laboring with Christ, disciples who give themselves to a spirituality of conversion would practice an asceticism inspired by Dietrich Bonhoeffer. His later, more mature theology, influenced by his experience of Nazi Germany, the solitude of his imprisonment, and his pastoral care of his fellow prisoners, reflects a meaningful ascetic practice in our postmodern context. In their analysis of Bonhoeffer's spirituality and moral leadership, scholars Geffrey B. Kelly and F. Burton Nelson reflect on the nature of this asceticism:

> Bonhoeffer . . . insisted it was the vocation of all who would be like Christ to share in Christ's own compassion, and to act, despite the dangers, and to be for those who suffer the embodiment of Christ's own liberating and redeeming love and his abiding presence in the service of others. Christians are expected to be moved not primarily by their own sufferings, "but by the sufferings of the brothers and sisters, for whose sake Christ suffered."
>
> Bonhoeffer's spirituality impelled him to embrace the Christian life as a call to suffer with and to respond with courage to those in whom Jesus Christ was experiencing a modern-day crucifixion. [For him] the liberating and redeeming words of Jesus Christ reach people through the preaching of God's Word . . . but that Word is also spoken in the Christ who has entered into communion with the most downtrodden and helpless of his brothers and sisters for whom, in the compassionate outreach of their fellow Christians, the cross of Christ has become what it has always been: the light shining in the darkness of human malevolence and personal tragedy.
>
> Sharing in God's own compassion, followers of Jesus Christ are called to an extreme sensitivity to human suffering. Their personal gifts are at the disposal of the most needy and, at times, the least grateful.[40]

This asceticism demands risking personal and communal discomfort. It involves the individual and the community making an intentional choice to be with others in their suffering. It challenges disciples to confront personal prejudices and fears. It calls forth new, more compassionate attitudes and behaviors that benefit the common good. This daily asceticism is practiced wherever we recognize and attend to the suffering Christ or the seeming absence of hope. As a source of formation, this asceticism brings us face to face with the suffering of others. It requires identifying and confronting unconscious defenses, fears, and prejudices that prevent the transformation that occurs when we are vulnerable to the pain and sorrow of others. It is making a conscious choice to immerse ourselves in the paschal mystery.

Romero practiced this asceticism. He often risked his life to travel to rural villages to be with the people and celebrate liturgy. He practiced it when he met daily with campesinos who walked miles to share stories of loss, tragedy, or hopelessness. He practiced it when he aligned the Church with the poor. It was Romero's incarnational Christology and social praxis that informed his asceticism and inspired his ministry of suffering with his people. The ability to enter into this praxis depends on another formative discipline central to a spirituality of conversion, the discernment of spirits.

How we relate to God depends upon our idea of who God is. One's personal experience and knowledge of God is foundational for discernment. Irenaeus revealed a God who is loving, understanding of our humanity, and accessible through our human experience. God is supportive and eager for the full development of our endowments and for our participation in the loving community of the Trinity. Embracing an image of a God who is compassionate, merciful, and understanding of the human condition makes discernment easier than images which cast God in more negative tones. Perceiving God correctly, we are more apt to drop our defenses and become supple to God's initiatives. Over time and through experience, we are then more apt to entrust ourselves with increasing confidence into the hands of God, whose thoughts and ways are in human terms unconventional and unpredictable.[41]

The context for discernment then abides in a covenant relationship with God. It is a partnership wherein making choices brings into existence God's gracious designs and hopes for us and the world. Discernment is not a pragmatic and efficient way of making choices, nor a utilitarian seeking out of God's will and responding accordingly. Rather, because it is based on mutual love, discernment is the quest to discover God's hopes and desires for us and a willingness to acquiesce to the mystery of God's wisdom.

Locating God's desires is often found in discovering our own deepest desire. Such desire energizes and empowers us. For the Christian, whose purest love and truest value is God, love of God directs us toward the God from whom we came. And it impels our existential longing to be reunited with God in that re-created form which only conversion brings about. On the critical role of desire in discernment, Michael Ivens has written,

> In the case of desire, it consists essentially in a testing of the immediate desire against the most fundamental and authentic of all our desires, those we experience at the deep level of ourselves where, in and through our own desires, the Spirit within us yearns for God. Discernment requires us therefore to become self-aware at this level and if, within this awareness, the meeting of our immediate desires and our Spirit-given desire for God brings harmony, this is indicative of the influence of the Holy Spirit in our immediate desires. Dissonance, on the other hand, indicates a "spirit" at variance with the Holy Spirit. [42]

The practice of constant discernment promotes living in relationship with God. It allows us to come closer to the Spirit who is at the core of who we are and, from there, it continues to re-create us into the likeness of the Son of God. Yet, the choice to respond to the grace of conversion rests with our freedom. In Lonsdale's words, "True freedom is the ability to become the person God destined us to be; the capacity to allow our relationship with God and hence the grace of God to determine and shape the direction of our lives."[43]

Through a spirituality of conversion, disciples and the whole community of disciples, motivated by a loving desire for God, engage this developmental process of recognizing and responding to grace intentionally. This provides the freedom to live in and with God regardless of cost or consequence. Discernment supports the Christian charism of conversion, as it enables disciples to abide in insecurity and unpredictability. It invites us to relinquish personal and communal dreams and expectations in favor of God's desires for us. It calls us to abandon the sure path of security and gradually to renounce all attempts to control God. In short, it assists in movement toward God, deferring to the Spirit who can lead us beyond what we thought was permanent to new and different horizons.

Personal contemplative prayer, the prayer of the community of faith gathered around the Word and Eucharist, an asceticism that recognizes and stands with God present in the suffering of the neighbor, and a constant discernment of good and evil spirits are formative disciplines that sustain a spirituality of conversion inspired by Irenaeus.

This is a spirituality of conversion. It is a paradigm of discipleship inspired by the writing of Irenaeus. Complementing the theories of conversion initiated by Bernard Lonergan and developed by other theologians, a spirituality of conversion offers a way of Christian living that is real, effective, and meaningful.

A spirituality of conversion is grounded in a theology of grace respected within the tradition and reflective of the vision of Vatican II. It is a way of discipleship that calls for a different way to be church. As a life lived in an intimate relationship with the Triune God, it is intended to be broad enough to be adapted by all Christians, yet custom-designed to bring about conversion at the very heart of our individual human reality.

There are four characteristics of Irenaeus's pastoral theology which inspire a spirituality of conversion. First, created with a capacity for God, a spirituality of conversion encourages disciples to pay attention to the movements of grace manifested in our "divinely appointed environment" constantly calling us toward true human authenticity and fuller union with God. Second, it calls us to healing and liberation. The context for conversion is the human heart where unnoticed gifts and unacknowledged woundedness are illuminated in the light of grace. Third, it inspires us to look for grace mediated through a community of love and service, and through the example of master disciples. Fourth, and most importantly, a spirituality of conversion emphasizes the importance of the struggle to be obedient to the grace of conversion. It is this soteriological struggle that has the potential to transform disciples into the likeness of the Son of God.

Because it has relevance to postmodern Christians, a spirituality of conversion is a dynamic path to holiness. Formed through personal contemplative prayer and communal worship in the liturgy of the Word and Eucharist, an asceticism that promotes solidarity with those who suffer, and the constant discernment of spirits with and among the loving community of disciples, a spirituality of conversion transforms disciples into the likeness of the Son of God. Embracing the struggle to be obedient to the grace of conversion, we are, throughout life, nudged deeper into the vision of God and the fullness of our endowed potentials.

Thus, in the fullness of our humanity and divinity, we too reflect, as did Oscar Romero, the glory of God.

NOTES

Abbreviations

AH: Irenaeus of Lyons, *Against Heresies*.

DSM: The American Psychiatric Association, *Diagnostic and Statistical Manual of Mental Disorders*.

SN: Romero, Oscar, *Spiritual Notebooks*.

Chapter 1

1. Woodward, *Making Saints: How the Catholic Church Determines Who Becomes a Saint, Who Doesn't and Why*, 40.

2. Dom Marmion (1858–1923) was abbot of Maredsous, the Benedictine Abbey in Belgium. He was regarded as an influential spiritual director and author on spiritual matters in the nineteenth and twentieth centuries.

3. *Spiritual Notebook* as cited in Delgado, *Oscar A. Romero: Biografía*, 18. *Spiritual Notebook* hereafter referred to as *SN*.

4. Ibid., 22.

5. Ibid., 12. See also Brockman, *Romero: A Life*, 34.

6. Luis de la Puente was born of Spanish noble blood in Valladolid in 1554. Admitted to the Jesuit novitiate in 1574, he was directed by Balthasar Alvarez who influenced Puente's desire and struggle for holiness. His religious life was spent in various Colleges of the Society in Spain; he served as rector, novice master, prefect of studies, and spiritual director. He is noted for his extraordinary love of God, his hard work, and his life of extraordinary penances. The corpus of his spiritual treatises include these: *Exposition on the Canticle of Canticles, Meditations on the Principle Mysteries of our Faith, Spiritual Guide*, and *Of Familiar Intercourse with God in Prayer.* Puente died at the age of seventy in 1624. In the introduction to *Of Familiar Intercourse with God in Prayer*, Alban Goodier, S.J., Archbishop of Hierapolis, wrote, "In some sense it might be said that what St. Thomas Aquinas was to dogmatic theology, that Puente was to mystical teaching, and what the *Summa Theologica* did for scholasticism, that the *Spiritual Guide* has done for mysticism." Puente, *Of Familiar Intercourse with God in Prayer*, v.

[7]. *SN*, February 4, 1943 as cited in Brockman, *Romero: A Life*, 38–39.

[8]. López Vigil, *Memories in Mosaic*, 29.

[9]. Brockman, *Romero: A Life*, 40.

[10]. Romero's notes from retreats made in 1966, 1970, and 1972 indicate that he was strongly influenced by the *Exercises*. *Spiritual Notebooks* I, II, III, (photocopy), Special Collection, John T. Richardson Library, DePaul University, Chicago, IL. Fr. James Brockman, who detailed the chronological divisions of the Notebooks for research and publication purposes, bequeathed photocopies of these notebooks to the Richardson Library.

[11]. The American Psychiatric Association, *Diagnostic and Statistical Manual of Mental Disorders IV*, 672–73.

[12]. Krauth, "Scrupulosity: Blackmailed by OCD in the Name of God," *Medscape*, http://www.medscape.com/viewarticle/587978?src=top10. See also Nelson, Abramowitz, Whiteseide, and Deacon, "Scrupulosity in Patients with Obsessive-Compulsive Disorder: Relationship to Clinical and Cognitive Phenomenon."

[13]. *SN* I, January 13, 1966. It is of interest to note that Romero uses the tools at his disposal (a spiritual plan) but was not yet aware of how even this perpetuated his OCPD.

[14]. Ibid., April 21, 1970.

[15]. Ignatius of Loyola, *The Spiritual Exercises of St. Ignatius*, 352–70.

[16]. Ashley, "Contemplation in Prophetic Action," *Christian Spirituality Bulletin* 8 (2002): 12, fn. 5.

[17]. *SN* I, June 8, 1970.

[18]. Ibid.

[19]. Delgado, *Oscar A. Romero: Biografía*, 44.

[20]. *SN* I, June 9, 1970.

[21]. Personal interview. Washington, DC. June 26, 2003.

[22]. *SN* I, November 17, 1971.

[23]. CIAS (Center for Social Investigation and Action) established the Society's commitment to social renewal. Provincials of the Society of Jesus, "The Jesuits of Latin America," May 1968, in Hennelly, Alfred T., ed., *Liberation Theology: A Documentary History*, 78.

[24]. Ibid., 80–81.

[25]. Delgado, *Oscar A. Romero: Biografía*, 53.

[26]. Ibid., 32.

[27]. Ibid., 59.

[28]. Ibid., 62. See also Diez and Macho, *En Santiago de María Me Topé con la Miseria: Dos Años de la Vida de Mons. Romero (1975–1977) ¿Años del Cambio?*

[29]. Ibid.

30. Ibid., 64.

31. Pope Paul VI, "On Evangelization in the Modern World," nos. 27, 29, 31, 34, 36, 37, and 58.

32. U.S. Ambassador Robert White, personal interview, June 26, 2003.

33. López Vigil, *Memories in Mosaic*, 101. For resources regarding Fr. Grande, see O'Malley, *The Voice of Blood: Five Christian Martyrs of Our Time,* 1–63; Cardenal, *Rutilio Grande: Mártir de evangelización rural en El Salvador*; Cardenal, *Historia de una Esperanza: Vida de Rutilio Grande*; Sobrino, *Archbishop Romero: Memories and Reflections*, 6–13; Martín-Baró, "El liderazgo de Monseñor Romero, un Analysis Psico-Social"; and Delgado, *Oscar A. Romero: Biografía*, 75–84.

34. Brockman, *Romero: A Life*, 257, footnote 41.

35. Martín-Baró, "El liderazgo de Monseñor Romero," 157–58.

36. Ibid., 160.

37. Lernoux, *Cry of the People: The Struggle for Human Rights in Latin America and the Catholic Church in Conflict with U.S. Policy*, 75–77, 80.

38. For a succinct treatment of this conflict, see James Brockman, "Oscar Romero: Paradigm of the New Latin American Church." Also see "Relations with the Nuncio," and "Relations with the Bishop's Conference," in "Romero's Letters to Cardinal Baggio," May 21, 1978, in Romero, "Brockman-Romero Papers."

39. Marcouiller, "Archbishop with an Attitude: Oscar Romero's *Sentir con la Iglesia*," 42–43. See also Romero, *Shepherd's Diary*, May 18, 1979.

40. Romero, *Shepherd's Diary,* June 21, 1978.

41. Unpublished letters in Romero, "The Brockman-Romero Papers."

42. Brockman, *Romero: A Life*, 112.

43. Romero, *Shepherd's Diary,* April 3, 1978.

44. Ibid., May 4, 1979.

45. Ibid., May 7, 1979.

46. Brockman, *Romero: A Life*, 246.

47. López Vigil, *Memories in Mosaic*, 217.

48. Las Casas, *Devastation of the Indies: A Brief Account*; *In Defense of the Indians: The Defense of the Most Reverend Lord, Don Fray Bartolomé de Las Casas, the Order of Preachers, Late Bishop of Chiapa, against the Persecutors and Slanderers of the People of the New World Discovered across the Sea*; and *Witness: Writings of Bartolomé de Las Casas*. See also Sobrino, *Memories and Reflections*, 16.

49. Romero, "La dimensión política de la fe desde la opción por los pobres," *La Voz de los Sin Voz: La Palabra Viva de Monseñor Romero*, 187.

50. Sobrino, *Memories and Reflections*, 72.

[51]. "The Easter Church," First Pastoral Letter of Archbishop Romero, Easter Sunday, April 10, 1977 in Romero, *Voice of the Voiceless*, 57.

[52]. Romero, *La Voz de Los sin Voz*, 457, homily of November 18, 1979.

[53]. A single Mass was held for Fr. Rafael (the fourth Salvadoran priest assassinated) after the prescribed nine days of mourning had been completed. Romero concelebrated this Mass on June 30, 1979 at noon with one hundred priests gathered with the faithful in the cathedral.

[54]. Sunday, February 24, 1980, as cited in Brockman, *Romero: A Life*, 232–33.

[55]. Account in *Noticias de la Provincia Centroamericana*, April 1980 (privately circulated) and in *Orientación*, May 11, 1980.

[56]. *SN* III, February 25, 1980.

[57]. Ibid.

[58]. López Vigil, *Memories in Mosaic*, 382–84.

[59]. An excerpt from a telephone interview given to José Calderón Salazar, the Guatemalan correspondent of the Mexican newspaper, *Excelsior,* and reprinted in *Orientación*, April 13, 1980. See also, Romero, *La Voz de Los sin Voz*, 461.

[60]. López Vigil, *Memories in Mosaic*, 396–97. Jorge Lara-Braud at the time was the United States representative to the National Council of Churches and the World Council of Churches.

Chapter 2

[1]. Irenaeus of Lyons, *Against Heresies* II, 2–4. This philosophical formula was common in the popular philosophical schools of the day and exercised a major influence on the development of several Christian doctrines. Subsequent citations from *Against Heresies* are referred to as *AH*. See Minns, *Irenaeus*, 33–34. (With regard to language in quoting Irenaeus, I retain the noninclusive language of the translation.)

[2]. *AH* IV.11.2.

[3]. *AH* I.22.1; II.30.9; III.8.3; III.24.2; IV.20.1–4; V.1.3; V.9.4.

[4]. Osborn, *Irenaeus of Lyons*, 196. See also von Balthasar, *The Glory of the Lord: A Theological Aesthetics*, particularly vol. 2, 31–94. Balthasar bases his argument for aesthetic theology on the poetic and aesthetic elements in Irenaeus.

[5]. Irenaeus of Lyons, *On the Apostolic Preaching*, 44.

[6]. *AH* III.24.1.

[7]. Tiessen, *Irenaeus on the Salvation of the Unevangelized*, 206.

[8]. Irenaeus sought to hold together the institutional and charismatic dimensions of the Church. See Donovan, *One Right Reading? A Guide to Irenaeus*, 93–94, 63–66.

9. *AH* III.3.1, .3–4. Kereszty, "The Unity of the Church in the Theology of Irenaeus," 207. See also Tiessen, *Iranaeus*, 190–201.

10. *AH* III.9.1–11.9, III.13.3–14.4. See Donovan, *One Right Reading?* 67–78.

11. *AH* I.9.4. See Tiessen, *Iranaeus*, 201–5; and Plumer, "The Development of Ecclesiology: Early Church to the Reformation," 27.

12. *AH* III.6.1. Donovan notes that Irenaeus sees the Father as God the anointer, the Son as God the anointed, and the Church as those who have received the grace of adoption (Rom. 8:15 and Gal. 4:5–6). *One Right Reading?* 68.

13. *AH* IV.33.8–9.

14. *AH* IV.38.3.

15. *AH* V.6.1.

16. *AH* III.20.2.

17. *AH* V, preface.

18. Lossky, *In the Image and Likeness of God*, 97.

19. *AH* IV.37.7.

20. *AH* IV.39.1.

21. *AH* IV.38.1.

22. *AH* IV.38.3.

23. *AH* IV.5.1.

24. *AH* IV.11.1–2

25. In Irenaeus's thinking, *Adam* refers not only to an individual, but to an archetype (a typical Platonic approach to Scripture), an emblem of all humankind, in terms of our collective personality that grows in history under God's providence through the Word and Wisdom. *AH* IV.38.1–2.

26. Hick, *Evil and the God of Love*, 214–15.

27. *AH* III.23.3, 4.

28. *AH* II.28.1.

29. *AH* IV.38.3.

30. Recapitulation is complex. One meaning, based on Paul, is the notion of correction or rectification of what has gone wrong from the beginning of human history. Christ returns to the point of error and replaces the wrong deed with the right deed, thereby rectifying the ancient fault. Another meaning, derived from the Gospels, is perfection. The perfection is *both* exclusive, in that it is God's unsurpassable perfection or the world's unsurpassable priority, *and* inclusive, in that it brings together all things within the Word of God, requiring the believer to put on the perfection of the head which is Christ. Osborn, *Irenaeus of Lyons*, 97–116, esp. 97–98, 100, and 104 .

31. Eph. 1:9–10.

32. *AH* III.11.8.

33. In regard to evil, I retain Irenaeus's term, *Satan*.

34. *AH* II.22.4.

35. *AH* V.21.1.

36. *AH* V.21.3.

37. Loewe, "Irenaeus' Soteriology: *Christus Victor* Revisited," 8.

38. *AH* III.19.2–6.

39. Wingren, *Man and the Incarnation: A Study of the Biblical Theology of Irenaeus*, 112.

40. *AH* V.21.3.

41. *AH* III.19.3.

42. *AH* III.20.2. The words in parentheses are that way in the original text.

43. *AH* IV.20.7. Deuteronomy 5:24.

44. *AH* IV.20.6.

45. *AH* IV.20.5.

46. Ibid.

47. *AH* IV.20.8.

48. *AH* IV.20.6.

49. *AH* IV.20.4.

50. Donovan, "Alive to the Glory of God: A Key Insight in St. Irenaeus," 296.

51. *AH* V.1.1.

52. *AH* IV.20.7.

53. *AH* IV.22.2.

54. Donovan, "Alive to the Glory of God: A Key Insight in St. Irenaeus," 297.

56. *AH* IV.20.7.

57. *AH* V.6.1.

58. *AH* IV.20.5.

59. *AH* V.28.4. The man Irenaeus refers to is Ignatius of Antioch.

Chapter 3

1. Dr. Millon's thinking is central to the classification and description of personality disorders, and much of the literature available refers to his work.

2. Millon, *Disorders of Personality: DSM III: Axis II*, 8.

3. Millon and Everly, *Personality and Its Disorders: A Biosocial Learning Approach*, 156–60.

4. Millon, *Disorders of Personality: DSM III: Axis II*, 237–40.

5. Weston and Heim, "Disturbances of Self and Identity in Personality Disorders," 650.

6. Beck, et al., "Obsessive-Compulsive Personality Disorder," 314–

17. See also Koran, "Obsessive-Compulsive Personality Disorders," 251–54.

⁷. Dean Brackley, S.J., has served on the faculty of the University of Central America (UCA) since 1990, replacing one of the six Jesuits murdered in 1989. Personal interview, July 2, 2003. Also see Brockman's account of Dr. Rodolfo Semsch, a clinical psychologist with whom Romero consulted during his time as Archbishop. Semsch offers a similar insight into Romero's mental state. Brockman, *Romero: A Life*, 49–50.

⁸. (Photocopy) June 24, 1978, unpublished letters in Romero, "The Brockman-Romero Papers."

⁹. Composing a program such as this was a formation practice in Romero's era. For more on "A Rule of Life," see Tanquerey, *The Spiritual Life: A Treatise on Ascetical and Mystical Theology*, 270–75.

¹⁰. Weisner and Riffle, "Scrupulosity: Religion and Obsessive-Compulsive Behavior in Children." The word *scruple* comes from the Latin, *scrupulus*, which refers to a hard pebble that was an annoyance if stepped on. Later it was used as an apothecary weight, one twenty-fourth of an ounce. It received a moral interpretation when related to a thought or circumstance so insignificant that it only affected a very delicate conscience. See also Greenberg, Witztum, and Pisante, "Scrupulosity: Religious Attitudes and Clinical Presentations," 29.

¹¹. Greenberg, Witztum, and Pisante, "Scrupulosity: Religious Attitudes and Clinical Presentations," 29. Also see Greenberg and Witztum, "Treatment of Strictly Religious Patients," *Current Treatment of Obsessive-Compulsive Disorder*; and Greenberg, "Are Religious Compulsions Religious or Compulsive? A Phenomenological Study."

¹². "Ascetical Theology is that part of spiritual doctrine whose proper object is both the theory and the practice of Christian perfection, from its very beginning up to the threshold of infused contemplation. We place the beginning of perfection in the sincere desire of advancing in the spiritual life. Ascetic Theology guides the soul from this beginning through the *purgative, illuminative* ways, as far as active contemplation or the *simple unitive* way." Tanquerey, *The Spiritual Life: A Treatise on Ascetical and Mystical Theology*, 5.

¹³. Ibid., 188. Italics are Tanquerey's.

¹⁴. Ibid., 196–97.

¹⁵. Ibid., 197.

¹⁶. Ibid., 198.

¹⁷. Marcouiller, "Archbishop with an Attitude: Oscar Romero's *Sentir con la Iglesia*," vi.

¹⁸. Brockman, "The Spiritual Journey of Oscar Romero," *Spirituality Today*, 313.

¹⁹. *SN* I, Retreats, January 13, 1966, November 1968, and February 16, 1972.

[20]. Personal interview, July 14, 2003. Archbishop Sáenz Lacalle concurs that Romero nurtured multiple practices of piety. See Sáenz Lacalle, "Homily of the Twentieth Anniversary of the Death of Monseñor Oscar Romero," 3.

[21]. Personal interview, June 26, 2003.

[22]. Jenike, "Psychotherapy of Obsessive-Compulsive Personality Disorders," 300–301.

[23]. Beck, et al., "Obsessive-Compulsive Personality Disorder," 321.

[24]. Ambivalence is the conflicting experience of wanting and not wanting at the same time. Evidence from Romero's *Shepherd's Diary* indicates that even as Archbishop, Romero consulted both men. See Romero, *Shepherd's Diary*, June 8, 1978.

[25]. Salzman, *The Obsessive Personality: Origins, Dynamics, and Therapy*, 40–41.

[26]. Ibid., 195–267.

[27]. Millon and Everly, *Personality and Its Disorders: A Biosocial Learning Approach*, 155.

[28]. Koran, "Obsessive-Compulsive Personality Disorders," 251.

[29]. *SN* I.

[30]. Brockman, *Romero: A Life*, 40.

[31]. Psychological exhaustion is a result of tremendous energy investment in self-control. Scrupulous persons have explosive episodes because they are fatigued from keeping their anger in check. Energy is used to repress feelings that might appear as sinful such as irritation, resentment, vulnerability, and a strong desire to love and be loved.

[32]. Personal Interview, July 14, 2003.

[33]. Koran, "Obsessive-Compulsive Personality Disorders," 252.

[34]. López Vigil, *Memories in Mosaic*, 67–69.

[35]. Van Ornum, *A Thousand Frightening Fantasies: Understanding and Healing Scrupulosity and Obsessive-Compulsive Disorder*, 25.

[36]. López Vigil, *Memories in Mosaic*, 69.

[37]. Brockman, introduction to the Aguilares homily, "A Torch Held on High," June 19, 1997 in "Romero's Homilies" (photocopy) in "The Brockman-Romero Papers."

[38]. Ibid.

[39]. Dooley, *Quest for Religious Maturity: The Obsessive-Compulsive Personality: Implications for Pastoral Counseling*, 88.

[40]. Personal interview, July 2, 2003.

[41]. Romero, *The Violence of Love*, November 6, 1977.

[42]. Marcouiller, "Archbishop with an Attitude: Oscar Romero's *Sentir con la Iglesia*," 37.

43. Ibid., 36.

44. *SN* III, January 9–13, 1978.

45. Romero, "Reflections on the Spiritual Exercises,"101.

46. Ibid., 104–5.

47. Ibid., 101.

48. Romero, "La Iglesia, Cuerpo de Cristo en la Historia," *La Voz de los Sin Voz: La Palabra Viva de Monseñor Romero*, 76.

49. Romero, "Reflections on the Spiritual Exercises,"101.

50. Ibid., 104.

51. Personal interview, June 26, 2003.

52. *SN* III, February 25, 1980.

53. López Vigil, *Memories in Mosaic*, 154. See also Romero, *Shepherd's Diary*, June 17–18, 1978.

54. López Vigil, *Memories in Mosaic*, 225. Also see Sobrino, *Memories and Reflections*, 51–52.

55. López Vigil, *Memories in Mosaic,*, 214.

56. *SN* III, February 25, 1980.

57. Ibid.

58. "Homily of the Twentieth Anniversary of the Death of Monseñor Oscar Romero," 3–4.

59. Marcouiller, "Archbishop with an Attitude: Oscar Romero's *Sentir con la Iglesia*," 37.

60. Millon, *Disorders of Personality: DSM III*.

61. Personal interview, July 14, 2003.

62. Van Ornum, *A Thousand Frightening Fantasies*, 30.

63. Jourard and Landsman, *Healthy Personality: An Approach from the Viewpoint of Humanistic Psychology*, 28–29.

64. Romero, *La Voz de Los sin Voz*, 458.

65. Romero, *Monseñor Oscar A. Romero: Su pensamiento*, Publicaciones Pastorales Arzobispado, vol. 5, 327.

66. Letter to Baggio (photocopy), May 21, 1978, unpublished letters in Romero, "The Brockman-Romero Papers."

67. López Vigil, *Memories in Mosaic*, 155–57.

68. Romero, *Monseñor Oscar A. Romero: Su pensamiento*, Publicaciones Pastorales Arzobispado, vol. 6, 106.

69. Romero, "La dimensión política de la fe desde la opción por los pobres," *La Voz de los Sin Voz: La Palabra Viva de Monseñor Romero*, 184.

70. Ibid., 186.

71. Regarding Romero's cautious political thought, see "Misión de la Iglesia en medio de la crisis del pais," *La Voz de los Sin Voz: La Palabra Viva de Monseñor Romero*, 123–72; and Brockman, "Oscar Romero on Faith and Politics," *Thought* 62 (1987): 190–204.

[72]. Romero, *Monseñor Oscar A. Romero: Su pensamiento*, Publicaciones Pastorales Arzobispado, vol. 1–2, 29. Also see "La Iglesia, Cuerpo de Cristo en la Historia," *La Voz de los Sin Voz: La Palabra Viva de Monseñor Romero*, 82–86.

[73]. Romero, *La Voz de los Sin Voz: La Palabra Viva de Monseñor Romero*, 461.

[74]. Romero, *Colección Homilías y Diario de Mons. Oscar Arnulfo Romero*, January 7, 1979.

[75]. Romero, *La Voz de Los sin Voz*, 453.

[76]. Ibid., 454.

[77]. Ibid.

[78]. Regarding this incident, Robert White told me that he had been instructed by the U.S. State Department to apply diplomatic pressure on the Vatican to "rein Romero in." White declined, saying the strategy would be ruinous to his diplomatic relationship with the Archbishop. Personal interview, June 26, 2003.

[79]. Romero, *La Voz de Los sin Voz*, 291–292.

[80]. (Photocopy) May 21, 1978, unpublished letters in Romero, "The Brockman-Romero Papers."

[81]. Romero, *La Voz de Los sin Voz*, 326.

[82]. Romero, *The Violence of Love*, 197.

[83]. Anaya, "Crónica del Mes, Mayo," *Estudios Centroamericanos* 6 (1979): 451.

[84]. (Photocopy) June 24, 1978, unpublished letters in Romero, "The Brockman-Romero Papers." See also Flannery, ed., *Christus Dominus*, no. 13.

Chapter 4

[1]. Millon, *Disorders of Personality: DSM III*, 241.

[2]. Millon and Klerman, eds., *Contemporary Directions in Psychopathology: Toward the DSM IV*, 705.

[3]. Brockman, *Romero: A Life*, 34. Romero's biographers and persons I interviewed could not offer any medical diagnosis for this illness. Brockman does say that this illness affected Romero's health, and restricted him from taking part in the normal play activities of children his age. I am inclined to think his time home alone with his mother, who was religious, may have contributed to this awakening.

[4]. Meissner, *Life and Faith: Psychological Perspectives on Religious Experience*, 194–202. Meissner suggests that hope, a realistic and helpful form of reassurance, is key to successful therapy, and is first conveyed to the patient through the therapist–patient relationship.

[5]. López Vigil, *Memories in Mosaic*, 159.

6. Ibid., 158–59.

7. Ibid., 280–82.

8. Eph. 1:4.

9. Flannery, ed., *Lumen Gentium*, no. 40.

10. Dooley, *Quest for Religious Maturity*, 55.

11. Jourard and Landsman, *Healthy Personality*, 380. See also Callahan, *In Good Conscience: Reason and Emotion in Moral Decision Making*; Patrick, *Liberating Conscience: Feminist Explorations in Catholic Moral Theology* ["Conscience at the Crossroads: Invitation to Radical Conversion," 40–71; and "Toward Liberating Conscience: Spirituality and Moral Responsibility," 170–99]; and Conn, *Conscience: Development and Self-Transcendence*.

12. Jourard and Landsman, *Healthy Personality*, 394. Pope John Paul II, "Sollicitudo Rei Socialis," December 30, 1987, 395–436, and "Centesimus Annus: On the Hundredth Anniversary of *Rerum Novarum*," May 1, 1991, 437–88. See also McCormick and Connors, *Facing Ethical Issues: Dimensions of Character, Choices and Community*; Hauerwas, "Character, Narrative, and Growth in the Christian Life,"; and Harak, "A Passion for Justice," 122–40.

Chapter 5

1. Conn, *Christian Conversion: A Developmental Interpretation of Autonomy and Surrender*, 215–16.

2. For Lonergan's interpretation of Aquinas's view of conversion, see Lonergan, *Grace and Freedom*.

3. Conn draws on the psychological developmental theories of Erik Erikson, Jean Piaget, Lawrence Kohlberg, James Fowler, and Robert Kegan. See Conn, *Christian Conversion*. See also "Merton's 'True Self': Moral Autonomy and Religious Conversion."

4. For Lonergan, self-transcendence is the inherent capacity of human consciousness that can only be achieved through conversion. In *Method in Theology*, he writes, "For a man is his true self inasmuch as he is self-transcending. Conversion is the way to self-transcendence. Inversely, man is alienated from his true self inasmuch as he refuses self-transcendence, and the basic form of ideology is the self-justification of alienated man" (p. 357).

5. "Christians are converted to Jesus. Conversion to Jesus then becomes surrender to the communal embrace of the Trinitarian God from whom Jesus cannot be separated. It becomes entering into what Greek Christianity has called divinization (theosis): our being taken up into God's life, made partakers of the divine nature (2 Peter 1:4)." Carmody, "The Desire for Transcendence: Religious Conversion," 71–72.

6. Rende, *Lonergan on Conversion: The Development of a Notion*,

186. To provide further understanding, Rende states, "The pure desire to know is the principle which underpins, penetrates, and promotes forward all of our cognitional operations. It is the principle which awakens questioning. It draws objects, events, and characteristics of ordinary living out of their initial contexts and into the context of elemental wonder. It frees the subject's memory and anticipation, conation and imagination from the routines of practical living and enlists them in the service of intelligent questioning. Again, it is the pure desire to know which poses and sustains the questions which lead to insight. It is the principle which guides the intellectual formation of insight into definitions, theorems, and systems. Again, it is the pure desire to know which promotes the subject from the level of intelligent formulation to the level of rational judgment. It is the principle which raises and sustains the critical question, 'Is it so?' and guides reflective understanding, the marshalling and weighing of evidence, and the rational proceeding judgment. Finally, it is the pure desire to know which orients us beyond all present cognitional achievements toward the distant goal of the totality of being." Rende, "The Development and the Unity of Lonergan's Notion of Conversion," 168–69.

[7]. "I would identify the transcendental notion of value with a dynamic state of freedom. It is such a dynamic state, not as a private possession, but rather as a possibility in which all persons are invited to share. Consequently, in moral conversion, the subject freely responds to the dynamic thrust toward freedom for itself and for others." Rende, "The Development and the Unity of Lonergan's Notion of Conversion," 166.

[8]. Rende, *Lonergan on Conversion*, 183.

[9]. Witherup, *Conversion in the New Testament*, 109.

[10]. See Dunne, *Lonergan and Spirituality: Towards a Spirituality of Integration*, 105–45 ("Love").

[11]. Conn, *Christian Conversion*, 226.

[12]. Lonergan, "Natural Right and Historical Mindedness."

[13]. Walter Conn and Donald Gelpi have made important contributions also. Conn blends theology with developmental theories. For him, affective conversion is a radical transformation of desire and self-giving triggered by the experience of falling in love. As the transformation of our deepest life of feeling, affective conversion is not merely associated with passions, feelings, and emotions; it includes deliberately making a decision for and commitment to another. It radically reorients our passionate desire from obsession with self-needs to the needs of others, and is crystallized in commitment to other-centered service. See Conn, *Christian Conversion*, 134–53. Gelpi's notion blends the psychologies of Carl Rogers and Carl Jung with theology. For him, affective conversion integrates responsibility for psychological well-being with the Christian ethos of responding to grace. It is the result of a conscious decision

to assume personal responsibility for emotional growth and development by deciding to integrate into the conscious personality the troublesome, unconscious negative emotions that motivate dysfunctional behavior. The agency of integration brings repressed negative emotions to conscious healing and liberation. See Gelpi, *The Conversion Experience*, 37.

14. William Johnston also esteems the *Spiritual Exercises* as a mode of emotional healing. In *The Mirror Mind: Spirituality and Transformation*, Johnston cites that Ignatian contemplation and discernment bring to conscious awareness our deep, subliminal feelings that we ordinarily ignore. Transformation occurs when we participate in the struggle to suffer through the process of dryness or emptiness prior to the emergence of a new level of feelings that Johnston calls interior or mystical affectivity. See pages 116–17.

15. Tyrrell, *Christotherapy II: The Fasting and Feasting Heart*, 17. This two-stage process is marked by a radical conversion and an ongoing conversion where a person is constantly turning toward what is constructive and integrative.

16. Tyrrell cites that rejection or extrinsic valuation (being loved for what one can do or what one will become) are the principal factors contributing to neurotic deformation, leading to feeling unlovable and worthless. See Tyrrell, "Psychological Conversion, Methods of Healing, and Communication," 243.

17. Tyrrell points to the Twelve-Step Recovery Program for the radical and ongoing schema he refers to. Steps one through three facilitate radical conversion; steps four through twelve, ongoing conversion. See Tyrrell, *Christotherapy II*, 21–23.

18. Tyrrell, "Passages and Conversion," 11–12. Also see Tyrrell, *Christotherapy II*, 145–233.

19. Doran, "Psychic Conversion," 236.

20. Doran, "Jungian Psychology and Christian Spirituality," 504.

21. Doran, "Subject, Psyche, and Theology's Foundations."

22. As an example, see Jamie Phelps, "Joy Comes in the Morning, Risking Death for Resurrection." Phelps discusses the effects of social sin upon the African American community in the United States.

23. Lonergan, *Insight: A Study of Human Understanding*, 218–42. See O'Keefe, *What Are They Saying about Social Sin?*, 76–84; and Lamb, "The Social and Political Dimensions of Lonergan's Theology," 255–84.

24. Rahner, "Concerning the Relationship between Nature and Grace," 310. In this essay, Rahner goes on to say, "Man should be *able* to receive this Love which is God himself; he must have a congeniality for it. He must be able to accept it (and hence, grace, the beatific vision) as one who has room and scope, understanding and desire for it. Thus he must have a real 'potency'

for it. He must have it *always*. He is indeed someone always addressed and claimed by this Love. For, as he now in fact is, he is created for it; he is thought and called into being so that Love might bestow itself" (p. 311). See also Rahner, *A Rahner Reader*, 176; Galvin, "The Invitation of Grace," 64–73, and Mascall, "Grace and Nature in East and West."

25. Laporte, *Patience and Power: Grace for the First World*, 231.

26. Similarly, Rahner advocates a mysticism of daily life. For him, the mystical experience is the courageous, total acceptance of life and of oneself. His mysticism is relational, first with Jesus, then with the world. Formed by Ignatian spirituality, Rahner's notion of mysticism is one of joy in recognizing God present in the world. His incarnational stance insists that grace mediated through created reality does not destroy or remove the immediate relationship of the graced person to God. God is in the here and now and can be found in all things. See Rahner, "The Ignatian Mysticism of Joy in the World."

27. See Teresa of Avila's teaching on prayer in *The Book of Her Life*, in *Collected Works*, chapter 11, and chapters 14–18. For contemporary explanations about the development of mature prayer, see Thibodeaux, *Armchair Mystic: Easing into Contemplative Prayer*, 151–59, and Cunningham and Egan, *Christian Spirituality: Themes from the Tradition*, 84–103.

28. See Sedgwick, *Sacramental Ethics: Paschal Identity and the Christian Life*, 38–52.

29. Hilkert, *Naming Grace: Preaching and the Sacramental Imagination,* 64. See also Radcliffe, "The Sacramentality of the Word," 133–47.

30. Hilkert, *Naming Grace*, 44. See also Janowiak, *The Holy Preaching: The Sacramentality of the Word in the Liturgical Assembly.*

31. Streeter, "The Role of Theological Communication in the Act of Preaching," 108. Italics are the author's.

32. Hilkert, *Naming Grace*, 45

33. Preaching first occurs through the testimony of the preacher's life, then through the preacher's vocation to interpret the power and presence of God in the community. See Burghardt, *Preaching the Just Word*, 20, and Hilkert, *Naming Grace*, 44–57.

34. Schillebeeckx, *Christ the Sacrament of Encounter with God*, and Schillebeeckx, *The Eucharist.*

35. "The two epicleses are harmoniously linked, even from a literary point of view. Furthermore, the first epiclesis, which asks for the Holy Spirit to be sent on the gifts so they may be transformed into the body and blood of the Lord is oriented toward the second one, which asks that the ones who are to receive communion receive the gifts connected with it. To paraphrase it very simply, 'Send your Holy Spirit upon US and upon these GIFTS to transform

them into the sacramental body so that WE, who are about to communicate, may be transformed into one ecclesial body.'" Giraudo, "The Eucharist as *Diakonia*: From the Service of Cult to the Service of Charity," 121.

[36]. Ibid., 131–32.

[37]. Asceticism is based on self-knowledge. It consists of employing any intentional practice whose goal is to eliminate any obstruction (psychological or spiritual) that hinders the communication—humanity to God, or God to humanity.

[38]. Astell, "Postmodern Christian Spirituality: A *Coincidentia Oppositorum?*" 1.

[39]. Wyschogrod, *Saints and Postmodernism*, xiii, 59. Also see Lakeland, *Postmodernity: Christian Identity in a Fragmented Age*; Wyschogrod, "Man-Made Mass Death: Shifting Concepts of Community"; and Sheldrake, "The Crisis of Postmodernity.".

[40]. Kelly and Nelson, *The Cost of Moral Leadership: The Spirituality of Dietrich Bonhoeffer*, 185.

[41]. For understanding the importance of the image of God in discernment, see Lonsdale, *Listening to the Music of the Spirit: The Art of Discernment*, 44–48.

[42]. Ivens, "Desire and Discernment," 33.

[43]. Lonsdale, *Listening to the Music of the Spirit*, 43.

SELECTED BIBLIOGRAPHY

Ackroyd, P. R., and C. F. Evans, eds. *Cambridge History of the Bible.* Cambridge: Cambridge University Press, 1970.

Alison, James. *The Joy of Being Wrong: Original Sin through Easter Eyes.* New York: Crossroad, 1998.

Altaner, Berthold. *Patrology.* Hilda Graef, trans. New York: Herder & Herder, 1960.

American Psychiatric Association. *Diagnostic and Statistical Manual of Mental Disorders IV.* Washington, DC: American Psychiatric Press, 1994.

Anaya, E. C. "Crónica del Mes, Mayo," *Estudios Centroamericanos* 6 (1979).

Apostolicam actuositatem. *Vatican Council II: Constitutions, Decrees, Declarations.* Austin Flannery, gen. ed. Northport, NY: Costello, 1996, 403–42.

Aschenbrenner, George. "A Check on Our Availability: The Examen," *Review for Religious* 39 (1980): 321–24.

———. "Consciousness Examen," *Review for Religious* 31 (1972): 14–21.

———. "Consciousness Examen: Becoming God's Heart for the World," *Review for Religious* 47 (1988): 801–10.

Ashley, Matthew J. "Contemplation in Prophetic Action," *Christian Spirituality Bulletin* 8 (2002): 6–13.

———. "Oscar Romero, Religion and Spirituality," *The Way* 44 (2005): 113–33, http://www.theway.org.uk/back/442Ashley.pdf.

Astell, Ann. "Postmodern Christian Spirituality: A *Coincidentia Oppositorum?*" *Christian Spirituality Bulletin* 4 (1996): 2–5.

Azcue, Secundo. *Orientación*, May 11, 1980.

Baer, Lee, and Michael Jenike. "Personality Disorders in Obsessive-Compulsive Disorders," in *Obsessive-Compulsive Disorders: Theory and Management*, 2nd ed. Chicago, IL: Year Book Medical, 1990.

Barth, Karl. "The Awakening to Conversion," in Bromily, G. W., and T. F. Torrance, eds., *Church Dogmatics*, Vol. 2: *The Doctrine of Reconciliation*. Edenburgh: T. & T. Clark, 1958, 553–84.

Beck, Aaron T. *Cognitive Therapies and the Emotional Disorders*. New York: International University, 1976.

———, et al. *Anxiety Disorders and Phobias: A Cognitive Perspective*. New York: Basic Books, 1985.

———, et al. "Obsessive-Compulsive Personality Disorder," in *Cognitive Therapy of Personality Disorders*. New York: Guilford, 1990.

Bernard of Clairvaux. "Selections from Sermon 50 on the *Song of Songs*," in *Bernard of Clairvaux: Selected Works*. G.R. Evans, trans. Mahwah, NJ: Paulist Press, 1987.

Berryman, Phillip. "The Oppression of the People: Archbishop Oscar Romero of El Salvador," in Chandler, Andrew, ed., *The Terrible Alternative, Christian Martyrdom in the Twentieth Century*. London: Cassell, 1998.

Billy, Dennis. "Ontic Evil and Equivocation: Revising the Terms of the Discussion," *Studies in Christian Ethics* 4 (1991): 73–79.

Black, Peter, "The Broken Wings of Eros: Christian Ethics and the Denial of Desire," *Theological Studies* 64 (2003): 106–26.

Bonhoeffer, Dietrich. *The Cost of Discipleship*. New York: Touchstone, 1995.

———. *Letters and Papers from Prison*. New York: Macmillan, 1971.

Bousset, Wilhelm. *Kyrios Christos: A History of Belief in Christ from the Beginning of Christianity to Irenaeus*. John Steely, trans. Nashville, TN: Abingdon, 1970.

Brackley, Dean. Interview by author. July 2, 2003. Internet correspondence.

———. "Rutilio and Romero: Martyrs for Our Times," in Pelton, Robert, ed., *Monsignor Romero: A Bishop for the Third Millennium*, 79–99.

Brennan, Margaret. "Christology and Spirituality," *Toronto Journal of Theology* 16 (2000): 27–38.

Brock, Rita Nakashima. *Journeys by Heart: A Christology of Erotic Power*. New York: Crossroad, 1988.

Brockman, James. "Oscar Romero on Faith and Politics," *Thought* 62 (1987): 190–204.

———. "Oscar Romero: Paradigm of the New Latin American Church," *Thought* 59 (1984): 195–204.

———. "The Pastoral Teaching of Archbishop Oscar Romero," *Spirituality Today* 40 (1988): 109–27.

————. *Romero: A Life*. Maryknoll, NY: Orbis, 1989.

————. "The Spiritual Journey of Oscar Romero," *Spirituality Today* 42 (1990): 303–22.

Brown, Peter. *The World of Late Antiquity, A.D. 150–750*. New York: Harcourt, Brace, Jovanovich, 1971.

Burghardt, Walter. *Preaching the Just Word*. New Haven, CT: Yale University Press, 1996.

Burke, Kevin. "Archbishop Oscar Romero: Peacemaker in the Tradition of Catholic Social Thought." Paper given at the Catholic Theological Society of America, New Orleans, June, 2002.

————. "The Future of the Church in the Memory of Romero," in Pelton, Robert, ed., *Archbishop Romero: Martyr and Prophet for the New Millennium*, 1–15.

Callahan, Sidney. *In Good Conscience: Reason and Emotion in Moral Decision Making*. San Francisco: HarperCollins, 1991.

Cardenal, Rodolfo. *Historia de una Esperanza: Vida de Rutilio Grande*. San Salvador: UCA Editores, 1985.

————. *Rutilio Grande: Mártir de Evangelización Rural en El Salvador*. San Salvador: UCA Editores, 1978.

Carmody, Denise Lardner. "The Desire for Transcendence: Religious Conversion," in Gregson, Vernon, ed., *The Desires of the Human Heart: An Introduction to the Theology of Bernard Lonergan*. Mahwah, NJ: Paulist Press, 1988.

Carrier, Yves. "Itineraire Pastoral de Msg. Oscar Arnulfo Romero." M.A. thesis, Faculte de Theologie, Universite Laval, 1996.

Casaldáliga, Pedro, and José María Vigil. *The Spirituality of Liberation*. Paul Burns and Francis McDonagh, eds. Maryknoll, NY: Orbis, 1994.

Cavada, Miguel Diez. "La autoridad en la Iglesia. Palabra y testimonio de Monseñor Romero," *Revista Latinomericana de Teologia* 40 (1997): 3–16.

Cavanaugh, William. "Dying for the Eucharist or Being Killed by It? Romero's Challenge to First-World Christians," *Theology Today* 58 (2001): 177–89.

Chadwick, Henry. *The Early Church*, vol. 1. New York: Penguin, 1993.

Chávez, Gregorio Rosa, "Archbishop Romero: A Bishop for the New Millennium," in Pelton, Robert, ed., *Archbishop Romero: Martyr and Prophet for the New Millennium*, Elizabeth Station, trans., 33–45.

Collins, Mary. "Spirituality Needs a Body: Symbolic Practices and Catholic Identity," *The Way*, Supplement 94 (1999): 54–68.

Comision de Derechos Humanos de El Salvador. *La Iglasia en El Salvador*. Salamanca: Loguez Ediciones, 1982.

Congar, Yves. *I Believe in the Holy Spirit*. David Smith, ed. New York: Seabury, 1983.

———. *Lay People in The Church: A Study for a Theology of the Laity.* Walter Attwater, ed. Westminster, MD: Newman Press, 1965.

———. "Sacramental Worship and Preaching," in Rahner, Karl, ed., *The Renewal of Preaching: Theory and Practice*. Mahwah, NJ: Paulist Press, 1968.

Conn, Walter. "Adult Conversion," *Pastoral Psychology* 34 (1986): 225–36.

———. "Bernard Lonergan's Analysis of Conversion," *Angelicum* 53 (1976): 362–404.

————. *Christian Conversion: A Developmental Interpretation of Autonomy and Surrender.* Mahwah, NJ: Paulist Press, 1986.

————. *Conscience: Development and Self-Transcendence.* Birmingham, AL: Religious Education Press, 1981.

————, ed. *Conversion: Perspectives on Personal and Social Transformation.* New York: Alba, 1978.

————. "The Desire for Authenticity: Conscience and Moral Conversion," in Gregson, Vernon, ed., *The Desires of the Human Heart.* Mahwah, NJ: Paulist Press, 1988.

————. *The Desiring Self: Rooting Pastoral Counseling and Spiritual Direction in Self-Transcendence.* Mahwah, NJ: Paulist Press, 1998.

————. "Merton's 'True Self': Moral Autonomy and Religious Conversion," *Journal of Religion* 65 (1985): 513–29.

Cooke, Bernard. *Sacraments and Sacramentality.* Mystic, CT: Mystic Press, 1994.

Crysdale, Cynthia. "Development, Conversion, and Religious Education," *Horizons* 17 (1990): 30–46.

————. *Embracing Travail: Retrieving the Cross Today.* New York: Continuum, 2001.

Cuéllar, Roberto, "Monseñor Romero: Human Rights Apostle," in Pelton, Robert, ed., *Monsignor Romero: A Bishop for the Third Millennium,* 35–46.

Cunningham, Lawrence. "Non Poena sed Causa: A Contemporary Understanding of Martyrdom," in Pelton, Robert, ed., *Archbishop Romero: Martyr and Prophet for the New Millennium,* 59–71.

Cunningham, Lawrence, and Keith Egan. *Christian Spirituality: Themes from the Tradition.* Mahwah, NJ: Paulist Press, 1996.

Curran, Charles. *Critical Concerns in Moral Theology.* Notre Dame, IN: University of Notre Dame Press, 1984.

———. *Directions in Fundamental Moral Theology.* Notre Dame, IN: University of Notre Dame Press, 1985.

———. *Themes in Fundamental Moral Theology.* Notre Dame, IN: University of Notre Dame Press, 1977.

Dear, John. *Oscar Romero and the Nonviolent Struggle for Justice.* Erie, PA: Pax Christi USA, 2004.

Delgado, Jesús. *Oscar A. Romero: Biografía.* Madrid: Ediciones Paulinas, 1986.

Demoustier, Adrien. "Ignatian Contemplation and the Contemplative Way," *The Way*, Supplement 103 (2002): 16–24.

Dennis, Marie, Renny Golden, and Scott Wright. *Oscar Romero: Reflections on His Life and Writings.* Maryknoll, NY: Orbis, 2000.

Derksen, Jan. *Personality Disorders: Clinical and Social Perspectives.* New York: Wiley, 1995.

Diaferia, Giuseppina, et al. "Relationship between Obsessive-Compulsive Personality Disorder and Obsessive-Compulsive Disorder," *Comprehensive Psychiatry* 38 (1997): 38–42.

Diez, Zacharias, and Juan Macho. *En Santiago de María Me Topé con la Miseria: Dos Años de la Vida de Monseñor Romero (1975–1977) ¿Años del Cambio?* Costa Rica: n. p., 1994.

Dilman, Ilham. "Self-Knowledge and the Reality of Good and Evil," in Gaita, Raimond, ed., *Values and Understanding: Essays for Peter Winch.* New York: Routledge, 1990.

Donovan, Mary Ann. "Alive to the Glory of God: A Key Insight in St. Irenaeus," *Theological Studies* 49 (1988): 283–97.

———. "Insights in Ministry: Irenaeus," *Toronto Journal of Theology* 2 (1986): 79–93.

———. "Irenaeus at the Heart of Life, Glory," in Callahan, Annice, ed. *Spiritualities of the Heart: Approaches to Personal Wholeness in Christian Tradition.* Mahwah, NJ: Paulist Press, 1990.

———. "Irenaeus in Recent Scholarship," *The Second Century: A Journal of Early Christian Studies* 4 (1984): 219–41.

———. *One Right Reading? A Guide to Irenaeus.* Collegeville, MN: Liturgical Press, 1997.

Dooley, Anne Mary. *Quest for Religious Maturity: The Obsessive-Compulsive Personality: Implications for Pastoral Counseling.* Washington, DC: University Press of America, 1981.

Doran, Robert. "Jungian Psychology and Christian Spirituality," *Review for Religious* 38 (1979): 497–510, 742–52, 857–67.

———. "Psychic Conversion," *Thomist* 41 (1977): 200–236.

———. *Psychic Conversion and Theological Foundations: Toward A Reorientation of the Human Sciences.* Chico, California: Scholars Press, 1981.

———. "Subject, Psyche, and Theology's Foundations," *Journal of Religion* 57 (1977): 267–87.

———. *Theology and the Dialectic of History.* Toronto: University of Toronto Press, 1990.

Downey, Michael. *Clothed In Christ: The Sacraments and Christian Living.* New York: Crossroad, 1987.

Dulles, Avery. "Fundamental Theology and the Dynamics of Conversion," *Thomist* 45 (1981): 175–93.

Dunne, Tad. *Lonergan and Spirituality: Toward a Spirituality of Integration.* Chicago, IL: Loyola University Press, 1985.

Dupre, Louis. "Evil—A Religious Mystery: A Plea for a More Inclusive Moral Theodicy," *Faith and Philosophy* 7 (1990): 261–80.

Eaton, Helen-May. "The Impact of Archbishop Oscar Romero's Alliance with the Struggle for Liberation of the Salvadoran People." M.A. thesis, Wilfred Laurier University, 1991.

Egan, Robert. "Jesus in the Heart's Imagination: Reflection on Ignatian Contemplation," *The Way*, Supplement 82 (1995): 62–72.

Eigo, Francis. *The Experience of Conversion: Persons and Structures in Transformation.* Villanova, PA: Villanova University, 1987.

Ellsberg, Robert. "The Mystery of Holiness," *Sojourners* 9/10 (1997): 24–27.

Endean, Philip. "The Concept of Ignatian Mysticism: Beyond Rahner and de Guibert," *The Way*, Supplement 103 (2002): 77–86.

———. "To Reflect and Draw Profit," *The Way*, Supplement 82 (1995): 84–95.

Equipo de Educacion Maiz. *Monseñor Romero: El pueblo es mi profeta.* San Salvador, 1994.

Erdozaín Plácido. *Archbishop Romero: Martyr of Salvador.* John McFadden and Ruth Warner, trans. Maryknoll, NY: Orbis, 1984.

Evans, Robert, and Thomas Parker, eds. *Christian Theology: A Case Study Approach.* New York: Harper & Row, 1976.

Faivre, Alexander. *The Emergence of the Laity in the Early Church*. Mahwah, NJ: Paulist Press, 1990.

Ferguson, John. *Pelagius: A Historical and Theological Study*. Cambridge: W. Heffer & Sons, 1956.

Fink, Peter. "Human Imagination and the God It Reveals," *The Way*, Supplement 94 (1999): 35–53.

Flannery, Austin, ed. *Christus Dominus. Vatican Council II: Constitutions, Decrees, Declarations*. Northport, NY: Costello, 1996, 283–315.

————, ed. *Gaudium et Spes. Vatican Council II: Constitutions, Decrees, Declarations*. Northport, New York: Costello Publishing Company, 1996, 163–282.

————, ed. *Lumen Gentium. Vatican Council II: Constitutions, Decrees, Declarations*. Northport, NY: Costello, 1996, 1–95.

————, ed. *Presbyterorum Ordinis. Vatican Council II: Constitutions, Decrees, Declarations*. Northport, NY: Costello, 1996, 317–84.

Fragomeni, Richard. "Conversion," in Downey, Michael, ed., *The New Dictionary of Catholic Spirituality*. Collegeville, MN: Liturgical Press, 1993.

Frost, Randy, and Patricia Marten DiBartolo. "Perfectionism, Anxiety and Obsessive-Compulsive Disorder," in Fleet, Gordon, and Paul Hewitt, eds., *Perfectionism, Theory, Research and Treatment*. Washington, DC: American Psychiatric Association, 2002.

Fuchs, Josef. "The Absoluteness of Moral Norms," *Gregorianum* 52 (1971): 415 – 457.

————. *Christian Ethics in a Secular Arena*. Washington, DC: Georgetown University Press, 1984.

————. *Christian Morality: The Word Becomes Flesh*. Brian McNeil, ed. Washington, DC: Georgetown University Press, 1987.

————. *Moral Demands and Personal Obligations*. Brian McNeil, ed. Washington, DC: Georgetown University Press, 1993.

Galvin, John. "The Invitation to Grace," in O'Donovan, Leo, ed., *A World of Grace: Introduction to the Themes and Foundations of Karl Rahner's Theology*. New York: Seabury, 1980.

Gelpi, Donald. *The Conversion Experience: A Reflective Process for RCIA Participants and Others*. Mahwah, NJ: Paulist Press, 1998.

————. "The Dynamics of Personal Conversion," in *Inculturating North American Theology: An Experiment in Foundational Method*. Atlanta: Scholars Press, 1988.

————. *Experiencing God: A Theology of Human Experience*. Mahwah, NJ: Paulist Press, 1978.

Gillespie, V. Bailey. *The Dynamics of Religious Conversion: Identity and Transformation*. Birmingham, AL: Religious Education Press, 1991.

————. *Religious Conversion and Personal Identity: How and Why People Change*. Birmingham, AL: Religious Education Press, 1979.

Gilson, Ann Bathurst. *Eros Breaking Free: Interpreting Sexual Theo-Ethics*. Cleveland, OH: Pilgrim Press, 1885.

Giraudo, Cesare. "The Eucharist as *Diakonia*: From the Service of Cult to the Service of Charity," in Pecklers, Keith, ed. *Liturgy in a Postmodern World*. New York: Continuum, 2003, 102–32.

Goodwin, Donald. *Anxiety*. New York: Ballantine, 1986.

Grant, Robert. "Irenaeus and Hellenistic Culture," *Harvard Theological Review* 42 (1949): 41–51.

———. *Irenaeus of Lyons*. New York: Routledge, 1997.

Greenberg, David. "Are Religious Compulsions Religious or Compulsive? A Phenomenological Study," *American Journal of Psychotherapy* 38 (1984): 524–33.

———, and Eliezer Witztum. "Treatment of Strictly Religious Patients," in Pato, Michele Tortora, and Joseph Zohar, eds., *Current Treatments of Obsessive-Compulsive Disorder*. Washington, DC: American Psychiatric Press, 1991.

———, Eliezer Witztum, and Jean Pisante, "Scrupulosity: Religious Attitudes and Clinical Presentations," *British Journal of Medical Psychology* 60 (1987): 29–37.

Gregson, Vernon. "The Desire to Know: Intellectual Conversion," in Gregson, Vernon, ed. *The Desires of the Human Heart*. Mahwah, NJ: Paulist Press, 1988.

Grenier, Yvon. *The Emergence of Insurgency in El Salvador*. Pittsburgh, PA: University of Pittsburgh Press, 1999.

Gudorf, Christine. "Admonishing Sinners: Owning Structural Sin," in Eigo, Francis, ed. *Rethinking the Spiritual Works of Mercy*. Villanova, PA: Villanova University Press, 1993.

Guider, Margaret Eletta, "*Sentir con la Iglesia*: Archbishop Romero, an Ecclesial Mystic," in Pelton, Robert, ed., *Monsignor Romero: A Bishop for the Third Millennium*, 73–89.

Guiver, George. "Prayer Rooted in Our Humanity," *The Way*, Supplement 94 (1999): 121–30.

Gula, Richard. *Reason Informed by Faith: Foundations of Catholic Morality*. Mahwah, NJ: Paulist Press, 1989.

Gutiérrez, Gustavo. *We Drink From Our Own Wells: The Spiritual Journey of a People.* Matthew O'Connell, trans. Maryknoll, NY: Orbis, 1984.

Haight, Roger. "Sin and Grace," in Fiorenza, Francis Schüssler, and John P. Galvin, eds. *Systematic Theology: Roman Catholic Perspectives.* Minneapolis, MN: Fortress, 1991.

———. *The Experience and Language of Grace.* Mahwah, NJ: Paulist Press, 1979.

Hall, Thelma. *Too Deep for Words: Rediscovering Lectio Divina.* Mahwah, NJ: Paulist Press, 1988.

Hamel, Ronald, and Kenneth Himes, eds. *Introduction to Christian Ethics: A Reader.* Mahwah, NJ: Paulist Press, 1989.

Hamm, Dennis. "Rummaging for God: Praying Backward through Your Day," *America* 170 (May 1994): 22–23.

Happel, Steven, and James Walter. *Conversion and Discipleship: A Christian Foundation for Ethics and Doctrine.* Philadelphia: Fortress, 1986.

Harak, G. Simon. "A Passion for Justice," in *Virtuous Passions: The Formation of Christian Character.* Mahwah, NJ: Paulist Press, 1993.

Häring, Bernard. *Free and Faithful in Christ: Moral Theology for Clergy and Laity.* New York: Seabury, 1978–1981.

Hassett, John, and Hugh Lacy, eds., *Toward a Society That Serves Its People: The Intellectual Contributions of El Salvador's Murdered Jesuits.* Washington, DC: Georgetown University Press, 1991.

Hauerwas, Stanley. "Character, Narrative, and Growth in the Christian Life," in *A Community of Character: Toward a Constructive*

Christian Social Ethic. Notre Dame, IN: University of Notre Dame Press, 1981.

————. "The Sanctified Body: Why Perfection Does Not Require a 'Self,'" in Powell, Samuel, and Michael Lodahl, eds., *Embodied Holiness: Toward A Corporate Theology of Spiritual Growth.* Downers Grove, IL: InterVarsity, 1999.

Haughey, John. *Housing Heaven's Fire: The Challenge of Holiness.* Chicago, IL: Loyola Press, 2002.

Haughton, Rosemary. *The Theology of Experience.* Paramus, NJ: Newman Press, 1972.

————. *The Transformation of Man: A Study of Conversion and Community.* Springfield, IL: Templegate, 1967.

Hausherr, Irénée. *The Name of Jesus.* Charles Cumming, trans. Kalamazoo, MI: Cistercian Publications, 1978.

Helminiak, Daniel. *The Human Core of Spirituality: Mind as Psyche and Spirit.* Albany: State University of New York Press, 1996.

Hennelly, Alfred T., ed. *Liberation Theology: A Documentary History.* Maryknoll, NY: Orbis, 1995.

Henriot, Peter. "Social Sin and Conversion: A Theology of the Church's Involvement," *Chicago Studies* 11 (1972): 115–30.

Hick, John. *Evil and the God of Love*, 2nd ed. New York: Macmillan, 1977.

Hilkert, Mary Catherine. *Naming Grace: Preaching and the Sacramental Imagination.* New York: Continuum, 1997.

————. ""Revelation and Proclamation: Shifting Paradigms," in *In the Company of Preachers.* Collegeville, MN: Liturgical Press, 1993, 113–38.

Hill, Rowena. "Poured Out for You: Liturgy and Justice in the Life of Archbishop Romero," *Worship* 74 (2000): 414–32.

Hitchcock, Montgomery. *Irenaeus of Lugdunum: A Study of His Teaching*. Cambridge: Cambridge University Press, 1914.

Holland, Joe. "A Postmodern Vision of Spirituality and Society," in Griffin, David Ray, ed., *Spirituality and Society: Postmodern Visions*. Albany: State University of New York Press, 1988.

Ignatius of Loyola. *The Spiritual Exercises of St. Ignatius of Loyola*. Louis Puhl, ed. Chicago, IL: Loyola University Press, 1951.

Irenaeus of Lyons. *The Demonstrations of the Apostolic Preaching*. J. Armitage Robinson, ed. London: Society for Promoting Christian Knowledge, 1920.

———. *Against Heresies*, vol. 1 of *The Ante-Nicene Christian Library: Translations of the Writings of the Fathers Down to A.D. 325*. American Reprint of the Edinburgh Edition. Buffalo, NY: The Christian Literature Publishing Company. 1885.

———. *On the Apostolic Preaching*. John Behr, ed. Crestwood, NJ: St. Vladimir Seminary Press, 1997.

———. *The Writings of Irenaeus*. Alexander Roberts and W. H. Rambaut, trans. London: Hamilton, 1958.

Ivens, Michael. "Desire and Discernment," *The Way*, Supplement 95 (1999): 31–43.

Jalics, Franz. "The Contemplative Phase of the Ignatian Exercises," *The Way*, Supplement 103 (2002): 25–42.

Janowiak, Paul. *The Holy Preaching: The Sacramentality of the Word in the Liturgical Assembly*. Collegeville, MN: Liturgical Press, 1989.

Janssens, Louis. "Norms and Priorities in a Love Ethic," *Louvain Studies* 3 (1977): 207–38.

———. "Ontic Evil and Moral Evil," in Curran, Charles, and Richard McCormick, eds. *Readings in Moral Theology, Number 1: Moral Norms and Catholic Tradition.* Mahwah, NJ: Paulist Press, 1979.

———. "Ontic Good and Evil: Premoral Values and Disvalues," *Louvain Studies* 12 (1987): 62–82.

Jenike, Michael. "Psychotherapy of Obsessive-Compulsive Personality Disorders," in Jenike, Michael, Lee Baer, and William Minichiello, eds., *Obsessive-Compulsive Disorders: Theory and Management.* 2nd ed. Chicago, IL: Year Book Medical Publishers, 1990.

———, and Marie Åsberg. *Understanding Obsessive-Compulsive Disorder (OCD).* Toronto: Hogrefe & Huber, 1991.

Johnson, Elizabeth. *Friends of God and Prophets: A Feminist Theological Reading of the Communion of Saints.* New York: Continuum, 1998.

———. *Truly Our Sister.* New York: Continuum, 2003.

Johnston, William. *The Mirror Mind: Spirituality and Transformation.* San Francisco: Harper & Row, 1981.

———. *Mystical Theology: The Science of Love.* Maryknoll, NY: Orbis, 2000.

Josephson, Stephen, and Elizabeth Brondolo. "Cognitive Behavioral Approaches to Obsessive-Compulsive-Related Disorders," in Hollander, Eric, ed., *Obsessive-Compulsive Related Disorders.* London: American Psychiatric Press, 1993.

Jourard, Sidney, and Ted Landsman. *Healthy Personality: An Approach from the Viewpoint of Humanistic Psychology*. New York: Macmillan, 1980.

Karl, John. "Discovering Spiritual Patterns: Including Spirituality in Staff Development and the Development of Psychological Services," *American Journal of Pastoral Counseling* 1 (1998): 1–23.

Keating, Thomas. *The Heart of the World: A Spiritual Catechism*. New York: Crossroad, 1981.

———. *The Human Condition: Contemplation and Transformation*. The Harold M. Wit Lectures, Harvard University Divinity School. Mahwah, NJ: Paulist Press, 1999.

Keogh, Dermot. *Romero, El Salvador's Martyr: A Study of the Tragedy of El Salvador*. Dublin, Ireland: Dominican Publications, 1981.

Kelly, Geffrey. "Bonhoeffer and Romero: Prophets of Justice for the Oppressed," *Union Quarterly Seminary Review* 46 (1992): 85–105.

Kelly, Geffrey, and F. Burton Nelson. *The Cost of Moral Leadership: The Spirituality of Dietrich Bonhoeffer.* Grand Rapids, MI: Eerdmans, 2003.

Kennedy, Eugene. *The Unhealed Wound: The Church and Human Sexuality*. Louisville, KY: Westminster/John Knox, 1996.

Kereszty, Roch. "The Unity of the Church in the Theology of Irenaeus," *The Second Century: A Journal of Early Christian Studies* 4 (1984): 202–18.

Kinast, Robert. *Let Ministry Teach: A Guide to Theological Reflection*. Collegeville, MN: Liturgical Press, 1996.

Knauer, Peter. "The Hermeneutic Function of the Principle of Double Effect," in Curran, Charles, and Richard McCormick, eds., *Readings in Moral Theology, Number 1*. Mahwah, NJ: Paulist Press, 1979.

Kolvenbach, Peter-Hans. "Images and Imagination in the Spiritual Exercises," *Review of Ignatian Spirituality* (CIS) 54 (1987): 11–32.

Koran, Lorrin. "Obsessive-Compulsive Personality Disorders," in *Obsessive-Compulsive and Related Disorders in Adults: A Comprehensive Clinical Guide*. Cambridge: Cambridge University Press, 1999.

Krauth, Laurie. "Scrupulosity: Blackmailed by OCD in the Name of God," *Medscape*, http://www.medscape.com/viewarticle/587978?src=top10.

LaCugna, Catherine Mowry. *God for Us: The Trinity and Christian Life*. San Francisco: HarperCollins, 1991.

La Espiritualidad de Monseñor Romero. San Salvador: Fundación Monseñor Romero, 2000.

Lakeland, Paul. *The Liberation of the Laity: In Search of an Accountable Church*. New York: Continuum, 2003.

———. *Postmodernity: Christian Identity in a Fragmented Age*. Minneapolis, MN: Fortress,1997.

Lamb, Matthew. "The Social and Political Dimensions of Lonergan's Theology," in Gregson, Vernon, ed., *The Desires of the Human Heart*. Mahwah, NJ: Paulist Press, 1988.

Laporte, Jean-Marc. *Patience and Power: Grace for the First World*. Mahwah, NJ: Paulist Press, 1988.

Lara-Braud, Jorge. "The Gospel of Justice: Monseñor among His People," *Christianity and Crisis* 40 (1980): 124–31.

Las Casas, Bartolomé de. *Devastation of the Indies: A Brief Account.* Translated by Herma Briffault. Baltimore, MD: Johns Hopkins University, 1992.

————. *In Defense of the Indians: The Defense of the Most Reverend Lord, Don Fray Bartolomé de Las Casas, the Order of Preachers, Late Bishop of Chiapa, against the Persecutors and Slanderers of the People of the New World Discovered across the Sea.* DeKalb: Northern Illinois University Press, 1992.

————. *Witnesses: Writings of Bartolomé de Las Casas.* Maryknoll, NY: Orbis, 1992.

Lawson, John. *The Biblical Theology of Saint Irenaeus.* London: Epworth, 1948.

Leahey, Thomas Hardy. *A History of Psychology: Main Currents in Psychological Thought.* Upper Saddle River, NJ: Prentice Hall, 1997.

Lernoux, Penny. *Cry of the People: The Struggle for Human Rights in Latin America and the Catholic Church in Conflict with U. S. Policy.* New York: Penguin, 1982.

Loewe, William. "Irenaeus' Soteriology: Transposing the Question," in Fallon, Timothy, and Philip Boo Riley, eds., *Religion and Culture: Essays in Honor of Bernard Lonergan, SJ.* Albany, New York: University of New York Press, 1987.

————. "Irenaeus' Soteriology: *Christus Victor* Revisited," *Anglican Theological Review* 47 (1985): 1–15.

————. "Myth and Counter-Myth: Irenaeus' Story of Salvation," in Kopas, Jane, ed., *Interpreting Tradition: The Art of Theological Reflection.* Chico, CA: Scholars Press, 1984.

Lonergan, Bernard. *Grace and Freedom: Operative Grace in the Thought of St. Thomas Aquinas.* J. Patout Burns, ed. New York: Herder & Herder, 1971.

———. *Insight: A Study of Human Understanding.* London: Longmans, Green, 1957.

———. *Method in Theology.* Toronto: University of Toronto Press, 1971.

———. "Natural Right and Historical Mindedness," *Proceedings of the American Catholic Philosophical Association* 51 (1977): 132–43.

Lonsdale, David. *Listening to the Music of the Spirit: The Art of Discernment.* Notre Dame, IN: Ave Maria, 1993.

López Vigil, Maria. Interview by author. July 14, 2003. Internet correspondence.

———. *Oscar Romero: Memories in Mosaic.* Kathy Ogle, trans. Washington, DC: Ecumenical Program on Central America and the Caribbean (EPICA), 2000.

———. *Piezas para un retrato.* San Salvador: UCA Editores, 1993.

Lorde, Audre. "The Use of the Erotic: The Erotic as Power," in Nelson, James P., and Sandra B. Longfellow, eds., *Sexuality and the Sacred: Sources of Theological Reflection.* Louisville, KY: Westminster /John Knox, 1994.

Lossky, Vladimir. *In the Image and Likeness of God.* John Erickson and Thomas Bird, eds. Crestwood, NY: St. Vladimir's Seminary Press, 1985.

Mambrino, Jean. "Les deux mains de Dieu" dans l'oervre de saint Irénée," *Nouvelle revue théologique* 79 (1957): 355–70.

Marcouiller, Douglas. "Archbishop with an Attitude: Oscar Romero's *Sentir con la Iglesia*," *Studies in the Spirituality of Jesuits* 35 (2003): 1–52.

Marmion, Dom Joseph Columba. *Christ, The Ideal of the Priest: Spiritual Conferences.* Matthew Dillon, trans. St. Louis, MO: Herder & Herder, 1952.

Martín-Baró, Ignacio. "El liderazgo de Monseñor Romero, un Analysis Psico-Social," *Estudios Centroamericanos* 36 (1982):151–72.

Mascall, E. L. "Grace and Nature in East and West," *Church Quarterly Review* 164 (1963): 181–98, 323–47.

McCormick, Patrick, and Russell Connors. *Facing Ethical Issues: Dimensions of Character, Choices and Community.* Mahwah, NJ: Paulist Press, 2002.

McCormick, Richard. "Current Theology: Notes on Moral Theology: 1983," *Theological Studies* 45 (1984): 80–138.

———. *Notes on Moral Theology: 1965 through 1980.* Washington, DC: University Press of America, 1981.

———. *Notes on Moral Theology: 1981 through 1984.* Lanham, MD: University Press of America, 1984.

McDonagh, Enda. *The Gracing of Society.* Dublin: Gill & Macmillan, 1989.

McKenna, Thomas. "Modern Spirituality," in Downey, Michael, ed. *The New Dictionary of Catholic Spirituality.* Collegeville, MN: Liturgical Press, 1993.

Meissner, William. *Ignatius of Loyola: The Psychology of a Saint.* New Haven, CT: Yale University Press, 1992.

―――. *Life and Faith: Psychological Perspectives on Religious Experience*. Washington, DC: Georgetown University Press, 1987.

Melloni, Javier. "The Spiritual Exercises and the Spirituality of the East," *The Way*, Supplement 103 (2002): 55–64.

Mendes de Almeida, Luciano. "Martyrs, Heroes, and the Contemporary Church: Latin America and the United States," in Pelton, Robert, ed., *Monsignor Romero: A Bishop for the Third Millennium*, 27–33.

Méndez, Juan, and Robert Pelton. "The Ongoing Legacy of Archbishop Romero," in Pelton, Robert, ed., *Monsignor Romero: A Bishop for the Third Millennium*, 113–18.

Miles, Margaret. *Practicing Christianity: Critical Perspectives for an Embodied Spirituality*. New York: Crossroad, 1988.

Millon, Theodore. *Disorders of Personality: DSM III: Axis II*. New York: Wiley, 1981.

―――, and George Everly. *Personality and Its Disorders: A Biosocial Learning Approach*. New York: Wiley, 1985.

―――, and Gerald Klerman, eds. *Contemporary Directions in Psychopathology: Toward DSM IV*. New York: Guilford, 1986.

Minns, Dennis. *Irenaeus*. Washington, DC: Georgetown University Press, 1994.

Moloney, Raymond. "The Person as Subject of Spirituality in the Writings of Bernard Lonergan," *Milltown Studies* 45 (2000): 66–80.

Moltmann-Wendel, Elisabeth. *I Am My Body: A Theology of Embodiment*. John Bowden, trans. New York: Continuum, 1995.

Moore, Sebastian. *Jesus the Liberator of Desire*. New York: Crossroad, 1989.

Morley, Jefferson. "Demoralizing D'Aubuisson," *The Nation*, May 1989, 624–46.

Muldoon, James, ed. *Varieties of Religious Conversion in the Middle Ages*. Gainesville, FL: University Press of Florida, 1997.

Nangel, Joseph. "Archbishop Romero's Challenge to U.S. Universities," in Pelton, Robert, ed., *Monsignor Romero: A Bishop for the Third Millennium*, 101–111.

Nelson, Elizabeth, Jonathan Abramowitz, Stephen Whiteside, and Brett Deacon, "Scrupulosity in Patients with Obsessive-Compulsive Disorder: Relationship to Clinical and Cognitive Phenomenon," *Journal of Anxiety Disorders* 20 (2006): 1071–86.

Nielsen, J. T. *Adam and Christ in the Theology of Irenaeus of Lyons*. Assen, Netherlands: Koninklijke Van Gorcum, 1968.

O'Brien, David, and Thomas Shannon, eds. *Catholic Social Thought: The Documentary Heritage*. Maryknoll, NY: Orbis, 2001.

O'Keefe, Mark. *What Are They Saying about Social Sin?* Mahwah, NJ: Paulist Press, 1990.

O'Keeffe, Terence. "Tillich, Ontology and God," *Irish Theological Quarterly* 49 (1982): 19 – 36.

O'Malley, W. J. *The Voice of Blood: Five Christian Martyrs of Our Times*. Maryknoll, NY: Orbis, 1980.

Orbe, Antonio. *Espiritualidad de San Ireneo*. Rome, Italy: Editrice Pontificia Universita Gregoriana, 1989.

Osborn, Eric. *Irenaeus of Lyons*. New York: Cambridge University Press, 2001.

Osborn, Ian. *Tormenting Thoughts and Secret Rituals: The Hidden Epidemic of Obsessive-Compulsive Disorder*. New York: Pantheon, 1998.

Osborne, Kenan. *The Christian Sacraments of Initiation: Baptism, Confirmation, Eucharist.* Mahwah, NJ: Paulist Pres, 1987.

Parker, Gordon. "On Modelling Personality Disorders: Are Personality Styles and Disordered Functioning Independent or Interdependent Constructs?" *The Journal of Nervous Mental Disease* 186 (1998): 709–15.

Pasquier, Jacques. "Examination of Conscience and *Revision De Vie*," *The Way*, Supplement 11 (1971): 305–12.

Patrick, Anne. *Liberating Conscience: Feminist Explorations in Catholic Moral Theology.* New York: Continuum, 1996.

Pauls, David. "The Role of Genetic Factors in OCD," in Fineberg, Naomi, Donatella Mazazziti, and Dan Stein, eds., *Obsessive-Compulsive Disorder: A Practical Guide.* London: Martin Dunitz, 2001.

Pelikan, Jaroslav. *The Christian Tradition: A History of the Development of Doctrine, Vol. 1: The Emergence of the Catholic Tradition (100–600).* Chicago, IL: Loyola University Press, 1971.

Pelton, Robert, ed. *Archbishop Romero: Martyr and Prophet for the New Millennium.* Scranton, PA: University of Scranton Press, 2006.

———, ed. *Monsignor Romero: A Bishop for the Third Millennium.* Notre Dame, IN: University of Notre Dame Press, 2004.

Phan, Peter, ed. *The Gift of the Church: A Textbook on Ecclesiology.* Collegeville, MN: Liturgical Press, 2000.

Phelps, Jamie. "Joy Comes in the Morning, Risking Death for Resurrection," in Townes, Emilie, ed., *A Troubling in My Soul.* Maryknoll, NY: Orbis, 1993.

Plumer, Eric. "The Development of Ecclesiology: Early Church to the Reformation," in Phan, Peter, ed., *The Gift of the Church: A Textbook on Ecclesiology in Honor of Patrick Granfield, O.S.B.* Collegeville, MN: Liturgical Press, 2000, 23–44.

Pollack, Jerrold. "Relationship of Obsessive-Compulsive Personality to Obsessive-Compulsive Disorder: A Review of the Literature," *The Journal of Psychology* 121 (1987): 137–48.

Pope John Paul II. *Sollicitudo Rei Socialis*, in O'Brien, David, and Thomas Shannon, eds., *Catholic Social Thought: A Documentary Heritage.* Maryknoll, NY: Orbis, 2001, 395–436.

———. *Centesimus Annus: On the Hundredth Anniversary of Rerum Novarum*, in O'Brien, David, and Thomas Shannon, eds., *Catholic Social Thought: A Documentary Heritage.* Maryknoll, NY: Orbis, 2001, 437–88.

Pope Paul VI. "On Evangelization in the Modern World," in O'Brien, David, and Thomas Shannon, eds., *Catholic Social Thought: A Documentary Heritage.* New York: Orbis, 2001.

Powers, David. *Irenaeus of Lyons on Baptism and Eucharist.* Nottingham, England: Hassall & Lucking, 1991.

Price, James Robertson. "Conversion and the Doctrine of Grace in Bernard Lonergan and John Climacus," *Anglican Theological Review* 62 (1980): 338–62.

Prokes, Mary Timothy. *Toward a Theology of the Body.* Grand Rapids, MI: Eerdmans, 1996.

Puente, Luis de la. *Of Familiar Intercourse with God in Prayer.* A Religious of the Order of St. Benedict, trans. New York: Benziger Brothers, 1932.

Quasten, Johannes. *Patrology.* Westminster, MD: Newman, 1953.

Quay, Paul. "The Disvalue of Ontic Evil," *Theological Studies* 46 (1985): 262–86.

Rachman, Stanley, and Ray Hodgson. *Obsessions and Compulsions*. Englewood, NJ: Prentice-Hall, 1980.

Radcliffe, Timothy. "The Sacramentality of the Word," in Pecklers, Keith, ed., *Liturgy in a Postmodern World*. New York: Continuum, 2003, 133–47.

Rahner, Karl. *The Church and the Sacraments*. London: Nelson, 1963.

———. "Concerning the Relationship between Nature and Grace," in *Theological Investigations*, vol. 1. Cornelius Ernst, trans. Baltimore, MD: Helicon, 1961.

———. "The Doctrine of the 'Spiritual Senses' in the Middle Ages," *Theological Investigations XVI*. David Morland, trans. New York: Seabury, 1979.

———. *Foundations in Christian Faith: An Introduction to the Idea of Christianity*. William Dych, trans. New York: Seabury, 1978.

———. "The Ignatian Mysticism of Joy in the World," *Theological Investigations,* vol. 3, 277–93. Karl-H. and Boniface Kruger, trans. Baltimore, MD: Helicon, 1967.

———. "Nature and Grace," in *Theological Investigations*, vol. 4. Kevin Smyth, trans. Baltimore, MD: Helicon, 1966.

———. *A Rahner Reader*. Gerald McCool, ed. New York: Seabury, 1975.

———. *Sacramentum Mundi: An Encyclopedia of Theology*. New York: Herder & Herder, 1969.

———. *Spiritual Exercises*. New York: Herder & Herder, 1965.

————. "The 'Spiritual Senses' According to Origen," *Theological Investigations XVI.* David Morland, trans. New York: Seabury, 1979.

————. *Theological Investigations*, vol. 15. Lionel Swain, trans. New York: Crossroad, 1982.

Rambo, Lewis. "Conversion: Toward a Holistic Model of Religious Change," *Pastoral Psychology* 38 (1989): 47–63.

Reid, Barbara. "Romero the Preacher," in Pelton, Robert, ed., *Archbishop Romero: Martyr and Prophet for the New Millennium*, 17–32.

Rende, Michael. "The Development and the Unity of Lonergan's Notion of Conversion," *Method: Journal of Lonergan Studies* 1 (1983): 158–73.

————. *Lonergan on Conversion: The Development of a Notion.* Lanham, MD: University Press of America, 1991.

Richard, Pablo. *The Church Born by the Force of God in Central America.* New York: New York CIRCUS, 1985.

Ricoeur, Paul. *The Symbolism of Evil.* Emerson Buchanan, trans. Boston: Beacon, 1967.

Roach, Richard. "Medicine and Killing: The Catholic View," *Journal of Medicine and Philosophy* 4 (1979): 383–97.

Robb, Paul. "Conversion as a Human Experience," *Studies in the Spirituality of Jesuits* 14 (1982): 3–52.

Rodríguez Maradiaga, Oscar Andres, "Monsignor Romero: A Bishop for the Third Millennium," in Pelton, Robert, ed., *Monsignor Romero: A Bishop for the Third Millennium*, 15–25.

Romero, Oscar. "The Brockman-Romero Papers," Special Collections Department, John T. Richards Library, DePaul University, Chicago, IL.

―――. *Colección Homilías y Diario de Monseñor Oscar Arnulfo Romero*. San Salvador: Arzobispo de San Salvador, 2000.

―――. "Homilies by Romero" (photocopy), 1977, Special Collections, John T. Richardson Library, De Paul University, Chicago, IL.

―――. *La Voz de los Sin Voz: La Palabra Viva de Monseñor Romero*. San Salvador: UCA Editores. 1980.

―――. "Letters of Romero for Possible Publication" (photocopy), 1977–1978, Special Collections, John T. Richardson Library, DePaul University, Chicago, IL.

―――. *A Martyr's Message of Hope: Six Homilies by Archbishop Oscar Romero*. Kansas City, MO: Celebration Books, 1981.

―――. *Monseñor Oscar A. Romero: Su pensamiento*. Publicaciones Pastorales Arzobispado, vol. 5. San Salvador: Imprenta Criterio. 1980–89.

―――. "Reflections on the Spiritual Exercise," *The Way*, Supplement 55 (1986): 100–106.

―――. "Romero: Cuaderno de Trabajo," 1971, 1972, 1973 (photocopy), Special Collections, John T. Richardson Library, DePaul University, Chicago, IL.

―――. *Romero: Martyr for Liberation. The Last Two Homilies of Archbishop Romero of San Salvador*. London: Catholic Institute for International Relations, 1982.

―――. "Romero's Diary in Rome 1937–1943" (photocopy), Special Collections, John T. Richardson Library, DePaul University, Chicago, IL.

————. *Roots of Faith: An Anthology of Early Christian Spirituality to Contemplate and Treasure.* Robert Van De Weyer, ed. Grand Rapids, MI: Eerdmans, 1997.

————. *A Shepherd's Diary.* Irene Hodgson, trans. Cincinnati, OH: St. Anthony Messenger Press, 1986.

————.*Spiritual Notebooks* I, II, III (Retreats) (photocopy), Special Collections, John T. Richardson Library, DePaul University, Chicago, IL.

————. *The Violence of Love: The Pastoral Wisdom of Archbishop Oscar Romero.* James Brockman, trans. and comp. San Francisco: Harper & Row. 1988.

————. *Voice of the Voiceless: The Four Pastoral Letters and Other Statements.* Michael Walsh, trans. Maryknoll, NY: Orbis, 1985.

Ross, Susan. *Extravagant Affections: A Feminist Sacramental Theology.* New York: Continuum, 1998.

Rossi de Gasperis, Francesco. "Ignatius of Loyola: The Man of the Experience of God," *Secretariatus Spiritualitatis Ignatae* (CIS) (1993): 27–54.

Roy, Paul. "Developing a Sense of Community (*Gaudium et spes*)," in Richard, Lucien, Daniel Harrington, and John O'Malley, eds. *Vatican II, The Unfinished Agenda: A Look into the Future.* Mahwah, NJ: Paulist Press, 1987.

Ruether, Rosemary Radford. "The Consciousness of Evil: The Journey of Conversion," in *Sexism and God Talk: Toward a Feminist Theology.* Boston: Beacon, 1983.

Ruffing, Janet K. "You Fill Up My Senses: God and Our Senses," *The Way* 35 (1995): 101–10, http://www.theway.org.uk/back/35Ruffing.pdf.

Ruiz García, Samuel. "Monsignor Oscar A. Romero: Martyr for the Option for the Poor," in Pelton, Robert, ed., *Monsignor Romero: A Bishop for the Third Millennium*, 65–77.

Sáenz Lacalle, Fernando. "Homily of the Twentieth Anniversary of the Death of Monseñor Oscar Romero: The Great Testimony of Faith," *Semanario Orientación*, April 1, 2000.

Salzman, Leon. *The Obsessive Personality: Origins, Dynamics, and Therapy*. New York: Jason Aronson, 1973.

———. "Psychoanalytic Therapy of the Obsessional Patient," *Current Psychiatric Therapy* 9 (1983): 53–59.

Schillebeeckx, Edward. *Christ the Sacrament of Encounter with God*. New York: Sheed & Ward, 1963.

———. *The Eucharist*. N. D. Smith, ed. New York: Sheed & Ward, 1968.

Schneiders, Sandra. "The Study of Christian Spirituality: Contours and Dynamics of a Discipline," *Christian Spirituality Bulletin* 6 (1998): 3–12.

Schüller, Bruno. "Direct Killing/Indirect Killing, " in Curran, Charles, and Richard McCormick, eds., *Readings in Moral Theology, Number 1*. New York: Paulist Press, 1979.

Schultz, Duane. *Growth Psychology: Models of the Healthy Personality*. New York: Van Nostrand Reinhold, 1977.

Sedgwick, Timothy. *Sacramental Ethics: Paschal Identity and the Christian Life*. Philadelphia, PA: Fortress, 1987.

Shannon, William. Personal interview. Rochester, NY, January 22, 2004.

Shano, Philip. "Resurrection and Imagination," *The Way*, Supplement 99 (2000): 140–50.

Sheldrake, Phillip. "The Crisis of Postmodernity," *Christian Spirituality Bulletin* 4 (1996): 6–10.

————. "Christian Spirituality as a Way of Living Publicly: A Dialectic of the Mystical and Prophetic," *Spiritus* 3 (2003): 19–37.

Shideler, Mary McDermott. *Spirituality: An Approach through Descriptive Psychology.* Ann Arbor, MI: Descriptive Psychology Press, 1992.

Shortell, Timothy. "Speaking a New Truth: Oscar Romero and the Salvadoran Church, 1977–1980." Ph.D. diss., Boston College, 1992.

Smith, William, and Henry Wan, eds. *Dictionary of Christian Biography, Literature, Sects and Doctrine during the First Eight Centuries,* vol. 4. London: William Clowes & Sons, 1887.

Sobrino, Jon. *Archbishop Romero: Memories and Reflections.* Robert Barr, trans. Maryknoll, NY: Orbis, 1990.

————. "Archbishop Romero: Model of Faith." London: Catholic Institute for International Relations, 1983.

————. "Monseñor Romero: A Salvadoran and a Christian," *Spiritus* 1 (2001): 143–55.

————. *Monseñor Romero Verdadero Profeta.* Spain: Editorial Desclée de Brouwer, 1982.

————. *Profeta y mártir de la liberación: Oscar Romero.* Lima, Peru: Centro de Estudios y Publicaciones, 1981.

————. "A Theologian's View of Oscar Romero," *Oscar Romero: Voice of the Voiceless.* Michael Walsh, trans. Maryknoll, NY: Orbis, 1985.

Stein, Andrew. "Religious Actors in El Salvador since 1992." Paper Presented at the XXI International Congress of the Latin American Studies Association, September 24–26, 1998, Chicago, IL.

Stein, Daniel, and Eric Hollander. "The Spectrum of Obsessive-Compulsive Related Disorders," in Hollander, Eric, ed., *Obsessive-Compulsive Related Disorders*. London: American Psychiatric, 1993.

Steinfels, Margaret O'Brien. "Death and Lies in El Salvador: The Ambassador's Tale," *Commonweal* 128 (2001): 12–20.

Streeter, Carla Mae. "Preaching as a Form of Theological Communication: An Instance of Lonergan's Evaluative Hermeneutics," in Farrell, Thomas, and Paul Soukup, eds., *Communication and Lonergan: Common Ground for Forging a New Age*. Kansas City, MO: Sheed & Ward, 1993, 48–66.

———. "The Role of Theological Communication in the Act of Preaching," in Siegfried, Regina, and Edward Ruane, eds., *In the Company of Preachers*. Collegeville, MN: Liturgical Press, 1993, 102–12.

Stull, Bradford. *Religious Dialectics of Pain and Imagination*. Albany: State University of New York Press, 1994.

Sudbrack, Josef. "Finding God in All Things: Christian Contemplation and the Ignatian Exercises," *The Way*, Supplement 103 (2002): 87–99.

Swanson, Tod. "A Civil Art: The Persuasive Voice of Oscar Romero," *Journal of Religious Ethics* 29 (2001): 127–44.

Swedish, Margaret. "Archbishop Romero and His Commitment to the Church," in Pelton, Robert, ed., *Monsignor Romero: A Bishop for the Third Millennium*, 2004.

Tanquerey, Adolphe. *The Spiritual Life: A Treatise on Ascetical and Mystical Theology.* Herman Branderis, trans. Tournai, Belgium: Desclée, 1930.

Tek, Cenk, and Berna Ulug. "Religiosity and Religious Obsessions in Obsessive-Compulsive Disorder," *Psychiatry Research* 104 (2001): 99–108.

Teresa of Avila. *The Collected Works of St. Teresa of Avila*, vol. 1. Kieran Kavanaugh and Otilio Rodriguez, eds. Washington, DC: Institute of Carmelite Studies, 1987.

Thibodeaux, Mark. *Armchair Mystic: Easing into Contemplative Prayer.* Cincinnati, OH: St. Anthony Messenger Press, 2001.

Tiessen, Terrance. *Irenaeus on the Salvation of the Unevangelized.* Metuchen, NJ: Scarecrow Press, 1993.

Timmerman, Joan. *Sexuality and Spiritual Growth.* New York: Crossroad, 1992.

Tombs, David. "Oscar Romero and Resurrection Hope," *Resurrection: Journal for the Study of the New Testament,* Supplement Series 186. Sheffield, England: Sheffield Academic Press, 1999.

Townsend, David. "The Examen and the Exercises—a Re-Appraisal," *The Way*, Supplement 52 (1985): 53–63.

Tyrrell, Bernard. *Christotherapy II: The Fasting and Feasting Heart.* Ramsey, NJ: Paulist Press, 1982.

———. "Passages and Conversion," in Lamb, Matthew, ed., *Creativity and Method: Essays in Honor of Bernard Lonergan, SJ.* Milwaukee, WI: Marquette University Press, 1981.

———. "Psychological Conversion, Methods of Healing, and Communication," in Lawrence, Fred, ed., *Lonergan Workshop*, vol. 6. Atlanta, GA: Scholars Press, 1986.

Urioste, Ricardo Bustamante. "Monseñor Romero: Martyr for the Magisterium," in Pelton, Robert, ed., *Archbishop Romero: Martyr and Prophet for the New Millennium*, Victor Carmona and Elizabeth Station, trans., 47–57.

Vacek, Edward. "Proportionalism: One View of the Debate," *Theological Studies* 46 (1985): 287–314.

Vaillant, George. *Adaptation to Life*. Toronto: Little, Brown, 1974.

Van Ornum, William. *A Thousand Frightening Fantasies: Understanding and Healing Scrupulosity and Obsessive-Compulsive Disorder*. New York: Crossroad, 1977.

Vest, Norvene. *No Moment Too Small: Rhythms of Silence, Prayer, and Holy Reading*. Kalamazoo, MI: Cistercian Publications, 1994.

———. *Bible Reading for Spiritual Growth*. San Francisco: HarperCollins, 1992.

von Balthasar, Hans Urs. *The Glory of the Lord: A Theological Aesthetics*. John Riches, ed. Andrew Louth, Francis McDonagh, and Brian McNeil, trans. New York: Crossroad, 1983.

Walsh, Michael. *Opus Dei: An Investigation into the Powerful, Secretive Society within the Catholic Church*. San Francisco: HarperCollins, 2004.

Ware, Kallistos. "The Power of the Name: The Jesus Prayer in Orthodox Spirituality." Fairacres: Oxford SLG, 1986.

Weisner, W. M., and P. A. Riffle. "Scrupulosity: Religion and Obsessive-Compulsive Behavior in Children," *American Journal of Psychiatry* 117 (1960): 314–18.

Weston, Drew, and Amy Kegley Heim. "Disturbances of Self and Identity in Personality Disorders," in Leary, Mark, and June Price

Tangney, eds., *Handbook of Self and Identity*. New York: Guilford, 2003.

White, Robert. Interview by author, June 29, 2003. Tape recording. Washington, DC.

Wingren, Gustaf. *Man and the Incarnation: A Study in the Biblical Theology of Irenaeus*. Ross Mackenzie, trans. London: Oliver & Boyd, 1959.

Wiseman, James. "The Body in Spiritual Practice: A New Asceticism," *Spiritual Life* 47 (2001): 200–215.

Witherup, Ronald. *Conversion in the New Testament*. Collegeville, MN: Liturgical Press, 1994.

Woodward, Kenneth. *Making Saints: How the Catholic Church Determines Who Becomes a Saint, Who Doesn't, and Why.* New York: Simon & Schuster, 1996.

Wright, Scott. "The Witness of Archbishop Romero: A Spirituality of Solidarity for Our Times," in *Central America/Mexico Report* (pp. 20–23). Washington, DC: Task Force on Central America and Mexico, January/February 2005.

Wyschogrod, Edith. *Saints and Postmodernism*. Chicago, IL: University of Chicago Press, 1990.

———. "Man-Made Mass Death: Shifting Concepts of Community," *Journal of American Academy of Religion* 58 (1990): 165–76.

Yaryura-Tobias, Jose, and Fugen Neziroglu. *Obsessive-Compulsive Disorders: Pathogenesis, Diagnosis, Treatment*. New York: Marcel Dekker, 1983.

Yates, Timothy. "Christian Conversion 1902–1993, William James to Lewis Rambo," *Mission Studies* 13 (1996): 306–19.

Zamora, Rubén. "The Empowering Spirit of Archbishop Romero: A Personal Testimony," in Pelton, Robert, ed., *Monsignor Romero: A Bishop for the Third Millennium*, 47–50.

INDEX